Television Drama

Other titles published by the authors

Sue Thornham

1996	*Media Studies: A Reader*, edited and introduced with Paul Marris
1997	*Passionate Detachments: An Introduction to Feminist Film Theory*
1999	*Feminist Film Theory: A Reader*
1999	*Media Studies: A Reader*, 2nd edition
2001	*Feminism and Cultural Studies*

Tony Purvis

2004	*Culture, Sexuality and Identity in the Fictions of Edmund White*

Television Drama

Theories and Identities

Sue Thornham and Tony Purvis

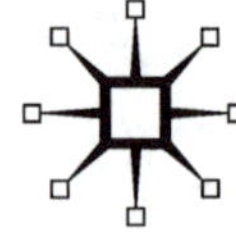

First published 2005 by
PALGRAVE MACMILLAN
Houndmills, Basingstoke, Hampshire RG21 6XS and
175 Fifth Avenue, New York, N.Y. 10010
Companies and representatives throughout the world

PALGRAVE MACMILLAN is the global academic imprint of the Palgrave Macmillan division of St. Martin's Press, LLC and of Palgrave Macmillan Ltd. Macmillan® is a registered trademark in the United States, United Kingdom and other countries. Palgrave is a registered trademark in the European Union and other countries.

ISBN 0–333–96887–5 hardback
ISBN 0–333–96888–3 paperback

This book is printed on paper suitable for recycling and made from fully managed and sustained forest sources.

A catalogue record for this book is available from the British Library.

A catalog record for this book is available from the Library of Congress.

10 9 8 7 6 5 4 3 2 1
14 13 12 11 10 09 08 07 06 05

Printed in China

Contents

Acknowledgements

We should like to thank the staff and students of Media and Cultural Studies at the University of Sunderland, who have been so important in working through the ideas in this book. Personal thanks go to Mike, Dan, Helen and Beth, and to Allan, Norma, Joe, and Sunny for their continuing support.

Introduction: Approaches to Television Drama

This book has three aims. First, it introduces the study of television drama to students and those interested in the study of media, culture and cultural theory. The book outlines key approaches useful in the study of television drama, and explores the ways in which these approaches have been employed in television criticism over the past 30 years. Second, these theoretical and critical approaches are considered in relation to specific case studies drawn from British and US television. Sometimes these case studies are woven into discussion of the critical approach being explored; on other occasions, a case study concludes a particular section or chapter. Finally, both television drama texts and the critical perspectives used to explore them are contextualised in terms of the changing identities, histories and discourses which have structured television's drama output and which inform how audiences and critics have read television dramas.

Chapter 1: 'Representing Television Drama' considers the way in which television drama has been discussed by critics and theorists. Sometimes this has involved a failure of critical engagement, as television drama becomes simply part of a generalised notion of 'television itself', and television in turn stands in metonymically for aspects of contemporary culture. From the 'spreading ooze' of mass culture envisaged by Dwight Macdonald in the 1950s to Jean Baudrillard's nightmare vision of the invasion of the individual by technology, television has been seen as signalling a collapse of values and of meaning. In other instances television drama has been singled out as standing apart from this general collapse – as offering a solid ground of meaning amidst the general flow of television. In contrast to both of these perspectives, Chapter 1 concludes by suggesting that television drama is more productively analysed as a primary generator and the most everyday source of narratives in contemporary culture. The narratives of television drama, it suggests, construct, mediate and frame our social and individual identities.

Throughout the chapters that follow, these narratives are considered in relation to the cultural identities upon which television dramas rely and which they help to construct. Yet these identities are not fixed or uncontested. Whilst some parts of the book consider the ways in which television drama can be seen to categorise social identities (as, for example, in the classification 'woman', 'working class', or 'gay'), other sections explore the ways in which identity is always relational, intersubjective and intertextual. Throughout, the emphasis is on television drama as a key site for exploring the usefulness of contemporary theories of identity, cultural change and representation. This is an approach which has been taken elsewhere in relation to film (Hollows and Jancovich 1995), and to television in general (Allen 1992; Holland 1997), but not in relation specifically to television drama. The critical perspectives mapped here offer a way of exploring these issues in relation to a range of television dramas spanning the late 1950s to the present time.

Identities can mean nations, subjects and citizens, but these same constituencies are also inflected by ethnicity, gender, sexuality and social class. Moreover, the discourses through which we represent these cultural categories and identities do not remain unchanged. The final chapter of the book traces the ways in which the 'nation' that was televised in the 1960s, with its stress on family values and consensus morality, contrasts – often starkly – with the postmodern society figured in recent output. Television drama, in its increasingly varied and hybrid forms, is seen always in relation to the conflicts of history, as well as to shifts in discourse, ideology and representation.

A key element in the study of any cultural text is to understand how that text has been structured and framed. Chapter 2 considers three concepts crucial to this understanding: *narrative, genre* and *realism*. The first of these draws first on the work of structuralist critics such as Roland Barthes to understand how *narratives* operate to structure meaning. But if the stories that circulate within culture work to construct our sense of who we are as individuals and social subjects, more recent critical approaches have drawn attention to the partial and incomplete nature of these narratives. In considering the stories which television dramas construct, we must also consider their contexts of production and reception, as ethnographic studies by Ien

Ang and David Morley, for example, have shown. Critics such as Michel Foucault and Pierre Macherey, too, extending and critiquing early structuralist methods, have shown how the texts themselves are unstable, always incomplete, subject to revision and rereading. Whilst it is argued, then, that narrative is one of the principal means by which personal, social and political identities are mediated, narratives are also contested, revised and called into question.

Popular television is often analysed in relation to the genres, formulas and devices that it employs to organise its stories. Popular genres are ways of structuring audiences, meaning and identity. 'Masculine' genres like police series, for example, have been contrasted with 'feminine' genres like soap opera. Popular genres, because of their 'formulaic' structure, have also been a focus for anxieties about the 'quality' and 'value' of television drama. But generic narratives, though they may serve to make some identities seem more appealing than others, are not so easily dismissed or disparaged. They are complex, shifting, and may be contested from within. Apparently 'fixed' genres may be subsequently reformulated in revised, hybrid and disruptive ways. Audiences, too, are not statically fixed in one tele-viewing position but work with a range of cultural repertoires in the viewing of popular genres and their narratives.

Realism, too, has been seen as a primary characteristic of television drama, and as such both criticised as inherently conservative and praised for its radical potential. The final section of Chapter 2 explores the varying meanings and values which have been attached to this term, and the ways in which it has been employed in the analysis of television drama. The concept of 'reality TV' has added to these debates. Television's supposed 'liveness' and ability to show us 'the real world' has always been drawn upon by the realism of television drama, whether this has been aligned with a conservative or an oppositional political perspective. 'Reality TV' seems to offer us the real as spectacle and story, and blurs the boundaries between the constructed and performed and the real. But it, too, is far from neutral. Finally, the techniques of 'reality TV' can in turn be appropriated by television drama, and this hybridity and blurring of boundaries can make us question what is meant by the 'real' and 'reality'.

It is the non-neutral and ideological status of television output which is considered in the remaining chapters of the book. Television dramas do not offer neutral or objective versions of contemporary realities. Gender, race, sexuality and social class are not only identities which are represented in television dramas but are also the cultural categories which structure how audiences decode dramatic representations. In the first section of Chapter 3, the concepts of *ideology, hegemony* and *discourse* are considered in relation to representations of race and power. The second section examines the usefulness of *psychoanalytic* theories to the analysis of televisual texts. If television is one of the most powerful agents in the construction of our sense of 'reality', then this is a matter not only of the ideological dimensions of its representations, but also of our subjectivities as individuals. The medium of television relies on a subject-audience who views images on television screens. These images are packaged in terms of narratives which render the world meaningful for us, but they are also encoded in relation to the dynamics of desire and pleasure. These images are never simply representative, mirroring some objective reality, but are mediated in terms of ideologies and desires. Television dramas are able to naturalise desire, concealing the devices and codes which make the artificial, the fictional and the ideological compelling because 'natural'.

The referential codes upon which television draws allude as much to popular pleasures and desires as they do to the dominant ways of seeing in any culture. Looking is not neutral, and the power to look is linked to forms of social power. *Gender* and *sexuality* are central in the relations of domination and subordination which looking can express. But looking not only links patriarchal ideology with the subordination of women in material and psychological ways. It offers pleasures – pleasures which are often mediated in terms of a (white) male heterosexual identity. More recent cultural critics, such as Judith Butler and Gayatri Spivak, have called into question the self-evident nature of categories such as gender, sexuality and race. Nevertheless, these categories continue to inform how television is produced and consumed. Chapter 4, then, in exploring approaches to the study of television drama which draw on gender and sexuality, also considers the usefulness of categories such as man–woman, masculine–feminine, and straight–gay in relation to the increasingly 'queer' spaces of television production and consumption.

In Chapter 5, the problems surrounding representation are discussed in relation to recent (postmodern) drama, postmodern theory and aesthetics. On the one hand, postmodern theory has been used to question the 'realities' which television constructs. If there is nothing behind the representation, no 'referent', or nothing to which the television image connects other than its own sign-system, then the references, codes and 'fictional' worlds of television drama allude to nothing other than themselves. On the other hand, television, in its mixing of the popular with the 'high', in its dismantling of public and private, and in its blurring of the categories of fact and fiction, appears now as the example *par excellence* of postmodern culture, with its dispersed and fragmented sense of identity. Postmodern and experimental dramas thus raise questions which are important not only in understanding how cultures are represented and understood, but also in relation to how 'television itself' functions within contemporary culture. In cultures that are so very different from those of the 1950s, from which the earliest case studies in this book are taken, what can we now understand the role of television drama to be, and how might it address its multiple constituencies?

Chapter 1

Representing Television Drama: Television Drama and its Critics

1.1 'Television Itself'

Any book which sets out to discuss television drama is faced immediately with problems of definition and demarcation. The first and most overwhelming of these relates to the issue of what Stephen Heath (1990: 282) calls 'the institution of television, the functioning, as it were, of television itself'. Television, with its 'interminable flow (of images and sounds, their endlessly disappearing present)' and its 'explosion of messages, signs, endless traces of meaning' (ibid., 267, 275) is so much a part of our everyday experience, so universally available, that it is this fact and its cultural significance which has tended to dominate discussions of the medium. The originator of this approach is Raymond Williams, whose comments have been so influential that they are worth quoting at length. Between 1968 and 1972 Williams wrote a monthly review of television for the BBC weekly journal *The Listener*, but it was, as he wrote in 1973, his first exposure to American television in 1972 which crystallised his view of the characteristic 'television experience':

> One night in Miami, still dazed from a week on an Atlantic liner, I began watching a film and at first had some difficulty in adjusting to a much greater frequency of commercial 'breaks'. Yet this was a minor problem compared to what eventually happened. Two other films, which were due to be shown on the same channel on other nights, began to be inserted as trailers. A crime in San Francisco (the subject of the original film) began to operate in an extraordinary counterpoint not only with the deodorant and cereal commercials but with a romance in Paris and the eruption of a prehistoric monster who laid waste New

York. Moreover, this was sequence in a new sense. Even in commercial British television there is a visual signal – the residual sign of an interval – before and after the commercial sequences, and 'programme' trailers only occur between 'programmes'. Here there was something quite different, since the transitions from film to commercial and from film A to films B and C were in effect unmarked. . . . I can still not be sure what I took from that whole flow. I believe I registered some incidents as happening in the wrong film, and some characters in the commercials as involved in the film episodes, in what came to seem – for all the occasional bizarre disparities – a single irresponsible flow of images and feelings. (1990: 91–2)

From this experience Williams develops the claim that 'in all developed broadcasting systems the characteristic organisation, and therefore the characteristic experience, is one of sequence or flow. This phenomenon, of planned flow, is then perhaps the defining characteristic of broadcasting, simultaneously as a technology and as a cultural form' (ibid., 86).

There are a number of points to note about this account. Most obviously, it is an account of 'television itself'. It is not simply that Williams does not discuss specific forms of television output or programming. For him, whilst such discussion 'can be useful, it is always at some distance from what seems to me the central television experience: the fact of flow' (ibid., 95). It is this 'apparently casual and miscellaneous flow' which, in constituting the 'television experience', also constructs 'the flow of meanings and values' of our culture, carrying its 'structure of feeling' (ibid., 118, 111).[1] Elsewhere, in 1974, Williams refers to this flow as specifically a *dramatised* flow. Drama, he writes, is, via television, 'built into the rhythms of everyday life':

Till the eyes tire, millions of us watch the shadows of shadows and find them substance; watch scenes, situations, actions, exchanges, crises. The slice of life, once a project of naturalist drama, is now a voluntary, habitual, internal rhythm; the flow of action and acting, of representation and performance, raised to a new convention, that of a basic need. (1989: 4, 5)

Within such an all-embracing view it is difficult, as Williams himself confesses, to find a framework within which to discuss something which is distinctively 'television drama'. Yet, in his *Listener* reviews and elsewhere, Williams does discuss particular television dramas. What happens at such times, as Stuart Laing (1991: 160) has pointed out, is that whilst he frequently refers to the concept of 'flow' in describing his viewing *experience*, when he turns to the structures, themes or 'structure of feeling' of specific dramas, he reaches instead for comparisons and continuities with earlier forms, primarily theatre and the novel. The result, as Laing argues, is that 'particular programmes are quite deliberately pulled out of the frame of general television experience and referred across to quite other media' (ibid.). There is clearly a tension, then, between Williams's sense of the centrality of 'flow' in any understanding of 'television itself', and the lack of usefulness of this concept for any discussion of *specific* television dramas.

The second point to note about Williams's account is its generalisation of the American television experience as *the* television experience. In *Television: Technology and Cultural Form* Williams is concerned to challenge what he calls '*technological determinism*', the idea that it is new technologies which produce 'social change and progress' (1990: 13). On the contrary, he insists, new technologies are *products of* specific social systems. They are also sites of struggle over the social uses that will be made of them, and the cultural forms they will take. Yet despite this emphasis on social struggle, it is the American experience, as Rick Altman (1986) has pointed out, which is taken as that towards which television – as both technology and cultural form – inevitably tends. In the account quoted above, Williams both raises the issue of national differences – American television disorientates him because it is so different from British television – and obscures them. If 'the *central* television experience [is] the fact of flow' (italics added), then British television, with its different history and structures, has simply not yet caught up. Once again, this has made it difficult to frame a discussion of specific national televisions and their dramas in relation to this central concept. Williams's own tendency to refer back to earlier national traditions of drama or narrative form in his discussions of particular television dramas again indicates the difficulty. The impression given is that these television dramas are either 'not really' television – as texts or as viewing experiences – or that they represent an 'earlier' form of television, not quite, or not yet, part of 'the *central* television experience'.

A third point to note about Williams's account is its tendency to conflate properties of the medium – the 'planned flow', which he argues is the defining characteristic of broadcasting's *textual* organisation – with patterns of audience use. A number of key phrases perform this blurring of boundaries. One is the 'flow of images and feelings', in which the first term (images) is a textual property, whilst the second (feelings) is a property of the viewer. A second is 'the television experience', which can only be the subjective experience of the *viewer* but which seems to be offered as an essential property of the *medium*. In Rick Altman's view, 'flow' is in fact not a characteristic of television itself, but of 'a specific cultural practice of television': American commercial television (1986: 40). It is the product of a system in which audiences are treated as commodities that can be measured and then 'sold' to advertisers, but in which audience size can be measured only by the number of sets switched on. Accordingly, programming must 'flow' to ensure that televisions remain switched on even when audiences are not watching. If this is the case, then the fact of programming flow in such a context tells us little about either the particular texts which might be embedded in such flow or the ways in which audiences in fact respond to them. Williams's blurring of boundaries in his concept of 'the television experience' serves to produce a slippage between textual organisation and viewing practices which tends to obscure the specificities of each.

A final point to note in Williams's account lies in the telling final sentence of the first quotation above: the television experience is of 'a single *irresponsible* flow of images and feelings' (italics added). John Fiske comments on this phrase that Williams's use of the word 'irresponsible' 'seems to derive from his literary desire for a named author to be responsible for a text, and for this responsibility to be exercised in the production of a coherent, unified text' (1987: 100). Williams, he feels, displays a 'lack of sympathy with the nature of television' (ibid.). Fiske's own very different view of television's 'flow' will be discussed below. His comment, however, draws attention to the way in which Williams's accounts of television bear the traces of the struggle over terminology – and hence over values – which John Caughie (1986) identifies as marking the emerging field of cultural studies. 'Mass culture' had been the term used by cultural critics of both left and right to describe contemporary mediated cultural forms. It suggested the loss of cultural value, which they identified with the emergence of contemporary 'mass civilisation', a development identified particularly with American 'commercial' culture. In opposition to a traditional 'high culture', 'mass culture' was variously defined as parasitic, exploitative, degrading: involving surrender to 'the cheapest emotional appeals' (Leavis 1994: 14) rather than the exercise of reason and discrimination. Unlike an older 'folk culture', 'mass culture' was seen as inauthentic, 'fabricated by technicians hired by businessmen' (Macdonald 1994: 30). Imposed upon rather than arising from 'ordinary people', its primary function was to ensure the continued passivity of its working-class audiences. For Dwight Macdonald, an influential proponent of this view in

America, 'mass culture' was 'a spreading ooze' that 'threatens to engulf everything' (1994: 34).

Raymond Williams offered a very different definition of culture, and a very different way of viewing contemporary cultural forms. Culture, he writes, is 'a description of a particular way of life, which expresses certain meanings and values not only in art and learning but also in institutions and ordinary behaviour. The analysis of culture . . . is the clarification of the meanings and values implicit and explicit in a particular way of life, a particular culture' (1965: 57). It reveals a society's 'structure of feeling'. Such a perspective insists that contemporary cultural forms – as 'popular culture' rather than the derogatory 'mass culture' – must be taken seriously. Indeed, in *Television: Technology and Cultural Form* he writes of television 'soap operas' that 'their persistence and popularity is significant, in a period in which, in so much traditionally serious drama and fiction, there has been a widespread withdrawal from general social experience'. 'Few forms on television', he adds, have 'the potential importance of the original serial' (1990: 61). Nevertheless, as John Fiske indicates, when Williams writes of 'television itself' rather than specific programmes, the traces of the 'mass culture' critique seem uncomfortably close. Between Williams's 'irresponsible flow' and Macdonald's 'spreading ooze' there seems little distance.

1.2 From 'Flow' to 'In-difference'

Williams's description of 'television itself' has been developed by a number of subsequent writers whose accounts, like that of Williams himself, are both important in any study of television drama and frustrating in their level of generality. Perhaps the most illuminating *and* the most frustrating is that of John Ellis, whose *Visible Fictions* was first published in 1982. Drawing upon Williams's concept of 'flow', Ellis is nevertheless critical of some of its underlying assumptions. For Williams, he argues, 'flow' is 'a liquid and even confusing process' in which separate texts become compromised by their random juxtaposition (1982: 117). The problem, he argues, is that Williams's model still assumes that the basic unit of television is the individual programme. In doing so, he 'underestimates the complexity of broadcast TV's particular commodity form, which has little to do with the single text' (ibid., 118).

Ellis's own model offers a number of important modifications to Williams's account. Instead of the single text, he argues, the basic unit of which broadcast television 'flow' is composed is the 'segment': 'small sequential unities of images and sounds whose maximum duration seems to be about five minutes' (ibid., 112). These relatively self-contained segments are organised into larger units, but the links between them are not ones of cause and effect, as in conventional narrative structures. Instead, in television's characteristic forms of the open-ended series and the continuing serial, segment follows segment with no necessary link between them other than that of 'vague simultaneity'. The news bulletin, magazine programme, drama, documentary and game show are all structured in this way, whilst the advertisement represents a single, self-contained segment. Unlike cinema, then, which characteristically gives us a single story told in compressed time, what television's segmented structure suggests is rather 'a continuous update, a perpetual return to the present' (ibid., 147). Formats, situations, places and casts of characters all remain the same, providing a constant background for the updated events of the week. This structure runs across and through all forms of television programming, whether fiction or non-fiction, news bulletin or soap opera. The complex interweaving of stories which characterises the soap opera narrative, for example, is assumed to be occurring in real time; it is not presented as an unfolding of events that have already happened.

Broadcast television, then, is marked by a sense of 'nowness' or immediacy, and this in turn is linked with a number of other characteristics. Television, of course, was originally broadcast live, and this sense of 'liveness' still haunts the medium. It means, for example, that television addresses viewers directly, simulating eye contact and assuming, as Ellis argues, that it and its viewers are 'held in a relationship of co-intimacy' (ibid., 132). This in turn means that the intensity of the cinematic gaze, in which the viewer is both immersed in and separate from the screen image, is replaced by an assumption of shared looking and eavesdropping. Television characters, argues Ellis, 'tend to become familiar figures, loved, or excused with a tolerance that is quite remarkable' (ibid., 139). They are also most characteristically presented to us in groups, whether the co-presenters of the magazine or news programme or the family, work or community grouping of the drama series, sitcom or soap opera. We, the viewers 'inside', isolated but connected in our domesticity, look 'out' at the world through them, but they also offer the comfort of confirmation. For these are groups which are assumed to be like us: they have shared values and they are organised in familial or pseudo-familial groupings.

Ellis's account of broadcast television, concerned as it is to distinguish television from cinema, offers important insights for a discussion of television drama. In particular, his insistence on the *difference* of television from cinema acts as a critique of assumptions about their continuity which were dominant in discussions of television drama in the 1970s. In 1974 Colin MacCabe had traced a continuity between the narrative structures, the constructions of discursive hierarchies and the use of realism from the nineteenth-century novel to cinema and television drama. The nineteenth-century realist novel, he argues, constructs particular forms of knowledge for its readers by framing all the actions and discourses of its cast of characters in relation to a central set of 'truths'. These 'truths' are carried by the storytelling itself (the novel's 'metalanguage'), which seems to be simply a transparent rendering of reality (MacCabe 1974: 10). In fact, he maintains, this 'classic realist text' offers a highly ideologically loaded view of the world.

In MacCabe's account, cinema continues this structure with one difference: the storytelling voice which in the novel offers 'direct access to truth' is in cinema replaced by the camera. The camera 'tells the truth against which we can measure the discourses' of the various characters (ibid.). It is therefore even more powerful as a carrier of ideology than the novel, because the camera's apparent capacity to record reality masks the processes of selection and construction which go into the production of a cinematic narrative. In articles that followed, MacCabe and others applied this critique of the 'classic realist text' to television drama, which also makes claims to truth-telling because of its dominant realist mode. Indeed, in television it can be argued that these claims are even stronger because of the tendency to merge drama and documentary forms, in plays like *Cathy Come Home* (1966 – Section 2.3) or more recently *The Navigators* (Loach 2002), or even in popular series like *Z Cars* (1962–78) or more recent docu-soaps.

Ellis's insistence on the *difference* of television's narrative structures contests this assumption of continuity. The greater fragmentation of the television text, its different relation to 'the real' and to time, the characteristic lack of narrative closure in its continuously updated narratives, the tendency of the television discourse to draw attention to itself through direct address to the viewer, and the lack of dominance of the image and greater importance of sound in television, all emphasise the need to consider television drama in a way which does not regard it as continuous with or dependent on film narrative. Nevertheless, as with Williams's account of flow, Ellis's account of 'television itself' tends to obscure differences: between fiction and non-fiction forms, and within the range of narrative forms and representational structures available across the medium, a range which has become far greater since the original publication of *Visible Fictions*.

Writers who have continued this focus on 'television itself' can be divided into two lines of development, inheritors in various ways of that conflict between a 'mass culture' and a 'popular culture' perspective with which Williams himself struggled rather uncomfortably. The more dominant perspective has been the pessimistic one. Jane Feuer, in articles written in the 1980s, picks up and develops a number of Ellis's points. Like Ellis, she insists that 'television as an apparatus differs in almost every significant respect from cinema' (1986: 101). Unlike cinema, it 'foreground[s] its discursive status', disseminating an 'ideology of presence that has its basis in the presumed "live" status of the apparatus' (ibid., 103–4). This assumption of 'liveness', she argues, is what constitutes its sense of 'flow'. A 'continuous, never-ending sequence in which it is impossible to separate out individual texts' (Feuer 1983: 15), it seems to replicate real life – to be, precisely, *alive*. This carefully constructed sense of flow and unity, however, serves an ideological function. Whole events, spatially fragmented and segmented, are reconstituted via narrativised commentary to offer a particular view of the world. 'Television itself', in other words, operates rather like soap opera, to offer us endlessly updated stories of 'the everyday'. Its 'foremost illusion is that it is an *interactive medium*', and its presumed interaction is with its ideologically positioned audience: the family. Its programmes persistently construct a dominant binary opposition between 'inside the family' and 'outside the family' (Feuer 1986: 106). All social and individual situations are referred to the family, where it is assumed they can be resolved. Even the soap opera, whose plots frequently centre on the internal rupturing of the family, contains its conflicts always within familial bounds; constantly disrupted, the family is at the same time endlessly reconstituted.

Feuer's theoretical framework is rather different from that of Ellis. Her focus is on television as an apparatus for producing ideologically positioned subjects. In addition to theories of ideology, she also draws on psychoanalytic theory, once again to distinguish television from cinema. Cinema, it has been argued,[2] positions its spectator in the position of voyeur, constructing sexual difference through the separation of masculine viewing subject and female object-of-the-gaze, and reinforcing the masculine ego through identification with the all-powerful camera. Television, on the other hand, assumes as its audience a family group whose gender and familial roles are already constructed, roles which it is the ideological business of television to reinforce. It is therefore above all, argues Feuer, a medium of *containment*. These arguments were to be developed in a number of ways by feminist critics of television narrative forms, including Feuer herself, as was the view, implicit in her argument that it constructs its spectators as domestic, familial subjects, that television is a despised medium because it is a *feminised* medium.

A more thoroughly pessimistic view is offered by Stephen Heath in 'Representing Television' (1990). Like Williams, he insists on the importance of trying to grasp and to represent 'television itself'. To see the analysis of television as 'just a question of more texts to be read, deconstructed' is to be complicit with that 'normalization' of television which the critic must contest (1990: 296). It is equally beside the point to argue that different national televisions are differently structured, or that individual viewers produce divergent readings. It is the American multinational television industry which dominates and absorbs across national boundaries, and 'the pursuit of plural readings' simply leaves this dominance 'intact, unthought' (ibid., 285). Heath's metaphors, then, intensify those of Williams and Ellis. Television is 'saturation, overloading, neutralization'; it offers 'a totalizing fragmentation, the television coherence of a moment-by-moment flow that relativizes any and every identity, meaning'. It absorbs the viewer into its network: 'I become part of the network, the circulation' (ibid., 292–3). The critic's task is 'to make the critical distance that television continually erodes in its extension, its availability, its proximity – all of which is played out on its screen from show to show in the endless flow' (ibid., 297).

For Heath, the threat that television poses is of saturation, excess of availability and proximity, and absorption; and the critic's task is to achieve separation, critical distance, and 'the forging of political meanings' (ibid.). We shall return to the implications of these metaphors later. But we can also contrast this dystopian view with a very different valuation of television's 'flow' and 'segmentation', which appears in more optimistic/utopian readings of 'television itself'. The chief proponent of this perspective is John Fiske, who draws on Roland Barthes's categorisation of texts into the 'readerly' and the 'writerly'. The former is rather like the definition of the 'classic realist text' offered by Colin MacCabe: it conceals its own processes of construction, purporting to be merely a transcript of 'reality', whilst in fact offering a highly controlled, ideological representation of the world (Silverman 1983: 243–6). The second draws attention to its processes of construction, resisting coherence and multiplying contradiction. No overriding meaning is imposed, and the 'writerly text replaces the concepts of "product" and "structure" with those of "process" and "segment" ' (ibid., 247).

For Barthes, the 'writerly' text seems less a different *kind* of text (though it has sometimes been seen as the *avant-garde* text)[3] than the text produced through a different kind of *reading*, a text which 'the reader or viewer has obliged to reveal the terms of its own construction', so that it no longer seems to be 'transparent' (Silverman 1983: 246). For John Fiske, however, 'process' and 'segmentation' are what – following Williams and Ellis – characterise the television text. Television, he argues, is not so much 'writerly' as 'producerly'. Rather than being a fragmentation of the world which is then bound together by an ideologically motivated 'flow', as Feuer argues, television's segmentation is for him a process which resists narrative closure and demands an active reader. The lack of connection between segments, the gaps and interruptions between segments and between episodes of a series or serial, and the ease with which viewers can switch channels, all contribute to making television 'the most open producerly text for it evades all attempts at closure. It is a form of scratch video that produces an individualized television text out of its mass-produced works' (Fiske 1987: 105). Rather than producing an ideologically positioned viewer, it is characterised by an 'excess of meaningfulness' (ibid., 92), which invites its viewers into a 'semiotic democracy' in which they can make their own meanings and pleasures (ibid., 95).

Television's presumed 'liveness', its direct address to and assumption of 'a relationship of co-intimacy' (Ellis) with the viewer, also receive a positive interpretation from Fiske. Television, he writes, is the inheritor of 'a popular culture in which orality plays a central role' (ibid., 105), and its popularity is partly due to 'the ease with which its programs can be inserted into those forms of oral culture which have survived in a mass, industrialized society' (ibid., 106). Television, then, is endlessly talked about, and, rather than being the antithesis of an earlier 'folk culture', it exhibits many of the qualities of that culture, with the additional virtue that, being a broadcast medium, it does not belong to a particular cultural group, but can be easily and differently incorporated into a wide variety of subordinate and resistive subcultures. In Fiske's account, the very qualities which make television such a culturally deadening medium for writers like Stephen Heath, become productive, not of an all-engulfing homogeneity, but of a liberating plurality and cultural diversity.

The *intertextuality* of television is another of the qualities that Fiske argues prevents any 'closing down' of its meanings. The television text, he argues, has always to be read in relation to other texts, both those within which it is embedded and to which it often refers, as part of television's 'flow', and those other 'secondary' texts – newspaper articles, publicity materials, magazines, radio shows, conversations – which inflect its meanings in a range of often contradictory ways. This is an argument also developed by Lawrence Grossberg, who argues that television programmes should be regarded not so much as texts to be read than as 'a space in which many different discourses, both serious and playful, appear' (1987: 31). Television is closer to the billboard than the story. It is, moreover, viewed always in the context of, and interrupted by, other social and media practices and domestic routines (reading, listening to the radio, chatting, cooking etc.), so that not only 'is it the case that the "same" text is different in different contexts, but its multiple appearances are complexly intereffective' (ibid., 34). Television, then, is not so much an ideological medium – its 'flow' makes it 'in-different' to ideology as it is to meaning – as an affective one. It appeals to the contemporary human subject whose identity is fragmented but constantly in process. Its 'democracy' is one of affect – of feeling – rather than of meaning, as Fiske proposes, but this 'democratic' quality makes it – as Fiske also argues – empowering for its viewers.

1.3 The Metaphors of Television

One of the most striking things about these accounts of 'television itself' is their highly metaphorical nature. In them, television is defined in a series of highly value-laden metaphors, and in turn becomes itself a metaphor, or metonym,[4] for contemporary cultural life. Peter Larsen defines one of the functions of metaphor as that of 'mapping'. Through spatial metaphors we ' "translate" complex situations into mental spaces; we divide troublesome phenomena into units; we "place" these units on various "locations" within a space' (1999: 118). In order to make sense of – to mentally 'map' – what Larsen calls an 'incomprehensible technology', then, we resort to spatial metaphors (flow, segmentation, the network, the billboard), and television in turn becomes the metaphorical space in which we encounter contemporary culture. We can identify three key forms which these metaphorical 'translations' of television take.

The first has been mentioned already. It is the use of television to stand in, in some way, for *America*. Both Williams and Heath see US television as the inevitable form of that 'totalizing fragmentation' (Heath) towards which television tends. In Grossberg's 'mapping of TV's affective economy' the key metaphor used to define television's functioning is that of the 'billboard to be driven past' on an American freeway: 'a space in which many different discourses . . . appear' (1987: 31). This is a metaphor carried even further by Margaret Morse, in whose account of 'television itself' it is the freeway itself, together with the shopping mall, that is analogous to television. The first of these analogies – with the freeway – picks up the metaphor of flow. The second – the comparison with the shopping mall – builds on the notion of segmentation: what Rick Altman has called the 'menu-driven' nature of television (1986: 45). Both metaphorically site television within the urban landscape of America. For Morse, all three of these cultural forms offer a form of 'derealized or *nonspace*' (1990: 197). The freeway is a displaced urban highway, disengaged from and seeming to 'float above' the American city which it crosses. The shopping mall, too, is 'completely separated from the rest of the world'. Unlike the city centre, which it replaces, it is a self-contained and privatised space whose spatial and temporal condensation offers the illusory promise of a journey through exotic spaces (the 'Mediterranean' village or the 'Indian' bazaar) and times past (the 'traditional' village square). Finally, television also offers this sort of dislocation from reality and 'derealized' experience. It, too, operates in a separated, dislocated realm and condenses – this time through audio-visually transmitted images – both space (television can 'take us' anywhere) and time (it offers representations of our past and our future). All three cultural forms are both highly regulated and privatised. In their consumer-subjects they create an experience of 'unanchored mobility', a sort of 'mobile subjectivity'. The state of mind produced by their dislocation from, but flickering engagement with, the reality 'outside', is one which 'can be described as *distraction*' (ibid., 202).

In Morse's description we can find echoes of a number of earlier accounts of television. The 'mobile subjectivity' which she describes echoes Raymond Williams's description of the phase of industrial development in which broadcasting appears as one of 'mobile privatisation' (Williams 1990: 26), and her account of the 'distracted' quality of the viewer's attention recalls John Ellis's description of television's 'regime of looking' as that 'of the glance rather than the gaze' (Ellis 1982: 137). For Morse, however, this conception of television is one which expands to take in the whole of contemporary American life. The analogues of television – the freeway and the shopping mall – she writes, 'are now undergoing a process of gradual convergence . . . with television itself'. Television screens, those purveyors of 'low-intensity dreams', are now found in malls and on the billboards that punctuate the freeway: 'It seems that soon one will have to speak of one great machine' (1990: 212).

Behind this identification of television with America we can already see the second of the metaphorical 'translations' referred to above: television as metaphor for postmodernity. Morse herself draws attention to this connection, comparing her own account of television's 'making the actual virtual and the virtual actual' to Baudrillard's postmodern 'simulations' (ibid.). Similarly, the theorists of the postmodern, Baudrillard, Lyotard and Jameson, provide the reference points in Stephen Heath's account of television. It is Baudrillard himself who makes this metaphorical function of television most explicit. Television is, he writes, 'the ultimate and perfect object for this new era' (1985: 127). In it, differences and distances are collapsed. There is no longer a separation between the real and representation; reality is orchestrated and produced by television. This is so not only in 'reality' shows like *Big Brother*, in which events, environment and relationships are constructed by, for and on TV. It is as true, argues Baudrillard, of the dramatic events played out on television news; these too 'are already inscribed in the decoding and orchestration rituals of the media, anticipated in their presentation and their possible consequences' (1994: 21). Representation, then, gives way to 'simulation' in which we have 'models of the real without origin or reality' (ibid., 1), and any reality which can not be absorbed into television seems like 'a kind of archaic envelope, a vestige of human relations whose very survival remains perplexing' (1985: 129). History is similarly effaced, becoming a random collection of images without cause or effect, absorbed into television's sense of 'total instantaneity' (ibid., 133). The separation of public and private is collapsed: 'the most intimate processes of our life become the virtual feeding ground of the media', whilst at the same time 'the entire universe comes to unfold arbitrarily on your domestic screen' (ibid., 130). Even the distance between subject and object is effaced, as we are absorbed into this world of the screen.

This nightmare vision of the collapse of the boundaries of the self, and the invasion of the body by technology in what Baudrillard calls a 'mutation of the real' (ibid., 30), is one which is familiar to us from the contemporary science fiction/horror film. David Cronenberg's *Videodrome* (1983), for example, presents precisely this scenario. Television, in the form of the brutally pornographic programme 'Videodrome', emits a signal which effects the double blurring of boundaries which Baudrillard describes. Its victims are rendered unable to distinguish hallucination from reality, but its effect on the film's hero is also to render him literally a 'switching centre'. In a bodily mutation, his stomach develops a slit into which a videocassette can be inserted and through which he can be penetrated/programmed. As Tania Modleski points out, this renders his body not only a postmodern 'terminal of multiple networks' but also a feminised body (1986a: 163). As she argues, this notion of the postmodern as a *feminised* culture is one which runs through all of Baudrillard's televisual metaphors. Here, then, is the third of the metaphorical 'translations' which characterise accounts of 'television itself': its use to describe a 'feminised' mass culture.

As Andreas Huyssen (1986) has pointed out, the identification of 'mass culture' with the feminine dates back to the nineteenth century. Indeed the substitution of the term 'popular culture' by cultural studies theorists, from Raymond Williams onwards, can be seen as an attempt not only to reposition contemporary cultural forms as the inheritors rather than the destroyers of earlier traditions, but also to rescue them from the stigma of feminisation by aligning them with a more 'robust' and masculine 'folk' culture. Huyssen himself concludes optimistically that '[m]ass culture and the masses as feminine – such notions belong to another age' (1986: 62), but it is clear that precisely such an equation is being made in the accounts of television described above. When Baudrillard describes the threat of the postmodern as 'too great a proximity, the unclean promiscuity of everything which touches, invests and penetrates without resistance' (1985: 132), he is describing the horror of a subject rendered feminine by television/postmodern culture. Similarly, the metaphors of 'ooze', 'flow' and 'saturation'; the accounts of television's 'menu-driven' nature and of its distracted, dreaming viewer; the descriptions of the suffocating closeness, the subject/object confusion, the excessive availability and empathy which it induces: all serve to identify television with an irrational, passive and consuming femininity.

In almost all of the accounts above, then, the task of the television critic is to reinstate distance and separation. As Jostein Gripsrud has observed, the 'flow' metaphor 'carries what seem to be two diametrically opposed images of the television experience: that of being swept away by an external force, and that of coolly and calmly regarding a river at a distance' (1998: 29). Although Gripsrud does not himself draw this conclusion, it seems that the first of these images invokes the threat of television, and the fate of that feminised 'other', its viewer. The second is the position assumed by its masculine critic – although he may occasionally also 'penetrate' the flow in his search for definitions. We can identify two exceptions to this critical stance. The first is exemplified by the work of John Fiske, whose accounts of television also attribute to it a feminine quality but who reads this as a subversive rather than a threatening characteristic (1987: 308). The second exception is provided by feminist critics, whose project has often been the investigation of the femininity ascribed to television. Thus Jane Feuer, Tania Modleski and Lynne Joyrich have all in different ways drawn attention to this ascription.

Tania Modleski has traced the identification of 'mass culture' with woman in the work of theorists from Marx to Barthes and Baudrillard, commenting that such an identification 'is hardly surprising since . . . mass culture has typically been seen as the realm of cheap and easy pleasure' (1986a: 163). In particular, she points to the way in which, for theorists of the postmodern no less than their modernist predecessors, the feminised 'masses' and the pleasures they embrace have served as an 'other' which is both 'monstrous' and endlessly fascinating and seductive.[5] The problem with this identification – even when, as in the work of John Fiske, it is presented as a theory of liberation or subversion – is, she argues, that it makes it 'much more difficult for women to interrogate their role within that culture' (1986b: 34). How, for example, can we analyse the varied and complex ways in which women are represented within television genres if television itself is seen as 'woman'? As Modleski comments, 'if women *are* the question, they cannot *ask* the questions' (ibid.).

For Lynne Joyrich, this identification between femininity on the one hand and television, consumerism and the postmodern on the other is one which pervades not only television criticism but also television texts. Women, she writes, 'are assumed to be the perfect consumers, devouring objects, images, and narratives just as they have been said to "devour" their loved ones' (1988: 145). But for Joyrich such an assumption is not confined to television critics and theorists. Television producers, too – who are overwhelmingly men – have a model of the audience-consumer as feminine.[6] Yet this is a model which can also invoke considerable unease, bringing with it as it does the 'threat of feminization' (1990: 163). In response, certain forms of television actively reject such a label, some seeking to 'achieve cultural status by mimicking the more respectable cinema' (ibid.); others celebrating within their narratives an excessive violence and 'maleness' which Joyrich calls 'hypermasculinity'. For Joyrich, then, the metaphors of femininity which have characterised accounts of television serve to obscure very real differences and contradictions within its texts.

1.4 Identifying Television Drama

Notions of 'television itself' have, then, posed quite specific problems for any discussion of television drama. The sense of 'nowness' that marks television has often seemed to assign an ephemerality to its texts which renders them unworthy of serious attention unless in the most general of terms. Until recently, indeed, television programmes were only rarely repeated, and many of the earliest examples were either not recorded or, where recordings did exist, not preserved. The continuous nature of television programming, its interrupted quality, and the dominance of the series or serial form, all add to this difficulty. How does the critic decide what constitutes the television text under discussion? Is it the single episode, the complete series (impossible in the case of soap opera and very difficult in that of the long-running series), the segmented, interrupted evening's viewing? In the case of the series or serial, how can textual meaning be ascribed when a long-running series or serial will employ teams of writers and directors whose composition will change?

This difficulty in determining the boundaries of the television drama text is compounded in other ways too. As writers from Raymond Williams onwards have observed, television's construction of a sense of a continuous updating is itself a form of *dramatised* flow. If all television output is, then, characterised by narrative and performance, or even, as John Fiske would insist, by 'fictionality' (1987: 308), how are the boundaries of 'television drama' to be drawn? In its own publicity, television is insistently generic, so that very few programmes are seen to fall outside established genre categories – 'drama', like 'sport' or 'news', is a category which is clearly marked. At the same time, however, television is also characterised by hybridity, so that new hybrid genres and sub-genres ('drama-documentary', 'docu-soap', 'comedy drama', the 'made-for-TV film') constantly appear. Such forms frequently blur the boundaries of 'fact' and 'fiction', the 'serious' and the 'popular', and television and film, in a way which has been seen by critics either as productive of contradictions and a potentially liberating polysemy (Fiske), or, alternatively, as erasing all differences in a stifling sameness (Heath). In either case, television drama as a specific object for analysis disappears.

If, then, as John Caughie has observed, writing about television has often been 'so caught by the fascination of the problem of "television itself" that it . . . cannot say anything about television in particular' (2000: 7–8), how have critics sought to identify a space for the analysis of something called television drama? One answer comes from a specifically British critical tradition. Julia Hallam has offered the following typology of approaches to the study of *British* television drama:

> Traditional critics trained in literary analysis tend to favour texts by acclaimed individual authors, works that provide a discrete focus for aesthetic commentary and stylistic examination; critics interested in politically challenging drama tend to focus on works that are in some sense oppositional to the general flow of popular generic products; and feminists trained in cultural and ideological critique who are interested in popular drama and its institutional contexts have favoured critical rehabilitation of 'feminine' genres such as soap and melodrama . . . (2000: 147–8)

We shall return to the question of feminist approaches later in this book. Here, however, we shall focus on the first two of Hallam's types of approach, for together they form a distinctively British response to the problem of constituting 'television drama' as a specific category for analysis.

As John Caughie and others have pointed out, the development of television drama in Britain has had a quite different history from that in the USA, protected as it has been by the ethos and regulatory framework of public service broadcasting. As a result, debates around possible definitions of 'quality' television, 'art' television or 'serious' drama have dominated discussions of British television drama. These are debates which have followed contours familiar from earlier – though still continuing – debates about British *cinema*. Just as British cinema was seen by critics of the 1940s to be a 'quality cinema', its 'quality' marked not only by the literary heritage upon which it draws but also, and more specifically, by the 'spirit of documentary'[7] which infuses it and which guarantees its 'realism', 'truth' and 'authenticity',[8] so British television drama has in turn been characterised as 'quality drama' in very similar terms. Just as the British documentary film of the 1930s was conceived of as both 'art' and 'social truth' (Grierson 1966: 215), so 'quality' television drama has been seen to embody both the creative vision of the individual artist and a politically oppositional and realist concept of 'truth'. And just as 'Hollywood' has frequently functioned as a synonym for all that 'quality British cinema' is seen to oppose and transcend, so American television, as we have seen, comes to represent the threat of saturation, flow and absorption against which British 'quality drama' must struggle. Writing in 1980, W. Stephen Gilbert makes precisely this case. For Gilbert, 'quality' television drama is the discrete single drama or 'teleplay', and such drama is threatened with disappearance. If this happens, he writes,

> [t]he loss to television will be incalculable. The slickness, conformity and blandness of television professionalism, 'giving the masses what they want', will have rendered television seamless. The unpredictability, unorthodoxy and disturbance of individual visions will no longer breach the schedulers' citadel. And there will be a loss to writing. Writers will no longer be able to address the nation. The 'true National Theatre', as the television play has been called, will be closed down. . . . And finally there will be a political loss. Where else on television can the diverse voices of others be heard? (1980: 43–4)

He concludes that with the loss of this 'unreverenced art form', British television will have abandoned its public service remit, with the inevitable result that the 'next metamorphosis will be the one that turns British television into American television' (ibid., 44).

There are a number of points to note in Gilbert's defence of this particular form of British television drama. First, its conception of 'art drama' is identified with the 'individual vision' of the writer, which is in turn aligned with a political seriousness and sense of public responsibility. Second, both stand opposed to the industrialisation and professionalism which mark the rest of television, a medium whose characteristics are presented in terms by now very familiar. Once again this form of television is 'mass' entertainment, slick, bland, predictable and above all 'seamless', a 'continuum'. What is different from the accounts of television 'flow' outlined earlier in this chapter, however, is that this form of television is seen here as an Americanised *other* to a specifically British television form which, though it may be situated *within* television's flow, is not *of* it. As in so many other accounts of television, Gilbert's metaphors invoke an opposition between solidity and flow. The British 'teleplay', he writes, will 'launch' its viewer on 'unfamiliar territory' (ibid., 36), outside the 'continuum' which is the rest of television. This form of television drama, it is implied, offers a refuge from the stickiness and fluidity of 'television itself', presenting television's virtual traveller with the solidity and materiality of dry land.

Such arguments are further developed in George Brandt's edited collection, *British Television Drama* (1981), a book which is, significantly, a collection of essays about television *writers*. Its contributors are concerned to rescue British television drama from the charge of trivialisation identified with television itself.[9] Such drama, they insist, 'matters. It is an important part of the culture of today. It merits critical attention' (Brandt 1981: 35). The argument has two aspects. First, the contributors seek to establish a distinctive television drama aesthetic. This has its key reference points both in the theatre (television drama 'retains an umbilical link with the theatre') and in cinema ('sometimes it's difficult to draw a clear distinction between films made for the large and those made for the small screen') (ibid., 32–3). Its distinguishing features are the sense of structure to be found in the single play, which distinguishes it from the rest of television output (ibid., 135), a 'sophisticated sense of dramatic values' (ibid., 32), and the ability to break free from the constraints of naturalism which television's insistence on 'nowness' imposes (ibid., 148). Thus the individual writer is celebrated for his ability (all these writers are men) to 'break the boundaries' (140), to disturb and 'make strange' established conventions, whether through stylistic excess, by an insertion of aspects drawn from non-drama traditions, or by the inclusion of non-realist elements. The most common point of comparison is the work of Brecht.[10]

The second aspect of this argument centres on the *seriousness* of such drama. Whatever means these writers use to disturb conventions – and many of them are seen to use comedy or music-hall traditions – they are characterised by their 'serious central intent' (Brandt 1981: 164). This 'ventilation of public issues' is viewed as 'one of the most valuable functions that television drama can perform' (ibid., 32). But the storytelling function of television drama, its ability to reach huge numbers of people, its capacity to get in close and to mix subjective and objective views, all combine to raise this concern with contemporary issues from mere commentary to something far more. The function of such drama, writes Brian Miller in relation to the work of Peter Nichols, 'is to help us to come to terms with life and its dangers', dangers such as the 'fragmentation of personality' or the contemporary division of life into 'self-contained and irreconcilable pieces' (ibid., 132).

Throughout these essays, then, we are presented with a narrative of the writer learning to move from being a servant of television, or an apprentice within it, into being 'its master' (ibid., 112, 143). In so doing, he creates a defined space for 'art' within television, a solid space within its flow, and it is this, and this alone, which is seen to constitute television drama. This is a vision which, not surprisingly, is shared by those writers who are the subjects of Brandt's book. Writing his own 'Preface' to his television plays in 1984, Dennis Potter comments that

> one of the many dilemmas of the would-be 'serious' playwright working in the small strand of television which still permits such things (and that's not in many places outside Europe, and no place as well as in Britain) is, straight away, how to show that there *is* a frame in the picture when most of the surrounding material is busy showing the picture in the frame. How, in short, to insist that a play is a play is a play: or how to *dis*orientate the viewer while he or she, and your work, is smack in the middle of the orientating process which television perpetually uses. (1984: 30)

A 'television play', he continues, 'is always in danger of collapsing into the ceaseless flux that surrounds it' (ibid.). Similar arguments were made by writers such as David Edgar, John McGrath and Trevor Griffiths, in a series of debates in the late 1970s and early 1980s which centred on the issue of how, exactly, to intervene effectively into the naturalised 'flow' of television. For Edgar and McGrath, the answer was to break the codes of naturalism, since, as McGrath argues, a naturalist form 'distorts what the writer is trying to say, contains it within safe limits' (1977: 105). For Griffiths, however, such techniques can only alienate the viewer, since when 'you're introducing fairly unfamiliar, dense and complex arguments into the fabric of the play, it's just an overwhelming imposition to present those arguments in unfamiliar forms' (1982: 39). Instead, it is the element of *performance* in the television play which, while pleasurable in itself, prevents the viewer from being drawn into any illusion of watching 'real life'. 'I have', writes Griffiths, 'to find ways both of allowing identifications and establishing critical distances from characters in action' (ibid., 40).[11]

Despite their differences, what unites these writers is a concern to *intervene in* the 'flow' of television. In a key phrase originating with Trevor Griffiths but also picked up by later critics,[12] what they seek to achieve is the 'strategic penetration' of television. The masculinity of the metaphor is not accidental. We have seen already how important metaphors of femininity have been in characterisations of television. In the critical tradition shared by Brandt's contributors and their subjects, television drama becomes a subject worthy of critical attention when it 'masters' or 'penetrates' that femininity. One result of this, as Madeleine Macmurraugh-Kavanagh and Julia Hallam have both pointed out, has been a virtual eradication of women from this category of 'quality drama', both literally, as Madeleine Macmurraugh-Kavanagh chronicles in her account of the exclusion of women writers from the flagship BBC series *The Wednesday Play* (1964–70) and critically, as Hallam has argued (see also Bignell et al. 2000). In Hallam's view, an emphasis on authorial innovation and intervention, together with the cultural status accorded to the notion of the 'playwright', has produced a British critical tradition in which female-authored drama is necessarily relegated to the margins, since it has so often tended to work with and through popular television generic forms and their pleasures, rather than in opposition to them.

It is a critical tradition which is marked not only by its exclusivity but also by its elegiac tone. This is particularly the case in Brandt's second edited collection, *British Television Drama in the 1980s* (1993), whose Introduction closes in Churchillian tones: 'British television drama will not disappear, nor will its quality decline overnight. But if some of the omens at the end of the decade are anything to go by, its brightest moments of glory in the eighties may prove to have been the golden glow of a setting sun' (1993: 17). Here the concern is not, as in the earlier volume, to make the case for *television* drama as an art form, but rather to distinguish *quality drama* from the rest of television. Once again, however, the definition is framed in both aesthetic and moral/educational terms: quality television drama is

> [d]rama as a mirror of life . . . ; as a reflection of real human concerns . . . ; able to relate individual experiences to an implicit moral structure and scale of values; able to broaden the viewers' sympathies beyond their normal confines, to lead them to a greater insight into interpersonal and social relationships, to educate their feelings (at all levels) through laughter, suspense, empathy or whatever, by means of images as well as words, and to do this in a form with a palpable beginning, middle and end. (ibid., 5)

The criteria for inclusion are wider in this second volume, with the 'authored' series dominating over the 'single play', and the popular series, the soap and the sitcom all making one appearance each. In these latter cases, however, the example chosen is marked by its 'serious' intent, and the focus is on the individual 'authored' episode. Only the essay on *The Lives and Loves of a She-Devil*, with its feminist stance and use of psychoanalytic, semiotic and postmodernist theory, strikes a discordant note.

A similar elegiac tone dominates a more recent collection of essays, *British Television Drama: Past, Present and Future* (Bignell et al. 2000), which brings together critical academic essays and contributions from writers, directors and producers of British television drama. There is a recognition here that '[c]ritical discourses on British television drama . . . have been constrained . . . by questions of authorship, realism and communicative effects', which has militated against its understanding 'in terms of other and more recently developed critical discourses' (2000: 81–2). Nevertheless – and despite the fact that individual essays do challenge these assumptions – the tone set in the Editors' Introduction is remarkably similar to that of Brandt's collection:

> At its best, television drama has provided not only a window on the world, but also a critical interrogation of it. Its willingness to say 'things that wouldn't normally get said',[13] however, meant ultimately that it signed its own death-warrant: it is no coincidence that the single play, the most radical form of television drama, disappeared from the schedules during the oppressively reactionary 1980s. (Ibid., 1)

Television drama is still for the most part identified with 'British television plays': the 'individual' authored text rather than the generic product; the 'elite' rather than the 'popular'; the British rather than the American. Its disappearance signals the loss of a 'Golden Age' of British public service broadcasting. The opposition is also – and again despite individual critical contributions – typically gendered. The writer David Edgar, for example, sets out what he sees as its defining characteristics: whilst 'free-standing non-genre single dramas and serials', he argues, work to 'keep the audience's muscles working', it remains the case that 'television drama has a natural tendency to biodegrade into soap opera' so that an otherwise active audience can 'on occasion . . . lie back and say I bring no agenda to this, do to me as you will' (2000: 77).

The most critically developed and sustained articulation of this British critical tradition is found in the work of John Caughie. As with the other writers discussed here, Caughie's concern is exclusively with 'serious drama', which he divides into three categories:

1. A category which derives from the theatre, and finds its classical form in the single play;
2. A category which is associated with cinema, and finds its most recognizable form in a number of the films commissioned by Channel 4;
3. A category which is more or less specific to television, and finds its forms in certain authored or adapted series and serials. (2000: 7)

Caughie acknowledges the problems associated with such a categorisation: the category of 'serious drama', he writes, 'operates to mark off a "legitimate" cultural territory within television from other areas which are not legitimated by the official discourses of cultural approval', and this can serve a cultural elitism (ibid., 3). His concern, however, is with the specific issues which this form of television drama raises, issues of 'the intellectual's relationship to the popular, the nature of authorship and creativity, the place of the text, and the possibility of a viewer who is neither distracted nor indifferent nor even resistant, but is engaged in both active and affective ways' (ibid., 6). Despite his caveats, however, the assumptions made here – about the relationship of 'authorship' to 'creativity', about the nature of a text, and about the kinds of texts which actively engage audiences – are familiar, as are the metaphors upon which he draws. Popular television is once again represented in terms of a journey through 'flow' ('voyages into strange environments'), whilst television drama becomes solid ground: 'a particular corner of the field of dramatic narrative' (ibid., 5, 8).

For Caughie, serious television drama was constituted as, and has remained, that which interrupts the flow of television: 'a kind of anchor-point within the evening (and perhaps within the week), which structured viewing in a different way and invited a particular kind of attention' (ibid., 34). Against a dominant form of television, which was identified by critics first with naturalism and then with postmodernism, (serious) television drama,[14] argues Caughie, is more properly viewed as modernist. Modernism, usually identified with the 'high art' of the early twentieth century, is characterised by its concern to disturb conventions in order to 'unfix . . . us from the conventions of the past'. Its disturbances are therefore at the level of both form and content, and it is marked by a 'current of ethical seriousness' which seeks to produce a critical distance in the spectator (ibid., 158, 167). As we have seen, precisely these aims have characterised British television playwrights and their critical advocates, though they have more usually identified them with 'realism' or 'non-realism' – or simply with 'quality'.

The modernism of television drama, however, takes a very different form from cinematic modernism, argues Caughie. In cinema both modes of identification and modes of disturbance are produced at the level of the visual and the spatial, through the image and the point-of-view shot, the cut or the montage sequence. But it is television's *temporal* conventions – its 'promise of endless flow' (2000: 138), its everydayness and segmentation – which are disturbed by television drama. Once again the difference between cinema and television is here seen as a gendered difference. Cinema, argues Caughie, has been theorised in masculine terms. Its pleasures and fantasies, its knowledges and prohibitions, its modes of identification – structured around desire and motivated by a sense of lack – have all been analysed using an Oedipal model drawn from psychoanalytic theory. Television's endless flow – 'providing, nourishing, invisibly mediating'– is in contrast maternal; its pleasures are those of the 'ornamental, the everyday and the feminine' (ibid., 138, 215). Typically, its narratives invite us, not into an intensity of identification and desire, but into 'flow and the interruptability of everyday space and time' (ibid., 139). A modernist disturbance of such modes, therefore, takes the form of creating in the spectator not a dislocation of identification but a 'detached engagement', 'the possibility of a space of engagement which is also a critical one' (ibid., 140, 139). Such possibility may be created through irony, through humour, through elements of the surreal, or – as Trevor Griffiths also argued – through an emphasis on acting as performance.

Whilst the medium may be feminine, however, the model for such a spectator, a model drawn again from Brecht, is revealingly masculine: it is 'a spectator who watches with the combination of engagement and detachment familiar to the aficionado of boxing – caught up in the conflict but able to assess the finer points' (ibid., 140). Caughie's project, then, is far from unthinkingly elitist: it is to reinsert television drama both into a wider British cultural history and into a set of theoretical concerns about the relationship of modernism to the popular. Nevertheless, its terms tend to restate a set of familiar oppositions: between television-in-general and that which is on but not of television; between television-as-flow and that which interrupts, anchors or 'penetrates' that flow; and between television-as-feminine, with its distracted viewer, and those 'authored' masculine interventions which invite a detached and critical engagement in the spectator.

1.5 Popular Drama

Other recent writers on television drama have sought to engage more fully both with the changing nature and multiplicity of forms of contemporary television drama, and with questions of audiences and the role they play in the production of meaning. John Tulloch's *Television Drama: Agency, Audience and Myth* (1990), as its title suggests, has precisely these concerns. For Tulloch *all* television drama should be viewed as a major site for the production of stories, or myths, about contemporary culture, and hence as a site of struggles over the meanings of that culture. It is this struggle, and the different ways in which it can be seen to operate within the institutions, the texts and the audiences of television, which is the focus of Tulloch's book. It is a struggle which he characterises as one between 'active agency' (whether of producers or of audiences) and the 'boundedness' of institutional structures which seek always to limit and contain (1990: 14).

For his definition of myth, Tulloch takes that offered by John Fiske. A myth, writes Fiske, is 'a story by which a culture explains or understands some aspect of reality or nature. Primitive myths are about life and death, men and gods, good and evil. Our sophisticated myths are about masculinity and femininity, about the family, about success, about the British policeman, about science' (1982: 93). The myths offered by popular television drama genres, argues Tulloch, act to complete the 'half-formed picture the viewer has of often unfamiliar sections of society' (1990: 69), and, as the villain is unmasked and order restored, they seem to resolve or dispose of social conflicts or contradictions in an ideologically acceptable manner. Popular genres, he argues, perform an ideological function in two ways. They allay anxieties about disturbing or potentially subversive aspects of contemporary society. But they also map out our social world in ways that conform to dominant ideological perspectives. Television drama 're-divides the social totality across differentiated bundles of genres' (ibid., 72), assigning some (the police series, the thriller, the legal or political drama) to the public sphere of masculinity, and others (the soap opera, the costume drama, the domestic comedy-drama) to the private sphere of femininity.

For Tulloch, however, such popular dramas are also the site of ideological struggle. This operates partly internally, in two ways. We can trace it first in the complexity and shifting quality of genres: the emergence of hybrid genres which cross public *and* private spheres and which feature strong female protagonists, for example, gives evidence of an 'unfixing' of concepts of gender roles. Secondly, it can be seen in the relationship between order and disorder which underlies the narrative pattern of each episode in the popular series. Excessive or disturbing elements may not in fact be fully excised with the return to order which marks each episode's close, but may leave us instead with a sense of problems unresolved. But such struggle can also operate in the relationship between popular dramas and their producers on the one hand, and, as Fiske would also argue, their audiences on the other. Even the most popular series, argues Tulloch, 'may offer institutional spaces for alternative or oppositional production voices; and action-dramas may carry an official discourse but be *read* differently' (ibid., 38).

Despite this shift in emphasis, however, roughly half of Tulloch's discussion is given to rather different issues of agency within the 'bounded' structures of television drama. Here again the focus is on the question of the 'strategic penetration' of these structures which can be made by the 'authored' television drama. The production processes of television drama, argues Tulloch, no less than their textual structures or audience interpretations, are 'the site of contestation and struggle *within and between* professional practices' (ibid., 181). Writers, directors, producers and actors may all contribute their 'signatures, working often collaboratively, sometimes in tension' (ibid., 185), with outcomes which may in turn do battle with the priorities of television controllers and schedulers – and much of the book is concerned to chart these struggles. Thus, despite his use of a Cultural Studies model, which sees television drama as *always* a site for cultural and ideological contestation, there remain the traces in Tulloch's book of an earlier set of oppositions. 'Authored' or 'quality' television drama still seems of a rather different aesthetic and political order from popular drama, a matter of conscious 'strategic penetration' rather than unconscious ideological struggle.

This sense is even stronger in Robin Nelson's *TV Drama in Transition* (1997), which is once again dominated by a sense of loss and an accompanying need to defend traditional criteria of artistic value: 'criteria of critical reflection on human life and its values in general' (1997: 230). Unlike earlier writers, Nelson takes the changing form of popular television drama as a central focus for his discussion. Such dramas are characterised by what he calls 'flexi-narrative':

> The cutting rate and the rapid turnover of narrative segments in all TV drama have increased exponentially. 'Flexi-narrative' denotes the fast-cut, segmented, multi-narrative structure which yields the ninety-second sound-and-vision byte form currently typical of popular TV drama. (Ibid., 24)

These dramas, he argues, have 'embraced the flexible sound-and-vision byte approach of the three-minute culture' (ibid.), and display all the hallmarks of postmodernity. Following the patterns established by advertising and the pop video, they raid both high and popular culture for their images, creating a 'collage of fragments' loosely woven into a segmented narrative which makes 'lifestyle' appeals to its consumer-audience. What is produced is 'flexiad drama', a 'circulation of signs' which 'appear to construct a recognizable world' but which in fact amount to 'nothing more than a simulation in Baudrillard's sense of copies for which there are no originals' (ibid., 86).

Viewers, segmented by lifestyle and targeted by market research, become consumers of superficial visual pleasures and vague nostalgia.

For Nelson, this postmodern 'flexi-narrative' is now the dominant form of television drama. Where earlier writers in the British critical tradition saw an unthinking naturalism as the 'flow' against which 'authored' drama must struggle, for Nelson this has been replaced by the visual and musical flow which characterises the 'flexiad' form. The opposing terms of value, however, remain unchanged from those set out by George Brandt or Dennis Potter. 'The very best TV drama', writes Nelson, 'makes you think. It stops viewers in their tracks, drawing their attention away from the knitting, the newspaper, the distractions of domesticity, to command attention' (ibid., 156). Using 'small but significant devices of dislocation', it distances viewers from their 'accustomed mythologies', submitting these to an 'ethic of truth-telling' (ibid., 157, 156, 147). Its focus is on social issues and its form is usually 'critical realism'; it is threatened with extinction with the disappearance of British television's 'public service ethos' (ibid., 231).

1.6 Identity and Television Drama

How, then, can we find a way of addressing television drama which pays attention to it *as* drama, not simply as 'television itself', but which avoids the kinds of value-laden dualisms (serious vs. 'flexiad'; British vs. American; critical realism vs. naturalism; modernism vs. postmodernism; 'strategic penetration' vs. feminised 'flow') that single out only certain kinds of drama as worthy of attention? The answer proposed by this book returns us to some of the ideas we encountered above, but within a framework that links them to concepts explored elsewhere in cultural, media and film studies over recent years.

John Fiske, as we saw, drew on the work of Roland Barthes to identify popular television narratives with myth as 'a culture's way of thinking about something' (1982: 93). Narrative, argues Fiske, is 'a basic way of making sense of our experience of the real' (1987: 128); it is a means by which we confirm or question our sense of social or individual identity. Elsewhere, Stuart Hall carries this idea further. Asked to think about his own sense of identity, he writes, 'I realise that it has always depended on the fact of being a *migrant*, on the *difference* from the rest of you'. As an immigrant to Britain, he adds, he was frequently asked, 'Why are you here?' His answer would take the form of a story – or rather, various stories, differing narratives of identity constructed for different audiences and at different times. The meanings and values attached to them would also shift, not only because they were told at different times, in different ways and to different people – with of course a different 'ending' each time – but also because of the ways in which they echoed or challenged more public narratives circulating at the time. Hall continues:

> Who I am – the 'real' me – was formed in relation to a whole set of other narratives. I was aware of the fact that identity is an invention from the very beginning, long before I understood any of this theoretically. Identity is formed at the unstable point where the 'unspeakable' stories of subjectivity meet the narratives of history, of a culture. (1987: 44)

This is true, he adds, for all of us: the public narratives which we encounter are always in some sense alien, not quite a fit with our own stories even as they invite us into the 'imagined communities'[15] which they construct. For all of us, then, accepting what Hall calls the 'fictional or narrative status of identity' (ibid., 45) means acknowledging that not only are our own identities constructed through narrativised representations (the stories we tell of and for ourselves, our fantasies, our memories). They are fixed and unfixed through our everyday encounters with public forms of representation: 'the narratives of a history, of a culture'.

As we have seen, television drama, in all its diversity and with all its hybridities, is a primary generator and the most everyday source of such narratives in contemporary culture. It is this fact which has produced anxieties about 'saturation', fear that firm identities and points of value are being lost, and the desire to rescue for serious critical attention that which is *not* fluid, unbounded and over-involving. It also, however, makes television drama a key site for exploring the usefulness of contemporary theories of identity, culture and representation. This is an approach which has been taken elsewhere in relation to film and to television in general,[16] but not in relation specifically to television drama. Boundaries, as we have seen, overlap and shift: film, theatre, sitcom, docu-soap and advertising have all been seen by the commentators we have examined as overlapping with television drama. This need not, however, be seen as a cause for anxiety or the occasion for a drawing of carefully policed boundaries. Rather, what it offers is the opportunity to examine the ways in which television drama – in all its diversity and complexity – can be theorised as a source of the public narratives which Hall describes: as constructing, mediating and framing our social and individual identities.

Chapter 2

Stories and Meanings

2.1 Narrative

Theories of Narrative

Narrative concerns the ways in which the *stories* of our culture are put together. The centrality of narrative to the study of culture and society is evidenced in the range of work in which narrative is considered pivotal. Structuralists such as Vladimir Propp, Tvetzan Todorov and Roland Barthes have emphasised the detailed study of narrative structures. Psychoanalytic approaches rely on narratives in order to interpret conscious and, more importantly, unconscious life. In Freudian and Lacanian clinical theory and practice, there is no past or unconscious without the stories which help this past to be understood. In the disciplines of genetics, history and medicine, narratives are associated with the method as well as with the object of research. Because 'narrative is such a fundamental cultural process', John Fiske suggests that 'it is not surprising that television is predominantly narrational in mode' (1987: 128).

Theories of narrative have become central – if often controversial – concerns in historical, political and scientific research. In the work of post-modern theorist and philosopher Jean-François Lyotard (1984), narrative has an *explanatory* function, providing a rationale for macro-global and micro-personal states of affairs. In some theories, gender and sex are understood primarily in relation to narrative. Ken Plummer's account observes how we all tell sexual stories (1995). And poststructuralist theorist Judith Butler sees gender and sex as linked to the conventions and performances of speech acts (1993, 1997a). Marxist critic Alex Callinicos acknowledges that there is no sense of history without some form of narrative (1997: 44–76). And in recent postcolonial theory, there are no identities without a story which gives a sense of shape, space and time to the people who embody the identities in question (Homi Bhabha: 1990). Narratives, as well as the *rhetoric* of narrative (its imagery, allusions and metaphors) allow the past to be understood (H. White 1975). Narratives can inform versions of the past and have the power to shape how the present might be understood in relation to them.

Stories and narratives *show* as well *tell of* the past. Without narrative, history becomes obscure, people less familiar, and space and time less clear. Narrative is not the past, and it does not make the past happen again. The BBC's *Dad's Army* is not the reliving of the Second World War; audiences do not live through the events of romantic-lesbian costume drama *Tipping the Velvet* (2002); and *The Buddha of Suburbia* (1993) is a reflection on, not a replication of, the 1970s. Nevertheless, narratives are the principal means by which the past is made intelligible in the present.

But narrative, because it is a human construction, and because it is something that is central to all social activity (we all tell stories), is also the principal means by which we understand the *present* time. 'Narrative is there', writes Roland Barthes, 'like life itself' (1977: 79). The understanding of the present also involves narrators and narratives. The fact that BBC Radio 4's *Today* is not quite the same as, for example, Radio 1's early-morning news bulletins, suggests that the events of *now* are presented to audiences in packaged and differently narrated (mediated) forms. Although 'live coverage' might give the illusion of seeing the events as they unfold, it is subject to processes of selection, editing, perspective, point of view, camera angle and institutional positioning. Two key dimensions of narrative, the syntagmatic and the paradigmatic,[1] mean that stories are placed in temporal sequences (syntagmatic selections) and located and peopled (paradigmatic selection) according to the demands of the genre and narrative aims. But these selections mean that live TV is never transparent or free of narrative conventions.

The Claims of Narrative

Before offering a summary of the elements in narrative structures,[2] we can note a number of key claims which have been made about narrative:

1. *Universality*: In 'Introduction to the Structural Analysis of Narrative' (1977), Barthes suggests that narratives are universal, common to all

societies, and take many different forms (oral, visual, filmic, televisual, written).

2. *Local and global*: Lyotard (1984) contends that narratives offer subjects and societies accounts of global-international, as well as local-personal states of affairs. Macro-narratives can take the form of explanatory accounts of the world, and micro-narratives can provide individual subjects with a sense of place, purpose, and meaning. But he also suggests that metanarratives or grand explanations of human experience (for example religious accounts) are giving way to a plurality of postmodern micro-narratives (personal voices from the margins).
3. *Structure*: Narratives or stories give a sense of shape to subjects' identities. They provide a sense of a beginning, a middle, an end, with endless junctions in between these three major time points. Yet narrative structures, because they are human constructions, can oversimplify the complexity and plurality of social life. There are only beginnings, middles and ends on the basis of the imposition of narrative, as opposed to natural, conventions.
4. *Identity*: The work of Jacques Lacan, particularly his 'The Function and Field of Speech and Language' (1989 [1977]: 33–125), suggests that it is in language that human subjects acquire a sense of identity. Although subjects always exceed narratives, language and narrative provide them with the means by which to make sense of identities. Yet the language of narrative can operate to undo identity, exposing its hybrid status.
5. *Diversity and difference*: No one narrative is able to contain the stories which make up a subject's personal, regional, national or international identities. Stuart Hall, drawing on deconstructive criticism, writes that 'identities are constructed through, not outside, difference' (2000: 17).
6. *Space, time and event*: The work of Edmund White (2001) and Michel de Certeau (1984) alludes to the ways metropolitan narratives and fictions give shape to how people live out their identities in space and time. Narratives are interested in the relations between time, space, sequence and causality. Yet narratives mean that events and time zones can be blurred, extended, reduced or ignored.
7. *Politics*: Postcolonial studies (Spivak 1987; Bhabha 1990; Said 1993) suggest that the 'universal' nature of narrative does not mean that stories are universal in their appeal. Some subjects are excluded, either by intention or by convention, from the narration of events. The

lives of some are narrated more than the lives of others. Some events are given more prominence in certain narratives than in others.

8. *Form and Fictionality*: Stories are not natural structures so much as they are social constructions which operate in relation to a whole range of narrative strategies. Stories assume a narrator and require a number of devices to take shape. Narratives always tell us about other narratives.
9. *Meaning*: Narratives are one of the principal means by which meanings are articulated. Frank Kermode (1967) writes of the necessity of stories and fiction in the understanding and construction of human cultures. If narratives promise meaning, post-structuralist and deconstructive criticism (Derrida 1978, 1991a; Butler 1993, 1997a) suggests that within narratives meanings are also *de*constructed; narratives break many of their promises; they remain incomplete; they require readers/viewers to produce meanings.
10. *Context*: The work of Valentin Vološinov (1996 [1919]) and Mikhail Bakhtin (1981, 1986) emphasises that narratives are made meaningful in relation to social, cultural, economic, political and personal situations. Similarly, the spheres of the economic, the public and the cultural are made meaningful in narrative forms. Feminist, as well as reception-based studies, have drawn attention to the importance of text on context, and vice versa.

Forms and Structures

Narrative, then, will concern a story and how that story is put together. But, as we have seen, this is not quite as self-evident as it might seem. Who tells the story (its *narrator(s)*) is distinct from the figure who wrote the story (its *author*). Within this basic scheme, further complications emerge. The author writes a story, but the readers and listeners are not the same ones who listen to or read the narrator's story. There will be an *addressee internal* to the narration (a *you* being addressed by the narrator), and an *addressee external* to the narration (an audience or reader), whose identity is never constant. This *literary* model is further complicated when it is mapped onto the study of television. Television does not use narrators as source of the narrative in the same way as novels. First- or third-person narrators in novels are usually more easily identified than their televisual equivalents. So camera angles, shots, sequences, and character perspectives will become important elements to identify in the television drama's narrative. Similarly, authors can be producers, institutions, scriptwriters, authors of a screenplay, and writing teams. Readers are viewers, listeners, audiences and researchers. Finally, if narratives aim at pleasure, as Barthes suggests, then these pleasures, too, are at some point encoded in the television narratives.

As with genre, much of the early work in the study of narrative is indebted to structuralist and formalist perspectives, particularly those associated initially with Ferdinand de Saussure (1974) Vladimir Propp (1968) and Tzvetan Todorov (1975, 1988), and later with Roland Barthes (1977) and Gérard Genette (1980). The more recent of these critics adopt an approach which pays attention to narrative in relation to how stories make *meanings* and how narratives operate to *encode* stories. Moreover, their work is interested in the impact that narrative structures have on the decoding of meaning. Barthes's work set out to highlight the details of the many components of meaning and narrative relations at work in texts. For Barthes, it is the narrative structures that give life and meaning to the text; and it is the text's internal dynamics, between plot, image and sequence, which connect with the text's systems of meaning.

Todorov's work helps us understand the dynamics of narrative structure. He proposes that all narratives operate according to a five-part structure, usefully deployed in the analysis of, for example, television police series, one-off dramas, and television science fiction. Beginning with what he refers to as *equilibrium*, a *disruptive* force destabilises the initial balance. This is followed by a recognition that the disordering event has taken place. Efforts are made at restoration, and a return to a different, as opposed to the same equilibrium, will be evident. This *resolution* indicates that *harmony* is restored. Whilst many genres no longer adhere to such straightforward or ideal structures, it can be seen that conflict and resolution inform many of the plots of popular genres or stories within genres. Much of the pleasure of soaps is their investment in climaxes, delays, deferrals and twists, which come between the beginning and the end of a story-line. Similarly, Vladimir Propp's categorisations of character (heroes, heroines, villains, fathers, helpers, donors, mentors) serve as labels in any schematic analysis of narrative and genre.

Further distinctions, especially those between the *content of the story* and its *shape* or *form*, are made by Vladimir Propp in his *Morphology of the Folk Tale* (1928a). Propp dissected and analysed the narratives of Russian folk tales into different morphological functions and spheres of action, and his narratological analysis still stands as a key method in the study of many cultural texts. In addition to the division between the content and shape of a story, Propp considers some key elements of the relations between character and action in narrative. In Propp's model, character is interesting not for the insights it provides into human psychology so much as for its *role* and *function* in initiating and establishing action or event. Whilst Propp's dissection of folk tales has been criticised for its functionalism, the formalism that characterises it is also implicit in the later work of European structuralism.

During the 1960s and 1970s, French structuralist and narratologist Gérard Genette, recasting earlier narratological distinctions, proposed three terms: *histoire* (story), *récit* (text) and *narration*. In the words of Rimmon-Kenan, *story* 'designates the narrated events, abstracted from their disposition in the text and reconstructed in their chronological order' (Rimmon-Kenan 1983: 3). *Text*, on the other hand, is 'spoken or written discourse which undertakes [the story's telling]' (ibid. 1983). In the text, 'events do not necessarily appear in chronological order . . . and all the items of the narrative content are filtered through some prism or perspective (focalizer)' (ibid.). *Narration* refers to 'the act or process of production' (ibid.). What these distinctions emphasise is that a story does not simply exist but is subjected to the formal changes imposed by a narrative (re)ordering of its elements, discussed in the analysis of *Tipping the Velvet* later in this section. Importantly, however, certain questions emerge for television studies: If narrative concerns *who* sees and tells the story's action, how is this realised in television?

'What', 'How' and 'Who' in Narrative

Genette's remains an important study of the analysis of narrative. He draws on a range of genres and shows how the key events of a story may be reordered by *narrative discourse*. The same story can be narrated in multiple ways so that there is no reason why the narrative discourse must start at the story's 'beginning'. 'Flashback' is a frequent device of television drama. In some popular television narratives (e.g. soaps, comedies), notions of beginnings and ends are problematic, even more so when viewed against the backdrop of television's constant flow. In telling a story, the sequence of the events may be changed, some minor events may be omitted, or the story may be shown from multiple as opposed to singular perspectives. BBC1 soap *EastEnders* famously had a number of versions for a story whose central element was the shooting of Phil Mitchell. The story, that Phil was shot, is not in doubt. *Who* shot him, *who* saw him being shot apart from soap's viewers, and *how* was this information divulged to audiences? These three questions indicate the appeal of narrative in popular drama.

Genette's work stresses the importance of *narrative position*, exploring how events narrated from one perspective are never quite the same when narrated from other positions. As with genre, narrative orderings of stories are never neutral, involving processes such as selection, deselection, cuts and edits. Sarita Malik, for instance, considers questions of selection in relation to the 'racialization of the black subject in television documentary' during the 1960s (2002: 35). Her argument that Black citizens were represented as undesirable neighbours, people who would bring a neighbourhood into disrepute (ibid., 35–55), has important bearing on this current discussion of narrative and narrative position. The audience, she writes, 'was encouraged . . . to read "the problem" [Black neighbours] from a White perspective', because the story's positioning was with the white neighbours (ibid., 47). Malik's points emphasise the ways in which audiences may be implicated in the persuasive power of narrative.

These observations can be considered in relation to *Tipping the Velvet* (BBC2: October, 2002; based on the novel of the same name by Sarah Waters[3]). The story concerns Nan, a young woman who falls in love with Kitty, an emerging music-hall star who is performing in Whitstable. Moving to London with Kitty and her manager, Nan realises that Kitty's feelings for her are not reciprocated. Nan instead finds love on the streets of London, first dressed as a man, and later living as a lesbian. The story as realised by the BBC is costume-based and draws heavily on the formulas and conventions of romance.

The distinctions between what, how and *who* narrates are not just matters of structural detail. Genett's notion of *narrating* is linked to 'who' narrates/tells the narrative. Who sees what happens, and are we invited to share their perspective? 'Who', then, can be thought of initially in terms of either (a) an *omniscient* or all-seeing perspective, or (b) a personal identity whose subjective perspective we share. Who audiences see and who they see *with* in narrative sequences such as those put together in *Tipping the Velvet* is thus of some importance, both in terms of *setting up* and *dismantling* identifications. To identify with an omniscient perspective is to share a different identity and position than if a perspective is limited to the gaze of a single character.

The audience's knowledge of any fictional world is, then, dependent on the telling of a story. Television drama both draws on and adapts the devices associated with written narrative fiction. Strategies such as voice-over, focalisation, montage, jump-cuts and long shots serve as visual replacements for techniques and strategies associated with fictional writing. In *Tipping the Velvet* the sense of an omniscient observer, or someone who can see the flow of the landscape at a glance, is achieved via the *establishing shots*, which present a picture of Whitstable. *Long shots* picture the coastline and more intimate *close-ups* introduce the characters who people this community.

The opening shots of the first episode immediately set up an opposition between this omniscient observer (represented by means of the silent long shots) and the first-person participant narrator (Nan). In order to generate the sense that audiences are accessing the public and the private spheres of Nan's world, the cameras use *eye-line shots*. In narrative fiction, a third-person narrator might represent the views and feelings of two characters in terms of their relations with each other. In television drama, eye-line shots perform the same function. In the opening two music hall scenes of Episode 1, the first shot shows Nan gazing at an object followed by a second shot in which audiences are shown the object of Nan's gaze, in this case Kitty. What is effective about eye-line shots is the way in which the first shot builds up a sense of anticipation and desire, and the second shot reveals the desired object. On the one hand, audiences 'share' Nan's view and subject position, and on the other, they are given the object of her gaze, the *other*. To 'share' Nan's view is not necessarily to agree with her or affirm her position. Rather, it is one of the ways in which television drama allows audiences to access the fictional reality and the dramatic action.

Barthes and the Analysis of Narratives

In his 'Introduction to the Structural Analysis of Narratives' (1977), Barthes details some of the key sequences and elements involved in the construction and reception of narrative. He makes clear that narrative and discourse, though not reducible to a 'sum of propositions' (1977: 85), are governed by units, rules and grammar (ibid., 82ff.). Like other analysts, he makes a key distinction between *what* happens (story) and *how* the happenings are represented (discourse). His work is considered here under five subdivisions.

1. *Information and action: vital and trivial*: Barthes distinguishes two kinds of action or information in narrative. What he refers to as '*nuclei*'

or 'cardinal functions' (ibid., 93) are *essential* pieces of information and action, necessary to the progression of the plot. *Catalysers* are what we might call satellite actions or information, elements which fill the space 'with a host of trivial incidents or descriptions' (ibid., 94). The connections which are built up between nuclei are thus of considerable importance, though what may seem trivial elements should not be dismissed. Consider the key pieces of data surrounding the shooting of Phil Mitchell in *EastEnders* (nuclei) and contrast this with information which, whilst it might not ultimately change the key events, is nevertheless relevant to our understanding and pleasure. Discussion of the narrative along these lines will be concerned with questions of substitution (asking how the action might change if undertaken by another character) and transposition (considering how the action might be viewed if seen through the eyes of another character).

2. *No characters without an action?* In Aristotle's theory of narrative, 'there may be actions without "characters" . . . but not characters without an action' (ibid., 104). Like Propp, Barthes considers characters not in terms of psychology but of the function, role or dramatic part they play in relation to narrative and plot actions (106–8). For Barthes, *character and action are inseparable*, the character all the time linked to a 'sphere of actions'. In *Tipping the Velvet*, the action is inseparable from the characters, principally Nan but including her family, her lovers, and how Nan perceives these relations.
3. *Reader–narrative relations*: The third level is narration itself (109). This part of Barthes's work is principally interested in the relations which the text sets up between producer (author, writer) and consumer (reader, viewer, spectator). In this third level of structural analysis, Barthes observes how the author, narrator and characters must not be confused or blurred as one entity. Fictional narratives are not dealing with real people but 'paper beings' (111), understood within the parameters set up by the narrative itself. That said, the world of nineteenth-century London as recreated in *Tipping the Velvet* is understood on the basis of Nan, and on the basis of her credibility as 'real' as opposed to her 'paper' status.
4. *Meanings*: The functions, actions and narration of the story and its discourse are not *outside* of society, even though characters and actions are fictional. 'Narration can only receive its meaning from the world which makes use of it' (115), writes Barthes. No fictional narrative is wholly separate from the realities of the world in which the narrative

circulates. And Barthes is in no doubts about the *political* and *ideological* zones in which narratives operate: 'Beyond the narrational level begins the world, other systems (social, economic, ideological) whose terms are no longer simply narratives but elements of a different substance (historical facts, determination, behaviors, etc.)' (115).

5. *Seeing*: In the final section of Barthes's analysis, he discusses the 'system of narrative' (117). The language of narrative serves the purposes of *articulation* (the joining and linking of actions) and *segmentation* (the separation and unlinking of actions). In narrative, he argues, actions and events 'may be separated by a long series of insertions belonging to quite different functional spheres' (119). He refers to this distance as the difference between *logical* and *real* time. Narrative 'does not show, does not imitate', argues Barthes (124). Narrative is not transparent; we do not 'see anything'.

This last observation of Barthes – that we do not 'see' in narrative – might seem odd: television is principally a visual and acoustic medium. However, Barthes's point is important. Television, though a 'visual' medium, does not picture the world in any straightforward sense. Rather, narrative offers meanings, codes and frameworks, and through its language (its systems of signs, images and internal references) narrative, in appearing to point to an external world, offers an interpretation of it. Television drama, then, is one way of 'seeing' the 'truth' of a story, but the story might well have been told as a documentary or as a news item. These problems of realism and reality in television are discussed in the final section of this chapter and in Chapter 5: 'Television Drama: The End of Representation'.

Narrative Complexities

Barthes's work sets out to highlight the details of the many components of meaning and narrative relations at work in texts. For Barthes, it is the narrative structures which give life and meaning to the text; and it is the text's internal relations, between plot, image and sequence, which connect with the text's systems of meaning.

Barthes is keen to stress that there is a connection between narrative and meaning on the one hand, and what, on the other hand, is referred to in later sections of *Image-Music-Text* as freedom and *jouissance* ([sexual] *pleasure*). But he stresses that narrative offers a limited freedom (1977: 123). Narrative's dual operations, its enabling and constraining dimensions, are taken up in the early work of Stuart Hall. The work of Hall (1973) and David Morley (1980) expands Barthes's model, showing how meanings encoded by producers are never simply decoded in any one way. Whilst these 'dominant' or preferred readings can never be ignored, there may be other readings which resist, contest or misinterpret the encoders' 'intention' as it is realised in the programme. The programme or narrative is subject to revisions which connect the decoding *context* of viewers with the encoded text.

However, during the period in which Hall and Morley were outlining and expanding their theoretical models, other observations about the function of television programmes reveal a growing concern about the negative impact of narrative. During the 1970s, B. N. Colby and N. M. Peacock (in John Honigman's *Handbook of Social and Cultural Anthropology*, 1973) expressed concerns about the *seductive* power of narrative. 'The subtle and undercover techniques of narrative as art, which do not obviously aim to control, may seduce people into letting their guard down', they write (Honigman 1973: 633). And they suggest that the 'rise of the mass media, which lend themselves more to stories than sermons' (ibid.), may well increase this power. Television's popular narratives are feared, then, for their seductive power: they 'might well assume increasingly important roles in social control' (ibid.).

During the 1980s, concerns about narrative were understood in relation to formulas, rituals and predictability. Sarah Kozloff's essay, 'Narrative Theory and Television' (1992: 67–100), notes some of the trends in American television narratives. She catalogues how the stress on formula and predictability limits narratives. Combined with appealing, pleasant, but standardised characters, functional settings, and narrative strategies which attempt to *naturalise* the discourse, narratives contain few if any surprises. She argues that American television functions like the fairytales analysed by Propp, where subject matter, situations and stereotypical characterisations have a nearly universal appeal (70–7). In the earlier version of her essay, she adds that it seems 'popular cultural forms are more rigidly patterned and formulaic than works of "high art" ' (in Allen 1987: 49).[4]

Anxieties about narrative are often related to questions of their effects on audiences, particularly their power to convince audiences of one reality above another. John Corner writes of the 'negative psychological, social, and political consequences often attributed to television narrative form' (1999: 50). He suggests that narrative structure in television 'frequently seduces the viewer into aesthetic relations with what is on screen (e.g. the pleasures of character, of setting, and of action' in ways which 'reduce critical distance' (ibid., 51). Narrative, he suggests, can oversimplify complexity, 'bringing into spurious unity what are more properly regarded as diverse elements of an issue' (ibid.). Finally, he contends that 'certain perspectives on events and circumstances depicted are given an epistemological privileging while others are subordinated, marginalized, or excluded' (ibid.). 'Engagement with the story and its characters entails a degree of alignment, however temporary, with dominant viewpoints' (ibid.).

There is no doubt that narrative is powerful. The mainstream narratives associated with the classic realist text (see Section 2.3), are often criticised for encouraging audience identification. Commentaries, often by way of letters to newspaper editors, suggest that identification with fictional characters in fiction and popular fantasies reduces 'critical distance': the world of the text, narrative or genre passes itself off as the only version of reality. Narrative can *seem* totalising, and observations about its liberatory potential ignore the ways in which narratives exploit identities. Soap operas, for instance, seem to offer no beginning or end and locate audiences in a permanent present. Despite differences amongst television dramas, standardisation is required because institutions, and not writers, set the terms of how the narrative will be put together for broadcast. Story-lines may be read in the same way, regulated by the form and not the readers or audiences.

The preceding arguments typify some of the criticisms of popular television narrative, and they have informed the research questions of a number of ethnographic studies that have sought to understand the relations between narrative, media form and audiences. Focus in this section, however, is placed on the extent to which the text itself is the site of its own deconstruction. Reader–audience relations are central to any deconstructive practice. Some evidence seems to suggest that texts themselves are never quite as formulaic or as overdetermining as the aforementioned criticism seems to imply.

Ien Ang's *Watching Dallas* (1985) shows how the American soap opera Ang discusses produces not uncritical readers, but ones who see in the television narrative a huge irony, something which opens itself up to mockery, and something which exposes rather than naturalises the workings of American capitalism during the 1980s. All texts can be read ironically, but the responses which Ang received in relation to her work suggest that any preferred reading the *Dallas* narrative might seem to demand was undercut by the text's implicit irony. Moreover, those groups who expressed 'hatred' for *Dallas* must surely count among those for whom the narrative was a seduction; the hatred must have been caused by something. If fantasy and narrative, writes Ang, do not 'function in place of, but beside, other dimensions of life (social practice, moral or political consciousness)' (1985: 135), then this seems to imply that texts – of all narrative kinds – are far less seductive and far more *provisional* in terms of their use, interpretation and circulation than criticism has suggested.[5]

The contradictions of the text (its narrative silences, its absences and its confusions) are discussed in the work of theorist Pierre Macherey (1978). He suggests, like Barthes, that texts are not secret puzzles, which contain final meanings. All texts, because of their very constructed status (in signs, images, visualisations), are read in terms of the permeable nature of these signs and not in terms of the centring hold of the author-producer. In all texts, Macherey argues, there is a 'conflict'. The conflict is not a sign of the text's 'imperfection' so much as it is evidence that the text, contrary to appearances, is 'generated from the incompatibility of several meanings' (1978: 80) What the text leaves unsaid, its 'unconscious', can in the reader's hands generate meanings. Rather than effacing ideology, narrative texts reveal its contradictions.

Television's narratives promote some versions of culture rather than others. Later chapters discuss how gender, race and sexuality have been represented. If we return, however, to Malik's observations about the representation of Black subjects in British documentaries of the 1960s, we can see that whilst they point to the dominant readings of 'race', she is also clear that these were being contested – albeit very slowly – inside and outside the media. The 'media space which Black people could potentially occupy', she writes, 'although highly regulated, had to be regarded as a significant site of struggle' (2002: 50). The television text is not a seamless whole able to *impose* its narrative so much as it is composed of competing – and often contradictory – elements.

Narrative Contradictions

This section concludes with a reading of *Tipping the Velvet*, where consideration is given to the ways in which all narratives set up their own contradictions. Although identification with narrators or characters might seem to offer the key means of entering the fictional world of narrative, the text's own narrative serves to deconstruct its naturalising appeal. Narratives, far from seducing audiences, set up more problems than they appear to solve.

The opening sequences of *Tipping the Velvet* employ a series of *jump-cuts*, where the editing creates a break so that the time and/or space is discontinuous. Continuity is provided by Nan's voice-over. She appears to prepare audiences for what is to be an intimate account of life in a fishing village. The scene is set for a romantic costume drama. Nan appears to ensure for herself a central place in the drama as its narrator and focaliser, someone with whom the audience will identify. In the opening three minutes, voices, songs, facial images, silences, blurrings of scenes, slow motion and dramatic anticipation establish that the space and time of the narrative are on one level uniquely the possession of Nan. They seem to ensure that it will be through Nan that audiences gain knowledge of this fictional world.

However, Nan and her story are only singular and unique when viewed alongside the multiple other narratives that compete with the story told in *Tipping the Velvet*. Insofar as the period being dramatised is set in the past, then Nan's story is a way of re-viewing and re-thinking this past, and understanding the culture of its subjects. A reading that attends to the text's reworking of the past might be interested in the text's historical accuracy far more than Nan's identity. But how accurate is this past if its central focus is not the nineteenth century but an account of lesbian sexual cultures? The 'accuracy' of the text's historical setting, moreover, is problematised by the impressionistic and surreal style of this BBC romance. The text's accuracy is in part reliant on, but also problematised by Nan. She is not in a position to 'see' everything. In identifying with Nan, audiences must now accept a limited and not a comprehensive insight into this fictional world. *Identification* with Nan also assumes *identifying* with her lesbian desires at some point. Even if this is also a narrative which describes nineteenth-century sexual cultures, is not any perspective a limited one? Identification with Nan on the basis of her views and motivations necessarily entails limitation: she is only *one* character in the narrative.

The drama's initial stress on identity (audiences learn fairly quickly that Nan is 'lesbian')[6] means that the costume-drama genre or historical periodisation might be less important than the sexuality and same-sex passion which the three episodes depict. Apart from anything else, Nan is only ever understood in the intersubjective field upon which the narrative relies. From the outset, this is a narrative which builds up an identity (Nan) only to make identification with her increasingly difficult.

Over-the-shoulder and point-of-view shots seem to ensure that audiences will feel and think from Nan's perspective. When Nan looks out from the carriage to the London buildings and streets, audiences 'see' Nan's view, almost as if looking over her shoulder. But Nan, now fast changing into the 'Tom' of Episode 2, wanders the streets dressed as a man; shots of Nan-Tom walking though London streets are mixed with Nan's voice-over commentary, but this is now a commentary which seems detached from the drama's 'real-time' action. With whom do audiences now identify? Which *characters* (Tom, Nan or the voice-over) seduce the audience? Are we seduced by a *lesbian* or a *rent boy*? Is the seducer finally a seductress, a disembodied voice, or the institution which made the programme?

These questions are not meant to trivialise how narrative identifications occur or to undermine critical work which stresses the degree to which narratives may seek to impose a particular world-view. But they do show how the text itself establishes its own difficulties. As the work of Barthes and Foucault shows, the text's formal features are themselves bound up with ideologies, histories and myths that are never neutral. But the particular inflections and emphases of the text's form (its signifiers) are always unstable, never able to contain a final meaning. Postcolonial theorist Gayatri Spivak, influenced by Marxist, feminist and deconstructive criticism, has suggested that all texts rely on metaphors or connections which also point to the gaps and fissures in the text. These gaps are as important as the apparent closures to which the text might seem to lead because they take readers and audiences in plural as opposed to singular directions. 'In the process of deciphering a text . . . we come across a word that seems to harbour an unresolvable contradiction', she writes (Spivak 1976: lxxvii). In attempting to locate or fix meaning, Spivak argues, we find only further 'concealment' 'self-transgression' and 'undecidability' (ibid.) Thus in all acts of decoding, audiences attempt to stabilise what a text means on the basis of gaps it leaves. Whilst audiences may exercise determination in the construction of meaning, this is always in relation to a text which is unable to establish its own completion.[7]

Tipping the Velvet, then, can be read as a costume drama, a historical romance, a story about women who love other women, a narrative about a history which has often been hidden from dominant accounts of Victorian Britain, or an account of middle-class and working-class lives in late-nineteenth-century England. Using formalist methods, we can analyse it in terms of story, discourse and narration. Judgements about narrative structures, as Barthes observes, also concern questions of viewer–narrative relations and meaning. Television narratives visualise and construct meanings, and they do so in relation to historical, social and political context. Finally we can note that they also solicit pleasures: of watching, of listening and of understanding. Some of these may function to confirm our sense of our own and society's identity. Others, however, may lead us in very different directions: towards unexpected identifications and unanswered questions.

2.2 Genre

Genres are one of the ways in which texts are made available to readers, viewers and listeners; they are one of the ways in which meanings are packaged and classified; and writers, directors and producers use genres in the fictional and factual representation of reality. Graeme Turner summarises genres as 'the product of a text- and audience-based negotiation activated by the viewer's expectation' (2001: 7). In the case of popular television genres, audiences know what to expect regardless of the inflections and twists in each genre variant. Working within the constraints of a genre, writers are required to follow a specific series of guidelines, and accompanying notes instruct 'authors' in the writing of the finer details of romantic, thrilling or domestic conflict.

The production and consumption of many *popular* genres (paperbacks, film, television) is connected to the changes in industrial production which occurred during the twentieth century. But genres themselves go back much further. Indeed, despite the criticisms to which popular genres have been subjected, none of the generic formulas discussed in this chapter are 'new'. The many contributors to *The Television Genre Book*, (ed. Glen Creeber 2001), as well as writers such as Patricia Holland (1997), Nick Lacey (2000) and James Watson (1998), all draw on traditions within early twentieth-century Russian, French and classical Greek criticism in their accounts. But mass production, as well as the increasing stress which was placed on the division of labour, specialisation and consumption, impacted on notions of good taste, literary quality, aesthetics and culture, and this has led many critics and commentators, including Q. D. Leavis (1978), Theodor Adorno (1997 [1944]) and Herbert Marcuse (1972) and, more recently, Jim McGuigan (1992), and Kate Soper (1999), to connect questions of genre with issues of *value*.

Definitions

Genre (meaning classification, group or type) is a term used to designate a specific *kind* of fictional, dramatic, filmic or visual-artistic text. *Genre* serves to categorise texts as, for example, situation comedy, science fiction, romantic comedy or police drama. Texts are not simply *texts* but come in bundles and groups, and these groups are laden with meanings and functions. Carolyn Miller (1984), for instance, argues that the more complex a society, the more compartments needed for genres. Film noir, soap operas, westerns, teenage gothic, and romantic comedies suggest something of the breadth of generic and subgeneric compartments. *Genre* also serves a critical purpose, operating as a way of *classifying* the text in question. Such logic implies that texts have to be formally classified, and that there are universal definitions both assisting and ordering our understanding of genre. This is not a new process and it is a heritage which television acknowledges in its own output. 'Each narrative genre has its own set of established conventions', writes Holland (1997: 125). 'Genre critics', writes Rick Altman, depend on 'careful adherence to classical standards, not only in terms of genre separation, but also in terms of rule-based creation' (1999: 16–17).[8]

Nick Lacey suggests that 'the best starting point' in identifying genres 'is to list the following: types of character, setting, iconography, narrative and style of the text and then consider whether it fits into any genre' (2000: 136). Similar listings and definitional outlines are proposed by Graeme Burton (2000: 86–94), Watson (1998: 137–42) and Holland (1997: 153–9). Though insisting on the complexities of genre, Altman and Steve Neale (2001; 2002: 1–10), both distinguished genre scholars, also suggest that classifications of genres are one of the necessary starting points for the understanding of televisual and filmic output. In *television drama* (as opposed to soaps, situation comedies, or children's entertainment) the contributors to *The Television Genre Book* (Creeber 2001) identify the single play, the western, the action series, the police series, hospital drama, science fiction, drama-documentary, the mini-series, costume drama, the teen series and postmodern drama as the key variants within this broad category.

Schemes and Structures

These schematic approaches, with their stress on the form, design and meanings of genres, are not being called into question here. But this chapter also underlines the problematic relationships genres set up and assume concerning *subjects* and *identities*. The identities of the audience, and the age, ethnicity, gender and sexuality of the subjects who constitute these audiences, are not solely connected to the marketing or production aims of institutions. Ethnographers and critical theorists of the media are interested in *why* people watch what they do. Television genres, moreover, are connected to debates surrounding the effects, rituals and activities associated with television viewing. The repeated naturalisation of one view of the world in popular genres can serve to depoliticise pleasure; genre boundaries offer closed worlds; and editing and selection mean that some groups never enter television's representational space. Media research of the last 25 years[9] has established that television is in a position to define social and political realities. Television genres, whether factual or fictional, matter because of their ideological power.

Television is classified in terms of genre, indicating its reliance on identity categories. Genres, moreover, are not extricable from the institutions that make and produce them, and the genre will easily be modified, changed or abandoned in the interests of market-led or market-shaping drives. 'Institutions act to interconnect funding, product [television genre], and use', writes John Corner (1999: 13). But media research also documents the complex interoperations between audiences and output (Radway 1987; Morley 1992). And the context in which the genre is being received or consumed will also be important in how it is used. Steve Neale draws attention to the 'systems and forms of publicity, marketing and reviewing that each media institution possesses' (Neale 2001: 1). Such processes play a 'key role in generating expectation [and] also in providing labels and names for its genres and thus a basis for grouping films, television programmes, or other works and texts together' (ibid.). However, the generic names and labels to which Neale refers criss-cross each other, and so an initial detailing of these features will be followed by discussion of the codes and controversies surrounding genre.

Some Key Features

In general terms genres are characterised by their repetitive and formulaic structures (see Altman 1999: 1–11; Neale 2001). The repetitive nature of the genre (and some popular narratives) suits production and institutional aims, though disruptions to these repetitions, or the construction of hybrid versions, can intensify market demands (e.g. docu-soaps, docu-dramas; see Corner 1999: 12–23, 70–9). Some genres have fixed or allocated timeslots in the weekly TV listings schedule, helping to generate and inform audience expectations. British terrestrial channels are associated with specific variants and attend to different audiences (e.g. Channel 4's *Hollyoaks*; ITV's *Coronation Street*; BBC1's *Neighbours*). An 'authored drama' (e.g. Lynda La Plante, Dennis Potter, Andrew Davies) will impact on audience expectations differently to popular generic forms (e.g. hospital drama). Narrative structures in authored dramas will tend to adopt more complex or extended structures than those in popular genres. Genres may adopt mini-series format (e.g. BBC's *The Buddha of Suburbia*, 1993), extend over two or three nights in succession (e.g. ITV1's *Prime Suspect* – discussed later in this book), or may be a two- or three-hour one-off production (see Creeber, *The Television Genre Book*, 8–43).

Popular genres (e.g. situation comedies, soap operas, some hospital dramas) occupy 30 to 60 minutes of air time, work with character stereotypes, and do not usually abandon the set times and days for the broadcast. Whilst some genres use institutional environments (hospitals or police stations) in order to anchor narrative, other genres (e.g. situation comedy) are sited in the home and revolve around plots and situations to do with class, gender or power conflicts (see Feuer 1992, 2001). In the case of comedy, but not exclusively so, characters are deployed on the basis of stereotype or oppositional character traits; narrative and plot operate with climaxes, critical twists or moments of suspense in order to ensure the success of the genre as well as the ritual associated with watching the next instalment. Comedy and romance tend to rely on social stasis or fixity, with little dynamism in terms of character, situation or relationships, though some variants adapt or radicalise the form in relation to these last three variables. Although tending to stay with genre-specific formulas, some genres will interweave elements of one form (e.g. tragedy) within the dominant mode of, for example, comedy (as in the final episode of BBC1's *One Foot in the Grave*, October 2000).

Genres construct characters who function in relation to *audience identifications* in both positive as well as negative, antagonistic ways. A traditional heroine or hero will not be flawless. Similarly, an antagonist, criminal or enemy will not be without redeeming features and thus will attract audience sympathies. Characters and the sphere of events are inseparable and are often constructed around plots, themes and identities which are informed by and exploit myths of everydayness, family values, morality and the potential for human goodness, connection and justice. Efforts are made at restoration, and a return to a different, as opposed to the same equilibrium, will be evident.

Codes: Roland Barthes and the 'Typology of Texts'

Roland Barthes's important discussion of codes in his *S/Z* (1970; trans. 1974) also draws attention to how codes operate in cultural texts. He suggests that five 'codes' shape how such texts are consumed. The *hermeneutic* code refers to the ways in which a narrative will always be concerned with establishing a 'question' (1974: 17). Detective series or soaps involve the resolution of an enigma or a personal relationship, and such tensions are pivotal to the programme's construction and pleasure. All genres revolve around some form of interpretive or decoding activity on the part of the audience; the hermeneutic code concerns how audiences discern and arrange the details of the text, usually with the aim of gaining some insight into the plot's resolution.

The *semantic* code refers to the ways in which a text sets up its own internal networks of meaning (connotations, metaphors, sets of reference). As Jonathan Culler writes, it 'provides cultural stereotypes (models of personality, for example) that enable readers to gather pieces of information to create characters' (1983: 84). Characters in the BBC's *The Royle Family*, for example, are linked to certain behaviours, actions, language and mannerisms which then trigger expectations amongst other characters as well as audiences.

Barthes's third code is the *symbolic* code. Barthes highlights how objects, colours, language and images become associated with certain characters. These links between symbol and character connect the symbolic representation of, for instance, morality or goodness with a character in the story. In Channel 4's *Queer as Folk*, specific tunes, objects and bars are associated with one character and not another. Stuart's car, his flat and his workspace are associated with consumer cultures, affluence, desire and pleasure. The symbolic domain of Stuart, however, contrasts with those linked to Vince, Nathan or Stuart's family.

The fourth category is the *proairetic* or action code. Here Barthes draws attention to the importance of what happens in stories, particularly in relation to sequence, logic, chronology and causation. The proairetic code enables audiences to draw on familiar models of behaviour or motivation (e.g. audiences are familiar with the dramatisation of the rituals surrounding a murder, a surprise party or bank robbery). It also reinforces generic conventions. It is unlikely, for instance, that a programme such as BBC1's *Spooks* (2002–), whose slogan 'MI5, Not 9 to 5' captures its interest in espionage, detection and national security, will have actors leaving government buildings in the manner of characters in comedy or musical genres.

The *referential* code is the last of Barthes's categories. It refers to how a text operates in explanatory, informative or illustrative ways, extending out beyond itself to point to all the cultural references upon which the text relies. The genre's referential or cultural code will offer explanations about culture and the (often) taken-for-granted practices of everyday life. But these referential codes also assume an authority outside the text. In BBC1's *Casualty,* for instance, a whole range of assumptions about the culture of hospitals as institutions, about the hierarchies among medical practitioners, and about the status of scientific knowledge are built into the genre.

Genre, Codes and the Meanings of Class

In all genres, these codes will be at work, providing initial and evolving clues as to the generic identity of the narrative. Their success or failure in constructing believable realities is measured by the way audiences respond to the genre. The genre and audience research of Ien Ang (1985), M. E. Brown (1994), E. C. Reid (1996) and Ellen Seiter et al. (1996) variously assess the impact genres have on subjects' lives. Despite concerns over the 'seductive' power of narratives and genres to 'reduce critical distance' (Corner 1999: 51), other evidence suggests that genre audiences 'commute with considerable ease between a referential and a purely fictional reading' (Seiter et al. 1996: 147). But Barthes's codes are not simply about understanding the genre so much as comprehending how these codes operate in relation to the encoding of cultural identities.

What is important, then, is *why* the codes of the genre matter in the first place. In Barthes's view, individual subjects are 'a plurality of other texts, of codes which are infinite' (1974: 10). If genre is concerned with the production and encoding of identity, then its codes take on greater significance because of the way all identities are implicated in society's power relations. Barthes's analysis underlines the ways cultural texts are encoded as containers of meaning. Meanings in culture invariably concern identity at some point. Identity categories arising from social class, ethnicity, gender, power, age and region will be figured in a genre in relation to setting, location, characters, voice, plot and so on. Institutions and producers rely on such generic classification. We can see how this works through a brief examination of BBC's *The Royle Family* (1998–2000). The popularity of this 'comedy' (written by Caroline Aherne, with Craig Cash,

Henry Normal and Carmel Morgan) ensured a swift move from BBC2 to BBC1. The series' downbeat setting, somewhere in Greater Manchester, is the Royles' terraced council house, audiences seeing one living room and a kitchen. The characters remain seated, the television is always switched on, and strained silences or lapses in conversation are filled by the television dialogue. Character dialogue always takes place with the television as intermediary. The camera position is invariably fixed, and the series is almost wholly shot without leaving the sitting room.

Questions about the identity of this 'working-class' family will relate to how the BBC deployed generic codes in order to make the family both credible and funny. Examination of the series' referential systems, or its way of drawing on cultural and semantic codes, will show how they represent class, gender and region. How different is the series from a docu-soap, for instance? How accurate is its picture of how working-class families live compared with a documentary format? Are 'Mams' and 'Dads' really like Barb (Sue Johnston) and Jim (Ricky Tomlinson)? Or is the series more concerned with how working-class families *used to* live? By focusing on questions of class identity, then, the series is, by implication, raising further questions about British identity. In addition, the series is necessarily implicated in discourses of gender and age, and patriarchy and sexism. Jim never really moves from his armchair, Barbara and teen-son Antony (Ralf Little) listening to his complaints and usually making his cups of tea. Daughter Denise (Aherne), and boyfriend (then husband) Dave Best (Craig Cash), complete the main characters in the family. Family antagonisms, between Barb and Jim, and between Denise and Antony, add to the series' domestic comedy.

The series' success is in part because of its deployment and encoding of the myths of northern and working-class life. But the show's location within the genre of comedy is crucial. Jim's coarseness and vulgarity, or Denise's laziness, would be subjected to alternative and possibly hostile audience readings if generically packaged in docu-soap or documentary. Jim sits all day; and Denise criticises her brother, repeatedly exploiting her mother's emotions. But these behaviours are acceptable because comic. At the same time, the scenes of personal intimacy which the series employs mean that its representations of class, gender and ethnicity do not raise the same sort of questions and concerns as, for instance, the 1960s–1970s comedy series *Till Death Us Do Part* (BBC1), on which *The Royle Family* is loosely constructed.

In *The Royle Family*, speech, accentuation and dialectal markers make clear the comedy's northern and working-class frames of reference. Its popularity is in part connected with *The Royle Family*'s reference to working class family values, domesticity and marriage. However, it also assumes knowledge of contrasting myths surrounding, in this case, the Royal family, *southern*, and *middle-class* identities and values. The setting is Greater Manchester, for example, and not Hyacinth Bucket's address in BBC1's *Keeping Up Appearances* (1990); the Royles' is a terraced council house and not the leafy-suburb location of the Edwardian terraced villa of *My Family* (BBC1, 2000) or the Southwark terrace of *This Life* (BBC2, 1996); and the spoken language inflects the north as opposed to Standard English and the hints of RP (Received Pronunciation) featured in the latter two series. Thus analysis of the series will be concerned partly with the accuracy of its representations of working-class life, but more importantly with the ways in which its use of comedy serves to naturalise some of the myths associated with white, working-class family values. The codes of genres are never simply about matters of style, and point to the political and ideological dimensions of genre.

Conflict over Genre

Some critics suggest that the traditional distinctions between genres are collapsing, making way for new classifications. Film theorists David Bordwell (1989) and Robert Stam (2000) point out the diverse, potentially endless ways films are categorised. Categories may relate to narrative structure and style (e.g. film noir), or to historical concerns (e.g. whether or not the film is *Reaganite*; Bordwell 1989: 146–8). Recently, for example, television output has been spoken of as *pre- and post-9/11*. For Stam (2000: 14–16), genres can be drawn from literature, may be story-based, or might be influenced by changes in technology (e.g. the musical), or changes in social structures (Stam cites 'Queer cinema'; see also Feuer's 'The Gay and Queer Sitcom (*Will and Grace*)', 2001). Moreover, both Bordwell and Stam suggest that any theme will do, no matter what the genre, subgenre or other division. Yet Patricia Holland (1997), commenting specifically on TV genres, seems to suggest that thematic categories are not as diverse as the work of Bordwell and Stam might imply. Although audiences may watch programmes in different genres, for programme makers and producers, 'the division is much more rigid. Jeremy Tunstall contends that "producers are locked into a genre-specific world" ' (in Holland, 1997: 18–19). What the film and television critics seem to agree on is that '[f]amiliarity with a genre means building up a set of expectations about a programme's style and content, both on the part of the producers and on the part of the regular audience' (Holland 1997: 19).

Historically, it was literary output that was grouped under the three key formal headings that divided drama, poetry and prose. Of course within these broad arrangements, further subdivisions existed. *Greek* drama, for instance, is *classically* described and defined as comic or tragic. Tragedy and comedy follow specific paths and pursue different aims. In Aristotle, the tragic plot is designed to arouse pity and fear, leading audiences to experience some kind of catharsis or cleansing. More commonly today, popular cultural texts are listed and promoted as thrillers, romances, soaps, sitcoms or horrors. Within these categories, further subdivisions proliferate: teen soaps (*Hollyoaks*), anicoms (*The Simpsons*), police psychological thrillers (*Cracker*), and so on. But television genres are also texts which provide pleasures. Barthes comments: 'There is supposed to be a Mystique of the Text. On the contrary, the whole effort consists in materializing the pleasure . . . in making the text *an object of pleasure*' (Barthes 1993b: 412).

Popular Genres and Popular Cultures

The pleasures of generic and narrative texts, as noted earlier, are not without controversy. Summarising some of the debates surrounding the pleasure of popular culture, Kate Soper (1999) suggests two lines of reasoning. On the one hand, and at its 'rudest and crudest', is the argument that 'the vast majority of programmes put out on TV [are] crap' (1999: 70). Since 'Adorno's day, the crap has got crappier, the banality more banal, and the ugliness uglier' (ibid.). On the other hand, she writes, is the argument:

> that talks about the problems attaching to the relativization of aesthetic value; of how, while recognizing the inadequacies of the erstwhile academic pieties about intrinsic literary merit and the eternal verities of the text, one may yet defend the fairly obvious literary merits of Hardy or Dostoevsky over James Herriot or Jeffrey Archer; of how to present a given text or artwork as more or less progressive from a feminist or post-colonial point of view if all conceptions of the good life are deemed to be on a par. (Ibid., 70)

In Soper's account, some versions of cultural study are figured as relativist: any text will do in the analysis of culture; its content and rhetorical structures do not matter if the text is able to bear (contain) some meaning – however unimportant – for audiences. Soper is anxious about theories of media and cultural production which privilege the *popular* (figured in her argument with Herriot and Archer) over and against the canonical (figured here as Hardy or Dostoevsky). Herriot writes according to popular formulas; Hardy writes in accordance with some sense of literary merit.

Soper connects this relativism with media manipulation. If the formulaic genres and narratives of popular television are not subject to critique, then media institutions are in a more powerful position to produce 'crap' programmes, manipulate audiences, and ultimately make money for a small group of media managers. Linking popular television, which is considered 'crap', with notions of media manipulation, Soper is concerned about the role of the media theorist and critic, and, by implication, about the function of media studies. She is deeply concerned by the 'extent to which *we* [students of culture and media] can consistently dispense with any theory of media manipulation and co-option, any *Ideologiekritik*, any "true"/"false" needs distinction, and still lay claim to be offering some professedly emancipatory engagement with cultural production' (ibid., 70–1; our emphasis).[10] In Soper's view, then, cultural criticism, media theory and the study of popular television *should* be tied to an emancipatory project in which cultural output is assessed on the basis of *form* and *content*. More specifically, Soper believes that it is the task of those involved in the study of media and culture to expose the workings of power in culture by analysing the texts, exposing the extent or not of media manipulation, and ultimately be in a position to adjudge which text best serves the purpose of cultural critique (described in her argument as *Ideologiekritik* and linked to cultural emancipation).

Soper's arguments surrounding popular television are persuasive. Adorno and Leavis, moreover, though approaching the debate from different angles, are similarly concerned by mass culture. More recently, work by Francis Mulhern (2000), Terry Eagleton (2000) and Rosemary Hennessy (2000) has argued for the continued importance of some form of *Ideologiekritik* in the analysis of culture. In the sphere of television drama studies specifically, critics such as John Caughie (2000: 1–24, 226–33), Robin Nelson (1997: 2–10, 30–2) and G. W. Brandt (1993: 1–18) present arguments which are underpinned by an apparent commitment to notions of quality, authorship, creativity and innovation. Brandt makes clear his central commitment is to 'the question of value' (1992: 3). Placing 'protective scare quotes around "serious drama" ', Caughie too invests in the 'question of value, judgement, and evaluation' (2000: 23). There is much to separate the above scholarship, and it does not constitute a specific trajectory of criticism. However, there is nonetheless a sense in which some cultural forms in these critical studies are figured ('valued') in terms of aesthetic eminence, literary merit and social critique, as if these were transparent features of the text, whereas other forms are part of a different – popular – order. On the 'crap' side as it is understood following Soper's logic, it is often popular genres which are singled out: soaps, police series, talk shows, home makeover programmes, American output and youth TV. What is the relationship between generic form and culture, and why is the relationship between the two antagonistic?

Using Genres

Attention to the form or shape of the signs of the television drama or genre are important not least because they are concerned with how genres are used by audiences. Robert Hodge and Gunther Kress, attending to the ways genres frame how audiences perceive reality, suggest that genres exist only 'in so far as a social group declares and enforces the rules that constitute them' (1988: 7). Within some criticism, genre is viewed in terms of its ideological functioning (see Chapter 3). Genres operate with representations which attempt to frame and naturalise one view of the world (Barthes's notion of 'myth'). Many of the essays, for example, in Curran et al. (1986) show how competing or alternative perspectives are excluded in the genre's ability to set the terms of *what* should be represented and *how* it should be represented. In the same collection, Stuart Hall is in no doubt that genre is an instrument of social control which reproduces the dominant ideology (1986: 5–14). Bernadette Casey notes that some genre commentators focus on how 'generically defined structures may operate to construct particular ideologies and values, and to encourage reassuring and conservative interpretations of a given text' (1993: 312). Audiences are interpellated, then, on the basis of the genre's mode of address, its way of encouraging audiences to believe one view of reality and not another.

Approaches that stress reader or viewer relations (the broad term *hermeneutics* [Iser, 1978] is linked with critical activities connected to reception studies, audience research, reader-response criticism and ethnography) contend that texts are never singular or monolithic in terms of their meaning potential. If genres are in part tied up in processes of communication, then one-way theories of communication are problematised as soon as messages are contested, misunderstood, or simply fail to provide the same information universally. Whilst no genre is outside of ideology, no one genre on its own can impose a world-view wholly successfully. The fact that the genre competes with other genres, and often critical acts of interpretation, serves to contest the text's attempt to present its 'realities' as neutral or natural. If different genres, as Sonia Livingstone claims, 'are concerned to establish different world views' (1990: 155), then genres are themselves part of a contradictory and ambivalent process where one genre serves to undermine another.

Whilst the form is never the final determinant of meaning (Corner 1998: 94–107), it remains an important part of cultural analysis, but always in a critical model which takes account of the 'interconnection with media production and consumption' (ibid., 95; see also Neale's discussion of films, 2002: 27–47). Genre is not so much what determines meaning but is concerned with how meanings take shape. Corner writes that form is 'the particular organisations of signification which constitute a given item as *communication*. . . . [S]uch signification is conventional, drawing on what may well be a large and complex range of conventions for doing what it tries to do' (ibid., 96). But formal analysis will be interesting in 'noting how [the text] might have been communicated differently and noting how different instances have been communicated similarly' (ibid., 97). Corner writes how form is central to all aspects of media analysis but he makes very clear that it is not so much an event or characterisation that matters as *how* the representation is achieved (ibid., 104).

Changing Genres

Models that draw on structuralist methods (Barthes) are clearly useful, if potentially limited, in the analysis of many popular dramas. The models, as suggested, are abstract. Moreover, recent television genres and subgenres exceed and transgress many of the formalist and structuralist templates. To connect one theme to a specific genre is also to limit how genre may be understood. It might be argued what is being done *with* and *to* genre is more important than any structuralist account can acknowledge. Hospital dramas are able to blend postmodern nostalgia (ITV: *The Royal*, 2002) with social and political critique (BBC: *Casualty*), and with romantic and erotic intrigue (BBC: *Holby City*). As David Bordwell notes, 'any theme may appear in any genre' (1989: 147).

Labelling genres is useful in that it allows programmes to be scrutinised in relation to structures, but what of the conditions and structures of reception? How is genre to be understood in relation to the hybridised versions of recent television output? Genre is not a *given* of everyday social experience so much as it is potentially a way of marking social change. Jane Roscoe's and Craig Hight's *Faking It* chronicles the changing shape of documentary and notions of realism (2001). Their analysis of parody (2001: 100–30) shows how notions of fact and fiction, and truth and falsity are blurred in mock documentary's subversion of factuality. And television dramas themselves demonstrate that the boundaries between, across and within genres are fluid and dynamic. The corruption, transgression and gradual corrosion of genres highlights something of the *permeable* qualities of genre. But it also suggests something about the relationship between viewing, definitional boundaries, and the textually based nature of social experience. Definitions and cultural identities can be overdetermining, so that anything outside an identity is excluded. But definitions and identities can also be limiting, so that an identity category fails to accommodate the breadth of social and subjective experience. Some dramas do not easily belong to one genre. In like manner, some people do not easily belong to one identity. Soaps, for instance, both transgress and supplement generic boundaries. And once themes and content are considered, then genre and form are complicated further. To remain without genre or identity definition impairs and impedes understanding and analysis (though there is not much evidence, writes Turner, 'that the term "genre" or any equivalent abstraction is actually used in [the] industrial process'; 2001: 5). To overdetermine what is expected of a genre's form and structure is also to limit and impair the multiple identities which contribute to a genre's innovation.

Michel Foucault

One way of understanding the relationship between genres, on the one hand, and the audiences who consume genres, on the other, is by linking genre and audience to cultural identitity. The work of Michel Foucault (1973, 1989 and 1995)[11] is useful in understanding the relations between discourse, discipline (or forms of social control) and subject or identity formation. In this current discussion, genre is being understood in relation to its ability to describe, but also to influence and inform the construction of cultural identities. Foucault argues that the construction of subjects involves methods of control, ways of *subject*-ing individuals in society. Identities in his thinking relate to complex regimes of representation, discourses and texts. Processes of *normalisation* require forms and practices which monitor how subjects behave in society. Though forms of control such as detention centres or CCTV camera constitute the more obvious means of surveillance, the media is in a unique position to inform behaviour and identity.

In his later work Foucault is interested in what it means to be part of a *way of life* or a culture, what it means to live according to expected patterns of behaviour, or conform to cultural norms.[12] At the same time as exploring these ethical questions, he is also concerned to expose which forms in the culture construct subjects, which narratives or knowledges encourage obedience, docility and acquiescence. Foucault concludes that it is impossible to avoid being subjected, and that subjects cannot *not* live without some sense of *subjectivity* (sense of self). However, he simultaneously observes the possibilities of resistance. Developing his claims around his notion of the 'care of the self', Foucault suggests that the cultural forms of a subject's society also provide an insight into the strategies which facilitate some resistance to that society. Simply stated, popular genres might seem to foster notions of social conformity, yet Foucault is suggesting that it is *within* and *against* the grain of these very popular genres that a subject may *counter* or question dominant discourses.

The implications of Foucault's work can be understood by mapping his notions of subjectivity onto the study of media. Recall that genre and narrative operate on the basis of codes and conventions (Barthes; Todorov; Propp). Some of the conventions concern the genre itself: in order to make itself meaningful, a genre works with certain expectations, certain structures, and so on (Barthes; Roscoe and Hight). Audiences expect genres to achieve certain things and not others. However, genre also has to make sense in relation to the context of its reception, within culture, and on the basis of certain social relations and not others. A whole range of popular programmes operate with notions of identity, offering models of subjectivity which continue to rely on dominant norms. But Foucault argues that it is important to discover how subjects are constituted through a multiplicity of representations. On this reading of Foucault, it might seem that genres operate to ensnare subjects, offering identity positions which only serve to reinforce an individual's subjection. But following Foucault, the analysis of genre would also want to grasp (take hold of) the role television plays in subjecting (giving an identity to) audiences. Rather than audiences or viewers coming to the television screen with already-formed identities, television genres, at least in Foucaultian logic, actually help to inform the identity in question.

Genres themselves are forced to stabilise identities in order to shape meaning. The appeal of popular genres is in part a result of the recognisable identities which stage the action and which people the dramatised space. But in working with those cultural texts (genres) which rely on identities, the subject is also in a position to call into question or *counter* its own identity formation. This countering of identity formation is tied to what Foucault calls *practices of the self*. These strategies are not simply invented by the subject but are, in the words of Foucault, 'the patterns that he finds in his culture and which are proposed, suggested and imposed on him by his culture, his society and his social group' (Foucault 2000a: 291). In order to interrogate the norms and conventions by which society makes subjects, then it is necessary to remain provisionally *within* some of these systems and representations in order to discover or invent ways which might thwart their very operations. To remain *inside* society, with its norms and conventions, is not the same as uncritically avowing the norms and identities that seem to keep this society intact. Foucault stresses, however, that an understanding of how the 'games of truth' are formulated (e.g. in the seductive power of genres, classic realism, or in narrative) is to begin to understand some of the ways in which society's 'games of power' actually operate (ibid., 298).

Genres and Difference

Something of the problematic nature of identity (both in terms of genre, narrative and audience, as well as the 'games of truth' (Foucualt) which posit some identities in more credible terms than others) is evidenced in recent popular output. The derivative and intertextual *Da Ali G Show* (Channel 4, 2000), *Goodness Gracious Me* (BBC, 1998) and *The Kumars at No. 42* (BBC, 2001) are examples of a number of contemporary programmes which rely on a textual as much as a multicultural and multi-ethnic history and context. Reliant on the conventions of dramatic output as well as the history of 'light entertainment', these programmes draw on a legacy indebted to popular media. *Goodness Gracious Me* takes its name from a song once sung by Peter Sellers, a one-off live show, and a radio series (which also included Sanjeev Bhaskar, Kulvinder Ghir, Meera Syal and Nina Wadia). *The Real McCoy* (BBC, 1991), and *The Fast Show* (BBC, 1994) also influenced the shape of *Goodness Gracious Me*'s sketch-show format. But *Goodness Gracious Me* is also *postcolonial* to the degree that it assumes a very different cultural context from programmes such as *Love Thy Neighbour* (ITV, 1972–6), *Mind Your Language* (ITV, 1977–9), or the period when the then-popular Charlie Williams hosted ATV's *The Golden Shot* (1967–75). Attentive to the symbolic and representational politics of ethnicity, and anticipating audience awareness of racial stereotypes, both *Goodness Gracious Me* and *The Kumars* are programmes which additionally (re)appropriate a well-established stage and television tradition (e.g., *The Black and White Minstrel Show*) in which white actors *blacked* up and played non-white characters.

The players in *Goodness Gracious Me* draw on a range of cultural and ethnic stereotypes in order to highlight the composite and generic features of all identities. And the cast of *The Kumars* exploit the intricacies of Standard English and RP in ways which far exceed the cultural and linguistic competencies of the 'native speaker'. Whilst an avant-garde or postmodern reading of the performative possibilities of earlier 'acting' might prompt audiences to consider the ideological and constructed nature of all racial identities, programmes such as *The Black and White Minstrel Show* were produced and consumed by white Britons, and were made with little attention to the fact that 'whiteness' is also a racially marked, though often invisible, cultural category. Broadcasting for (as opposed to by) ethnic minorities was grounded in a didactic tradition which saw English-language acquisition and education in (British) cultural competency as central aims. As the discussion of *Man from the Sun* suggests (Chapter 3), Asian and black communities have often been subjected to a generic logic which figured the 'non-white' citizen in terms of exclusivity and exceptionality. Moreover, the predominance of Received Pronunciation and Standard English at this time was also connected to a cultural past in which the centrality of the Church of England, the canon of English Literature, the Houses of Windsor and Parliament, and the BBC served to homogenise nation and commonwealth around a common culture. More recently, the BBC1 costume drama *Rhodes* (1996), following in the traditions of Granada/ITV's *The Jewel in the Crown* (1984), continued to present an image of empire in terms of heroism, (white) personal struggle, and non-white silence.

It is alongside genres such as costume dramas, documentaries and 'English as a Second Language' programmes, with their limited notions of both ethnicity and identity, that the identities staged in 'hybrid' genres make sense. *Goodness Gracious Me* and *The Kumars* go some way in highlighting how British culture is itself composite, reliant on models of cultural coherence which disintegrate, revealing, in effect, the synthetic and hybrid aspects of all identities. For some (Homi Bhabha 1990; Stuart Hall

1990, 2000) *hybridity* is a key marker of cultural identity in the postmodern world. In Hall's work, subjects discover identity in a multiplicity of relational or subject positions. For Bhabha, all subjects are bound to a process of narrativisation, telling (new) stories about dispersed nations and diasporic cultures. But in the work of Bhabha and Hall, the subject is problematically tied to a relational network (texts, narratives), at once enabled by discourse but potentially disabled by its breadth. Media texts do not facilitate agency, then, so much as they expose the structures which offer the promise of agency or autonomy.

Perhaps, however, *Goodness Gracious Me* and *The Kumars* foreground how all identities are tied to, but not wholly restricted by, mediated images, genres and social contexts. Foucault's work suggests that one cannot *not* have an identity. But Foucault is interested in the function of identity, the exploitation of identity, and why a particular identity should assume the importance it does in the first or last instance. Throughout *Goodness Gracious Me* and *The Kumars*, the satire and the comedy are often directed at singular notions of British identity. Yet the satire is only meaningful within the context of a culture whose attempts at homogenisation seem always to reverberate the multiple and hybrid origins of identity. Indeed, what is at stake in *The Kumars* is the whole concept of a stable identity. More so than many 'mainstream' shows, both *Goodness Gracious Me* and *The Kumars* address audiences whose understandings of 'national identity' are more complex than the sanitised (white) versions of early broadcasting. Undoubtedly, contrasting and ambivalent images of identity, or attention to the hybrid natures of both genre and identity, are always understood in relation to a climate in which individual and institutional instances of racism and sexism, for instance, are never finally ameliorated as a result of television dramas. Sarita Malik contends that:

> A point that might help break through the ambivalence [in 'racist' representation] is to consider that not all racisms work in the same way. Alf Garnett's [*Till Death Us Do Part*] is different from Bill Reynold's [*Love Thy Neighbour*], Bernard Manning's different from Kenny Lynch's. Whilst there is clearly a new climate of racial sensitivity, we also need to consider how Black and White audiences have themselves changed and ask what it says about the traditions of British television that a central tenet of its comedy programming has been so obsessed with . . . racist humour. (2002: 106)

It is these very ambiguities and contradictions which make genre and narrative all the more central to any analysis which considers the relations between television drama and cultural identity. Citing the work of Kobena Mercer, Malik notes how 'wider manifestations of ambivalence' raise important questions for the study of texts. 'Ambivalence functions as a complex "structure of feeling" experienced across the relations between authors, texts and readers – in relations that are always contingent, context-bound, and historically specific' (cited in Malik, ibid.). Genres, then, whilst they might seem formulaic and governed by convention, are also the spaces in which identities are represented. But it is also clear that the image on the screen is always a form of misrepresentation. The genre, necessary in the framing of narrative, also frames reality on the basis of inclusion and exclusion, presence and absence, and certainty and ambivalence. It is this inside/outside logic which informs later discussion of television drama's 'realities'. 'Realism', discussed in the following section, considers how reality is framed in the form of the classic realist text.

2.3 Realism

'Realism', as critics from Raymond Williams (1976) onwards have pointed out, is a slippery and often confusing term. In relation to television, it has proved to be so confusing that John Corner, for example, has suggested that it might be better abandoned as a critical term. Yet, as Corner goes on to point out, 'realism' has also been seen as 'television's defining aesthetic and social project' (1992: 98). It is, moreover, a term which, in popular as well as critical usage, makes certain claims to *value*, however vague or shifting its definition might be. Given the importance of the term as a criterion of value, then, it is important to understand both why it has been so central within television drama criticism, and why its meaning has been so variable and so contested.

Realism and Naturalism

Raymond Williams, in his accounts of the development of the term (1976, 1977), provides a historical background to the confusing variability of its meaning, as well as some very useful definitions. Williams points out that we use the term 'real' in two quite contradictory senses, senses whose early origins lie in a disputed sense of where 'reality' lies: in the material or in the spiritual or ideal world. Thus on the one hand we use 'real' to contrast with 'imaginary', to refer to something which has material existence, as in 'the *real* world'. On the other hand, we use 'real' to contrast with 'apparent', to refer to a truth which lies hidden *below* the level of the material, as in 'the *real* truth of the situation'. Both of these meanings recur in the various ways in which the terms 'realism' and 'realistic' have been applied to television drama. Either could be implied in the characteristic ambition of realism to 'show things as they *really* are'.

As applied to representations, the term 'realism' dates from the mid-nineteenth century, when it was used to describe art, theatre and the novel. Williams argues that from its beginnings its use combined two elements: an attitude, or world-view, and a method, or set of conventions. Its inherent world-view is characterised, as Christine Gledhill writes, by a belief that 'the world is capable of both adequate explanation and representation' (1987: 31). Realism, that is, depends on a belief in an objective reality which we can experience accurately, represent authentically, and understand. For Williams, this generates three characteristics of realism. It has a contemporary setting; it is concerned with 'secular' action – that is, with actions that have causes, and are played out, wholly in the social and material world; and it involves a movement towards 'social extension' – that is, towards the representation of 'ordinary people' and subordinate social groups. This last characteristic leads to a fourth element which Williams sees as applying to much realist drama, particularly that identified with 'social realism' or 'progressive realism': it is 'consciously interpretative in relation to a particular political viewpoint' (1977: 68). That is, its claim to accurately represent the 'real world' and its social subjects is also a claim about how we should understand that world.

Realism's method, or conventions, then, can never be wholly a matter of description, since it seeks to offer us understanding as well as depiction of the real. As John Fiske comments, realism is defined 'by the way it makes sense of the real, rather than by what it says the real consists of'(1987: 24). Here we can turn to another distinction within understandings of the term which began at the end of the nineteenth century but has continued into discussions of television drama: that between realism and naturalism. Naturalism was seen as an essentially descriptive method, positioning us as *observers* of the material details of reality. Realism, on the other hand, particularly in the Marxist critique of Georg Lukács, was seen as a more dynamic method, using narrative to position us with 'typical' characters, whose confrontations with 'world events, objects, the forces of nature and social institutions' (Lukács 1970: 124) would allow us to *experience* these events and struggles through the characters. Naturalism thus gives us the surface of social life, whilst realism allows us to understand its contradictions and causes; naturalism is implicitly fatalistic, accepting what is there, whilst realism assumes the possibility of struggle and change. Such arguments were deeply influential amongst early practitioners and critics of British television drama, underlying, for example, the attacks by Troy Kennedy Martin and John McGrath in the 1960s and 1970s on the 'old' television naturalism and their demand for a new, more dynamic realism. In line with the definition suggested by Raymond Williams, this was to be a shift in form – away from static cameras and close-up shots and towards an emphasis on 'action, pace, narrative drive' (McGrath 1977: 103).

Realism and Film

Early theories of realism were formed, as we have seen, in relation to theatre and, even more centrally, the novel. Whilst many critics have emphasised the continuity between these forms and the narrative structures of film and television, there are clearly also crucial differences. The ability of film to capture the world through the photographic image extended across time, and later through sound recording as well, seems to give it a more immediate and direct relationship to reality than earlier media forms. Indeed critics such as André Bazin, writing in the 1940s and 1950s, and Siegfried Kracauer in the 1960s, argued that the true nature of film lies in its ability impartially to reveal the world to us, an impartiality guaranteed by the mechanical nature of the camera's recording process. For Kracauer, 'Film is essentially an extension of photography and therefore shares with this medium a marked affinity for the visible world around us. Films come into their own when they record and reveal reality . . . [and] are true to the medium to the extent that they penetrate the world before our eyes' (1965: ix). Despite the fact that its origins lay at least as much in the 'pictorial sensationalism' of nineteenth-century melodrama as in photographic realism, cinema, as Christine Gledhill writes, came to be seen as 'an inherently realist medium' (1987: 27, 34). Its most prestigious forms, whether European 'art cinema' or Hollywood's 'classic genres', were identified as realist; melodrama came to be seen as the province of a 'feminised' mass culture, epitomised by the 'woman's film'.

For Colin MacCabe, writing in the 1970s, the differences between the Italian 'neo-realist' cinema which André Bazin was writing about and post-war Hollywood cinema were less important than their commonalities of attitude and form. Both assumed that reality could be effectively represented by film, and both aimed for a 'transparency of form' (1976: 9): the creation of an illusion that what unfolds seamlessly on the screen is a transparent rendering of reality. For this reason, MacCabe's category of the 'classic realist text' is very wide-ranging, wide enough to include *The Sound of Music* as well as *Bicycle Thieves* (MacCabe 1974, 1976). 'Classic realist texts', argues MacCabe, share two key characteristics. First, they consist in a hierarchy of discourses in which it is the 'visual discourse' – what the camera shows us, not what the characters tell us – which 'guarantees truth' (1976: 11). Second, they invite identification with key characters, inscribing spectators within their narratives so that the journey to knowledge which the film enacts is our journey too, and at its close we accept the 'knowledge' which the film provides of how things 'really' are, a knowledge which was 'implicit in it from the beginning' (ibid., 19). For MacCabe, then, *any* claim to represent the real is suspect, however progressive its vision of reality might be, because it hides its own constructedness and masks its ideological position behind a myth of transparency.[13] Those forms of realist narrative which for Lukács guaranteed the *active* involvement of the reader, for MacCabe produce precisely the reverse: a spectator who passively accepts the messages of the text.

Other critics, however, have sought to make distinctions between different kinds of realist project: those which seek to be *about* the real – Williams's 'social realism' or 'progressive realism' – and those which aim instead for 'verisimilitude' or being *like* the real (see Corner 1992). First used by Tzvetan Todorov and applied to film by Steve Neale (1990), 'verisimilitude' is a term which means 'having the appearance of truth'. Verisimilitude, then, indicates the extent to which a text conforms, not to reality itself, but to our expectations or understandings of reality. Following Todorov, Neale makes a further distinction: between *cultural verisimilitude* and *generic verisimilitude*. Cultural verisimilitude means conformity with the norms, values and expectations of the social world outside the text – with what we might call society's 'dominant ideological discourses'. It acts to confirm an audience's commonsense notion of 'how things are'. Generic verisimilitude operates within this broad sense, but is on the one hand narrower – it involves conformity with the rules of a particular genre – and on the other hand broader – it allows a play with fantasy which might seem to be outside our expectations of 'reality'. Thus for example, confrontation with vampires will be within the scope of a horror film but not of a soap opera (generic verisimilitude), but in their construction of character and values both will conform to cultural or ideological norms and expectations (cultural verisimilitude).

These distinctions allow us to get a rather clearer perspective on some of the confusingly contradictory definitions we have examined. What we mean when we say that a film or TV drama is 'realistic' is usually a combination of photographic realism and cultural and generic verisimilitude. Both of the latter were in play, for example, among Ien Ang's viewers of *Dallas*, some reading the serial primarily in terms of cultural verisimilitude – how far it conformed to their cultural norms and expectations – and some accepting its conformity to the generic conventions of melodrama or soap opera. But both are a matter of convention – the codes and conventions through which an accepted and acceptable sense of 'how things are' is produced. Both will be contested by that form of realism which, to use John Corner's distinction, seeks to be '*about* the real': to be progressive, in Raymond Williams's sense, by opening up new areas of society to our view and offering new interpretations of that world. Such an impulse, as we saw with Troy Kennedy Martin and John McGrath, will come from an oppositional political perspective, and will seek to break with existing forms and conventions in what Christine Gledhill calls its 'relentless search for renewed truth and authentication' (1987: 31). Of course, the resulting new stylistic and narrative forms will in turn become accepted codes of cultural verisimilitude, as John McGrath indicates when he complains that after the success of the early *Z-Cars*, with its 'emphasis on narrative – society, real and recognisable, but *in motion*', the series was 'taken over by forces beyond [our] control', becoming 'just another lot of naturalistic dramas' (1977: 104). Realism, then, will always be a contested term: claimed both by forces seeking to challenge the status quo ('showing things as they *really* are') and by those defending it (protesting that the new forms are 'unrealistic').

Television and Realism

All of these debates – about the difference between realism and naturalism, about the progressive potential of realism, about the 'classic realist text', and about the relationship between cultural and generic verisimilitude – have been carried over into arguments about television drama. But if television drama represents, in both its photographic realism and its narrative forms, a continuity with film, television as a medium also brings with it certain assumptions which attribute to it both a different relation to the real and a different cultural value from the medium of film.

Television, as we have seen (Chapter 1), is characterised by a presumed 'liveness' or immediacy, and an assumption of co-presence with its viewers. Its news technology, as John Ellis writes, 'has been driven by the demand that it should provide ever more instantaneous material, to the extent that flexible digital video formats plus satellite technology are moving us towards an era of "real-time" news in which we can see events more or less as they happen' (1999: 56). But this sense of immediacy and contingency is not confined to news: sports programming, game shows, chat shows, 'reality TV' and 'docu-soaps' are all driven by this sense of liveness, contingency and interactivity. In television, argues Bill Nichols, 'Everything is up for grabs in a gigantic reshuffling of the stuff of everyday life' (1994: 43). 'Reality', then, in all its rawness, disorderliness and excess, is a quality which characterises television in a way that simply does not apply to film, whose more focused narratives concern events which are assumed to have been already completed before the film begins. At the same time, however, television narrativises everything. 'Story telling', writes Bill Nichols, 'is television's forte. . . . Everything . . . is subject to interpretation by television as a story-telling machine' (ibid.). What Nichols points to here is a contradiction inherent in television's demand for realism. It is a contradiction which we have seen throughout the history of the term but one which television's ubiquitous sense of 'nowness' makes even more urgent. On the one hand, television must approximate the real; that is, it must be seen to give us unmediated access to both the everyday and a world beyond our immediate experience. On the other hand, it must give us explanations of the real in the form of narratives which will shape the disorder of reality into forms which are recognisable, meaningful and safe – forms, in other words, which comply with the requirements of cultural and generic verisimilitude. Such narratives characterise all the television formats listed above. Television's realism, then, is always unstable, its need to adequately represent and interpret the real in conflict with the requirement to 'make safe' the unruly and contingent nature of reality.

The second assumption about television as a medium which differentiates its relation to the real from that of film is its status as a 'feminised' medium. As we saw in Chapter 1, television's status as 'mass culture', together with its characteristic fluidity and apparent formlessness, have meant that it has been persistently identified with the feminine, often in contrast to the more coherent, structured – and prestigious – narratives which typify film. As Christine Gledhill writes, from such a perspective, 'all mass entertainment is inferior, and is associated with qualities that are inherently feminizing, while the cultural gold standard of realism is drawn

Table 2.1 The gendering of cultural forms

Mass culture/entertainment	*High culture/art*
Popular genre conventions	Realism
Romanticized stereotypes	Rounded psychological characterization
Glamour	Severity
Emotions	Thought
Expressive performance	Underplaying/understatement
Talk about feelings	Taciturnity/decisive action
Fantasy	Real problems
Escapism	Coming to terms
Private domesticity	The public world
Pleasure	Difficulty
Femininity	*Masculinity*

Source: From Gledhill (1997: 349).

into an alignment with values characterized as masculine' (1997: 349). She illustrates the point in Table 2.1, which shows culturally opposed characteristics.

To exemplify the two sets of characteristics, Gledhill chooses soap opera, identified with both television and the feminine, and the western, identified with film and the masculine. Equally, however, we might choose examples from within television itself, for, as we have seen, those forms of television which have sought to identify themselves as 'serious', as concerned with 'quality', as producing 'difficult knowledge' rather than 'easy entertainment', have sought on the one hand to identify themselves with realism and on the other to distance themselves from the general 'flow' of 'television itself', with its 'trivialising' tendencies.[14]

Documentary Realism and Documentary Drama[15]

For Gledhill, realism's world-view can be defined as a belief that 'the world is capable of both adequate explanation and representation' and it is identified with reason or 'thought', with 'real problems', and with 'the public world'. Following this definition, we can see that one form of realism which *has* been identified with television is 'documentary realism'. Documentary, of course, began with film, and with the desire of documentarists like John

Grierson in the 1930s[16] to create a socially responsible cinema of record, which would contrast with Hollywood's focus on fantasy and individual desire (Corner 1995; Kilborn and Izod 1997), but it has since become the almost exclusive province of television, where it has had a particular status in relation to television's claims to social responsibility. In Britain in particular it has been identified with television's 'public service' remit, its requirement to produce programmes which would inform and educate and not merely entertain: programmes which would focus on serious public issues in an objective and authoritative way (see Kilborn 1996). It thus potentially fulfils both the terms of Christine Gledhill's definition of realism, and Raymond Williams's idea of 'progressive realism': a realism which will be *about* rather than simply *like* the real. In many ways, of course, the claims which documentary makes in relation to the real are quite different from those made by drama. As Bill Nichols has written (1991), documentary claims to offer us access to *the* world, not to *a* fictionally constructed world; it is structured around *arguments* about the real world, not stories set within an imaginary world, however realistically constructed; and it invites us to look *at* that world rather than drawing us into it through continuity editing and point-of-view shots – its organisation of sound and image is designed to construct *evidence* rather than character or plot. Yet at the same time, documentary too is reliant on narrative structures, as was clear even in John Grierson's 1933 definition of documentary as 'the *creative interpretation* of actuality' (Grierson 1966: 13, italics added). Documentary, like fiction, produces an interpretation of the real via narrative; it is as much part of television's 'story-telling machine' as is drama, and as much dependent on generic conventions, however much its conventions seek to establish a distance from those of drama.

Unlike the conventions of realist drama, those of documentary do not seek to render the camera invisible, so that we seem to be watching a piece of reality unfold before us. Instead, the acknowledged *presence* of the camera serves as a guarantor of authenticity: the use of hand-held camera and natural lighting, of often barely audible location sound, of interviews and montage editing, all testify to the documentary maker's presence at a scene which s/he has not constructed, but is simply observing. John Caughie refers to these two sets of realist conventions as the 'dramatic look' and the 'documentary look'. The first is that familiar to us from Colin MacCabe's notion of the 'classic realist text': eye-line match, shot/reverse shot, point-of-view, all of which serve to position us in relation to the characters and the narrative, ordering the world 'into a readable hierarchy'

(Caughie 1980: 26). The documentary look, on the other hand, is a look *at* its object, 'fixing the object rather than putting its look into play, the object looked at but only itself looking on' (ibid., 30). In documentary, the camera follows its subjects; we never share their visual point of view and are always positioned outside them, as observers.

Given the status given to the documentary form within television as a guarantor of seriousness, 'truth' and 'authenticity', in contrast to what have been seen as the 'trivialising' tendencies of television as a medium, it is not surprising that those makers of television drama who have sought to produce 'serious' or 'progressive' realist drama have often borrowed from the conventions of documentary. The result, the hybrid form of the drama-documentary, has been described as 'the most institutionally potent but at the same time problematic of the small screen's programme categories' (Kerr 1990: 75). If we look at the series of BBC dramas produced under the heading of 'The Wednesday Play' and 'Play for Today' between 1964 and 1972, for instance, we can see that a number of them, particularly those made by the Ken Loach–Tony Garnett partnership, fall into this category.[17] The goals of such dramas, as described by Tony Garnett, are those of Raymond Williams's 'progressive realism'[18]: 'We wanted to go out into the world where we could capture the physical conditions of people's lives, how people actually lived, and bring that material back to create a dramatic document. The drive was political as much as aesthetic' (2000: 17–18). The method was described by Loach in a 1994 interview: the challenge, he says, was 'to put something in front of the camera which was absolutely authentic', and he denies any distinction between documentary and drama in this respect: 'I don't think you can justify putting something in front of the camera that is just sloppily researched' (*Face to Face*, BBC2: 19.09.94). The techniques of documentary, then, were borrowed to give drama the status of 'authenticity' and 'truth' which is generally attributed to the well-researched 'document'. In a context in which the 'authored' single play or mini-series is permitted, even encouraged, to offer unorthodox views as part of television's public service remit, so long as those views are clearly marked as the 'personal' views of a recognised 'author',[19] Loach and Garnett's insistence that they were not making 'art' but rather a 'dramatic document', and their use of documentary conventions to 'give a voice to those who are often denied it' (Loach, ibid.), can be seen as a way of claiming for their dramas a status as 'truth' which is usually afforded only to the documentary.[20] At the same time, in their choice of a few representative figures on whom to centre their narratives, they refer us back to debates about the difference between realism and naturalism. As John Caughie points out (1980: 26–7), the 'documentary look' can be seen as the inheritor of naturalism's aim to position us as (critical) *observers* of the material details of social life. The 'dramatic look', on the other hand, can fulfil the aims of realism by placing us *with* the characters, so that we experience social oppression and struggle through them. The combination of the two, often in order to attack the political status quo, has frequently produced unsettling dramas which have attracted the wrath of politicians and government.[21]

Cathy Come Home (1966) is perhaps the most famous example of 'progressive realism' achieved through the form of the drama-documentary. It traces the story of Cathy from the moment she hitches a lift to London, through courtship and marriage to Reg, the birth of three children, and through the descent into homelessness and enforced separation, first from her husband and then from her children. The final shots see her as she began, hitching a lift. Over a close-up of her face are printed the words, 'All the events in this film took place in Britain within the last eighteen months. 4,000 children are separated from their parents and taken into care each year because their parents are homeless. West Germany has built twice as many houses as Britain since the war.'

The narrative is episodic: writer Jeremy Sandford recounts a working method which involved filling a folder with 'bits of quarto paper which had the headings of the various sections of the film on them such as "Happy Days", "Life in the Slums", "The Luxury Flat" . . . work[ing] from a very large number of newspaper clippings that I had accumulated over the years, transcripts of tape-recordings that I had made, notes about people I had met . . .' (1984: 18). Shot on newly available portable 16 mm cameras previously considered suitable only for news, not drama, it is told partly through improvised drama – and camera – techniques. Partly it is told through Cathy's voice narrating her story over documentary shots which serve, in John Corner's words, to open up 'documentary space around the storyline' (1996: 106), recording the social conditions which are the background to her story. Finally, it is told through a range of other voices, some belonging to characters who appear briefly, from the unsympathetic middle-class civil servants and officials to the fellow-homeless, who recount their stories either to Cathy and Reg or direct to camera, some disembodied, recounting statistics or official views. The effect is to position us both with Cathy and outside her. Use of close-ups is frequent, and we share the intimacy of her life in a way not available to documentary; at the same time, however, whilst Cathy may speak *to* us directly, there is no use of eye-line match or shot/reverse shot – we do not look through her eyes. The subjective techniques of drama are refused; instead we are all too often aware of the camera as it follows the characters, often to find its (and our) access to them blocked, barred or obscured.

If we consider *Cathy* in terms of the arguments about realism outlined above, we can make a number of observations. It exemplifies both the belief underpinning realism, that the world can be both explained and authentically represented, and the political purpose which Williams identifies as a key characteristic of 'progressive realism'. Its combination of 'authenticity' and conscious political intention did result in changes in the real world outside the text.[22] At the same time, however, its use of the 'documentary look' and absence of point-of-view shots, its constant cluttering and blocking of the screen, seem to rob the characters of agency. They themselves offer no analysis of their situation and are never in narrative control: they are simply victims with whose inevitable narrative descent we are invited to empathise. In Colin MacCabe's terms, this 'transparent' rendering of reality is in fact – despite its oppositional political intentions – highly ideologically charged, repressing potential contradictions within its representations of class (all middle-class characters are unsympathetic, all working-class characters sympathetic), race (all black characters are victims) and gender.[23] In its representation of the family and gender roles, in particular, it conforms to conventional ideological values. Reg and Cathy are a conventionally 'happy family' whose bourgeois dream simply cannot be fulfilled. Cathy herself conforms wholly to conventional notions of (white) femininity: passive, domestic, lacking desire, roused to angry reaction only in defence of her children. In the end, *Cathy Come Home* illustrates both the problems with realism and its strengths. In its claims to 'truth', realism must always be suspect, constituted as it is, as John Ellis writes of documentary, 'on the basis of a fallacy and as the result of a desire' (1999: 61). Yet as a tool for bridging the gap between the text and the world, for producing dramas which, in John Caughie's words, 'have the capacity to be events as well as texts' (1980: 34), it can be highly effective.

New Realisms?

Realism implies a belief that the world can be adequately represented and explained. Yet, as we have seen, its demands are inherently contradictory, requiring both the 'authentic' rendering of reality *and* its ordering into coherent narrative form. Contemporary television, with its huge capacity for the instantaneous capture of the 'raw data' of everyday life, has massively increased both our ability to access 'the real' and our need to make sense of it through narrative forms. One result has been the growth of hybrid forms which blur the boundaries between fact and fiction, and between representation and the real. Such forms, as John Ellis (1999) suggests, make sense of the disorderly stuff of reality through narrativisation, but their narratives are in the present tense, inconclusive and open-ended. The relentless drive to *explain*, which underpins realism, can no longer be so confidently maintained.

Yet realism, as Nichols points out (1994: xi), is not so easily abandoned or extinguished. Just as the television drama of the 1960s drew on documentary conventions in its drive towards authenticity, so contemporary drama has raided the techniques of 'reality TV' in its search for new forms of 'progressive realism'. The work of Tony Garnett, producer of 'The Wednesday Play' in the 1960s, and most recently of *The Cops* (1998–2001) exemplifies this. The US series *The Cops*, first launched in 1989 and now in its fifteenth season, was one of the first reality TV shows. Bill Nichols uses its mix of 'patrol-car footage, drug-dealer arrests and potential shoot-outs' to illustrate his argument that such shows operate to 'recuperate' the 'potential subversion and excess' of the disorderly reality which they present, by positioning us with the police whose function is to patrol not only the city streets but also our sense of the boundaries of normality. Through them, writes Nichols, the potentially strange and threatening is rendered banal, woven into inconclusive narratives of the everyday, devoid of social or political purpose (1994: 43–6).

It is this style which – together with the title – Garnett's series appropriates. The first episode opens without a credit sequence, the music we hear revealed to be a disco beat. The sound is confused, the lighting natural and the image grainy. In the disco toilet we watch as a girl snorts coke and drinks beer. Our view is repeatedly obscured by passing figures. In the sequences that follow, a moving, unsteady camera follows her as she runs into the police station. Takes are long; the camera swings sideways to catch the latest speaker, or zooms quickly, losing focus; there are close-ups, but no point-of-view shots. Characters speak over each other. The style is described by Garnett as ' "being there". What is on the screen actually happened and a camera was around to make a record of it. And here it is' (world-productions.com/cops 2000). But this is, as he adds, a 'conceit, the little game the audience is in on'. Not only is the structure of the episode a familiar dramatic one – we are introduced to a number of characters, including a new sergeant, and a story-line which will continue; we end the episode as we began it, with the probationer Mel, now at the end of her shift and with decisions about her future to make – but the aim is firmly that of realism. But it is a realism whose didactic edge has been tempered since Garnett's early productions.

Realism, then, continues to reinvent itself, despite its own inherent contradictions and despite our increasing loss of faith in the ability of the camera to capture objectively some fundamental social truth. Its boundaries are unclear, its conventions constantly shifting, and its terrain a contested one. But if, as John Ellis writes, television now 'acts as our forum for interpretations' of the world (1999: 69), then realism, with its relentless search for 'the authentic', continues to be a means by which the 'truth' of those interpretations is both claimed and evaluated.

Chapter 3

Power and Subjectivity

3.1 Ideology, Hegemony and Discourse

Ideology and the Media

The term 'ideology', as used in contemporary media and cultural studies, has its origins in Marxism and its contention that all systems of ideas, beliefs, meanings and values are determined by the social and economic structures of the society which produces them. Ideology, in this definition, is the shared set of meanings and values through which a society makes sense of its own structures and processes and their relationship to the material world. These meanings and values do not exist simply as sets of ideas or beliefs, however; they are embodied in and circulated through specific social institutions like the Church, the education system, the family and cultural and media institutions. They also exist at the level of 'common sense' – the everyday conceptual frameworks which people use to make sense of the world and its events. But since society is structured according to relations of power, these systems of meaning and value, and all the ways in which they are communicated and expressed, are not neutral. Those which circulate most widely and are most dominant produce explanations of the world which originate in, and serve the interests of, society's most powerful groups. Ideology, then, is the process of making the world *mean*, but ideological power is the power of ensuring that those meanings structure our lived experience. As Terry Eagleton puts it, it is 'not just a matter of meaning, but of making a meaning *stick*' (1991: 195).

It is easy to see why this concept assumed such importance in the emerging field of media and cultural studies. It links issues of the social and the material – issues of economics and power – with issues of representation – the narratives, images and forms which render the world meaningful. And it links a concern with social and cultural *structures* with a concern for how *individuals* both represent those structures to themselves and make sense of public representations of them. Ideology, then, is bound up with power relations and embodied in social institutions, but it operates through *representations* and, because the meanings we give our lives constitute our sense of individual identity, at the level of the individual. As Kathryn Woodward argues, 'Representations produce meanings through which we can make sense of our experience and of who we are.' They establish 'individual and collective identities' and 'provide possible answers to the questions: who am I?; what could I be?; who do I want to be?' (1997: 14).

It was the French Marxist philosopher Louis Althusser who developed this particular definition of ideology. Ideology, writes Althusser, 'represents the imaginary relationship of individuals to their real conditions of existence' (1984: 36). It operates through what he calls 'Ideological State Apparatuses': institutions such as religion, education and the media which, whilst not necessarily controlled by the state, operate in its interests, maintaining its power not through force, as with 'Repressive State Apparatuses' like the army or police force, but through systems of values and beliefs and their related practices. As individuals, we have our identities constituted through ideology: we can become *subjects* – makers of meaning and authors of our actions – only by being *subjected*, by operating within the conceptual frameworks or 'maps of meaning' (Hall 1977: 330) which ideology constructs for us. In this way, we are 'interpellated' – called into the subject position which we learn to occupy – by ideology. Althusser argues that in the pre-capitalist period there was one dominant Ideological State Apparatus, the Church, whose various aspects – education, the family, publishing and communication – have now acquired independent status (1984: 25). What Althusser calls 'the communications apparatus' – 'the press, the radio and television' – has now become in itself a massively powerful ideological institution. Stuart Hall develops this point further. The transformation of Western societies which comes with the move to industrial-urban capitalism from about the 1880s – the phase of advanced 'monopoly' capitalism – is also, he writes, 'the phase in which the modern mass media come into their own, massively expand and multiply, install themselves as the principal means and channels for the production and distribution of culture, and absorb more and more of the spheres of public communication into their orbit. . . . They have progressively *colonized* the cultural and ideological sphere' (1977: 340).

If the mass media can be seen as the most powerful form of 'ideological apparatus' in contemporary society, television has been the most important focus for analysis in these terms. Television, as we have seen, offers a sense of 'liveness' or 'nowness', its constant flow of images seeming to transmit and record everyday reality, giving us a constantly updated 'window on the world'. It is, moreover, a supremely domestic medium, addressing us directly as individuals and members of family groups, in the privacy of the home which is assumed to be the space in which our identity as individuals is most fully expressed and preserved. Yet, as Stuart Hall remarked in 1975, the '*transparency* of the television screen is an illusion' (1975: 8); what television offers are images, representations and narratives about the world, not reality itself. It can be seen as a massively powerful carrier of ideology. Hall suggests three forms of 'ideological work' performed by television in contemporary society. The first, in an increasingly fragmented society, is to provide images and representations of 'the lives, meanings, practices and values' of social groups unfamiliar to us. The second is to provide a means of ordering this 'social imagery', by providing classification labels for, ways of making sense of, these unfamiliar groups. Finally, it is to 'shake into an *acknowledged order*' what has thus been 'made visible and classified', to produce an ideological consensus about how the world works and what it means (1977: 340–2). In short, the ideological work of television 'fills in' our picture of the world through its representations, classifies these representations, and works to secure our consent to the 'imaginary unity or coherence' it thus constructs.

Before turning to the ways in which this approach to the analysis of television was applied to television drama, a further element of the argument needs to be explored. The work of Louis Althusser was influential in media studies because, as Mimi White says, it defines ideology 'in terms of both systems of representation and individuals' relation to their material world' (1992: 169). But Althusser's concept of Ideological State Apparatuses leaves little room for conflict or struggle. If as individuals we are *subjected* to ideology in the process of becoming human *subjects*, if our conceptual 'maps of meaning' are provided by 'dominant ideologies', then it is difficult to see how these can be contested, at least at the level of representation itself. Althusser himself argues that the 'ruling ideology' is always engaged in conflict with other ideologies in a social formation, ideologies emerging from exploited and subordinate class groups. As he presents it, however, this social conflict seems to be merely reflected, not enacted, at the ideological level, and in any case, the operation of the 'ideological apparatus' as he describes it is so effective in positioning us as subjects that it would seem to exclude conflict or struggle.

Yet the images we 'read', the terms we use, the representations of the world which we are offered and which we make and remake, and the identities which we construct through such representations, do not seem to be fixed in this way. When, in 1979, two feminists responded to a billboard advertisement for a Fiat 127 car which proclaimed, 'If it were a lady, it would get its bottom pinched' by adding 'If this lady was a car she'd run you down', they were contesting the meaning of this representation at the level of the representation itself – 'taking over the poster', as one argued – and in so doing asserting an identity for women (as active, assertive, witty) in direct conflict with that affirmed by the advertisement itself (Posener 1982: 12–13). Similarly, the terms 'black', 'gay' and 'queer', and the representations within which they have been embedded, have all been subject to contestation over recent years. It seems clear, then, that a conception of ideology which accounts for such contestation and struggle is needed if it is to be useful in media analysis.

For Stuart Hall in the 1970s, it was Antonio Gramsci's concept of 'hegemony' which supplied such an account. For Gramsci, the processes through which dominant social groups win the consent of subordinate groups (hegemony) are always processes of struggle – struggle at the level of ideology, of representations, but struggle which is never completed. Hegemony is at best an 'unstable equilibrium' (Hall 1977: 334); every ideological sign or representation is a potential point of struggle over meaning. It was this concept that underpinned Hall's essay, 'Encoding and Decoding in the Television Discourse' (1973, 1980). Events, real or fictional, are not simply transmitted by television, argues Hall; they are assigned meaning or 'encoded' by being placed in a structured context, and this meaning is open to contestation. In the 1973 version of this essay[1] Hall uses the example of the television western series to illustrate his point. The TV western, 'with its clear-cut, good/bad Manichean universe, its clear social and moral designation of villain and hero, the clarity of its narrative line and development, its iconographical features, its clearly-registered climax in the violent shoot-out, chase, personal show-down, street or bar-room duel' (1973: 5), is structured according to generic codes (see Section 2.2). Its actions, however violent, are coded according to well-established ethical rules (the hero always draws fastest and shoots straightest, but he never draws first; the 'bad', that is, sexually promiscuous woman may be redeemed but she must always die), and its characters and events have meaning only in relation to the overall meaning-structure constructed by the genre. That genre emerges at a particular historical moment and plays out in narrative form the problems and concerns of American society at that moment, but in a displaced, 'encoded' form. The genre, its patterns and the 'solutions' to the problems it proposes – problems of violence, of law and order, of gendered identity – shift according to historical change. Its meanings, though structured according to 'dominant' ideology, are not given once and for all. They are open to contestation both within the various and shifting embodiments of the genre itself and in the readings made by viewers who, coming from a different cultural background or class position, may 'decode' the programme according to 'meaning-frameworks' quite different from those 'preferred' by the programme or its makers.

Ideology, Hegemony and Television Drama

In the 1970s and 1980s a number of more extended attempts were made to apply ideological analysis to television drama. One originates in Colin MacCabe's application of Althusser's theories to the analysis of literary and visual texts in his concept of the 'classic realist text' (1974). MacCabe, as we have seen,[2] argued that the nineteenth-century realist novel, Hollywood cinema and popular television drama all construct particular forms of 'social knowledge' by framing the actions and discourses of their cast of characters in relation to a central set of 'truths'. These 'truths' are carried in the case of the novel by the storytelling itself (the novel's 'metalanguage'), and in the case of cinema and television by what the camera shows us. Both seem to offer 'direct access to truth', a transparent rendering of reality against which we can measure the discourses and actions of the various characters. In fact, their apparent realism or transparency masks the ideological work of the narrative, whose seeming 'truth', that of 'common sense', is the 'truth' of the dominant ideology. In accepting the conclusions – the 'social knowledge' – to which the narrative leads us, we accept in turn our positions as subjects within that ideology.

In the debates which followed publication of MacCabe's article, a key focus for discussion was popular historical drama on television. Colin McArthur makes the key point when he argues that 'all television (including drama) fulfils an ideological function and that there will be a relationship between the popularity of a programme and the extent to which it reinforces the ideological position of the majority audience' (1981: 288). Contrasting popular series like *Upstairs, Downstairs* (1971–6) with the

Allen/Loach/Garnett series *Days of Hope* (1975), with its radical focus on working-class history, and comparing the public reception of the two, McArthur concludes that the 'lesson to be learned, of course, is that programmes which support the dominant ideology are regarded as natural and the few which do not are regarded as political' (ibid., 297).

What was not agreed upon by critics taking an ideological approach, however, was whether a series like *Days of Hope*, which employs a conventional narrative and characters and the techniques of realism, but with politically oppositional intent, can ever disturb dominant ideological discourses. McArthur argued, tentatively, that it could, partly because its *subject matter* is in contradiction to the dominant ideology, so that it has a disturbing effect on an audience which is used to the techniques of realism being employed to present a quite different view of the world, but more particularly because, whilst the series employs many of the techniques of realism, it breaks with others in not privileging a particular point of view through its characters. What characters *say* in a particular scene may be at odds with what we see happening, so that the narrative is able to present its audience with ideological contradiction. MacCabe disagreed, arguing that such a scene *always* ascribes 'truth' to what we *see*, because the camera is presumed to have privileged access to reality, so that the contradiction which McArthur describes, between what a character says and what we see occurring, has always already been resolved within the narrative. We 'know', because of the conventions of realism, what to regard as 'truth'. What both writers agree on is that ideology operates within television drama not simply through content – the kind of view of the world we are given – but even more importantly through form. The more 'closed' a narrative is, the more it conforms to conventions of realism and genre, the less possibility it offers for ideological questioning and contradiction.

Such a view was also taken by Philip Schlesinger, Graham Murdock and Philip Elliott in their book *Televising 'Terrorism'* (1983), which deals with television's treatment of 'terrorism' in both its non-fiction and its fictional genres. Arguing that the series format is in general more closed than the serial form, the authors explain that in the series:

> The plots always revolve around the central characters. They are the heroes. They are on screen for most of the time and the action is seen from their point of view. The villain's function is to disturb the social and moral order and present the heroes with problems to solve. The villains do not have to be rounded characters to fulfil this role. They simply have to personify threats to the established order

> in a readily recognisable form. They appear abruptly at the beginning of an episode and are purged at the end. (1983: 79)

The world of the popular series is therefore the world of the dominant ideology, and its hegemonic project is to organise consensus around both dominant ideological conceptions such as nation, community or the masculine ideal, and dominant ideological responses to contemporary anxieties. In the case of the action series *The Professionals* (1977–83), with which Schlesinger et al. deal at some length, we can see the series responding to contemporary anxieties about threats to order and democracy posed by terrorism in a way which promotes the legitimacy of official violence. The potential contradictions in such a stance – the difficulties of distinguishing 'acceptable' violence from 'terrorist' violence and the threat to democracy posed by a secret state force which uses the same tactics as its opponents – are resolved by displacing the opposition between state and terrorist violence on to that between order and disorder, between law and criminal, between Britishness and 'foreignness' and even between the natural and the unnatural (many of the most evil terrorists are women, who are seen to be betraying their 'natural femininity').

Here again, then, the popular television drama series is seen as dealing with contemporary cultural anxieties but in a way which displaces the actual issues and contradictions inherent in the contemporary situation onto narrative threats which can be resolved – which, indeed, have in one sense always *already* been resolved through the very format of the series. As with the arguments made by MacCabe and McArthur about the historical drama series, too, ideological 'closure' is identified with a closure of form. Schlesinger et al. contrast the 'tight' format of the popular series, with its stable cast of representative character types and repetitive narrative structures, with the 'looser' space of the single play which, whilst it may not guarantee ideological openness or questioning, does give 'added scope for personal viewpoints and openness to alternative or oppositional viewpoints' (ibid., 77).

The most sustained application of this approach to television drama in the 1970s and 1980s came in the analyses of the popular police series carried out by Geoff Hurd, Alan Clarke, James Donald and others. In 1972 Ashley Pringle proposed a methodology for the analysis of the television drama series which describes the operation of such series in terms very similar to those in which Stuart Hall presents the 'ideological work' of television as a whole. The drama series, writes Pringle, provides 'images of others, pictures of (perhaps) unfamiliar sections of society', completing 'what the experience of the viewer only half-glimpses or suspects in a rather vague way'. These images are used to 'fill in or explain away otherwise unresolved contradictions in contemporary society, by locating themselves at points of tension and consummating them in the most consensually acceptable way' (1972: 119).

The popular television drama series, despite its appearance of realism, functions as myth, transposing actual social contradictions into 'timeless' oppositions between good and evil through a narrative structure of disruption/quest/restoration (or its contemporary form of crime/pursuit/arrest). As such it is seen as inherently ideologically conservative. Such a view has been taken by a number of writers, particularly in relation to the police series. The police series is a genre which deals overtly with threats to public order and with marginalised or threatening social groups. It is also a genre which makes explicit claims to realism; indeed, when it seems to step outside acceptable realities of contemporary policing it is often subject to public criticism from the police themselves.[3] Yet, as Geoff Hurd argues, the oppositions around which it is structured are the stuff of myth. In an analysis originally applied to *The Sweeney* (1975–8) but subsequently widened to include other police series, Hurd cites the oppositions shown in Table 3.1 as being important within these series, with the series' central characters lined up with the terms on the left of the list:

Table 3.1 Binary opposition in police series

police	crime
law	rule
professional	organization
authority	bureaucracy
intuition	rank
masses	intellectuals
comradeship	rank

Source: From Hurd (1981: 66)[4].

Discourse and Ideology

James Donald's 1985 analysis of *The Sweeney* focuses on rather different aspects of the series, centring on the troubled masculinity of its central character, Regan. Looked at from this point of view, he argues, 'the series is as much concerned with the crisis in male self-confidence that marked many films of the period . . . as with the politics of law and order' (1985: 133). His comments suggest a problem with the concept of ideology as we have considered it so far. Originating in Marxism, it was developed in relation to a central problematic of class. Stuart Hall's concept of 'encoding', for example, assumes that however complex that field may be, events can be coded according to a 'preferred meaning' which operates within the field of a 'dominant ideology'. This meaning will be 'decoded' differently only by individuals differently positioned within the social formation. James Donald's perspective, however, a perspective initiated within feminism (see Section 4.2), suggests that a range of different axes of power may be in operation within a single text (in this case the axes of gender and sexuality as well as that of class) and that they may operate in complex relationship to each other. In one reading of *The Sweeney*, Regan may be seen as the upholder of a class-based ideological consensus; in another as a troubled figure within a patriarchal order. The two orders may overlap, but they are not the same, and in some series, for example those which feature a female police detective, they may be brought into contradiction.

Stuart Hall's later discussions of representation, therefore, replace the concept of 'encoding' with that of 'discourse'. This concept of discourse comes from the work of Michel Foucault, who argues that all discourses are infused with power relations. A discourse according to this definition is 'a set of statements or beliefs which produce knowledge that serves the interests of a particular group or class' (Hall 1992a: 292). In this sense discourse, or 'discursive formations', can be said to operate in a very similar way to ideology, but discourse can not be aligned with a single axis of power. Medical discourse, for example, operates to produce particular ways of understanding – 'knowledges' or 'truths' about – the human body and mind. It is bound up with and serves the interests of a specific social institution – that of medicine – and is embodied in specific practices and rituals. It carries discursive power – the power to define, to deem valid or invalid our sense of our own bodies – but also material power, the power to enforce our compliance. But whilst it is part of the circulation of power, or 'power/knowledge' as Foucault terms it, both within its own institutional settings and within society in general, it can not be simply equated with the power of a dominant class or group. It is *specific*, and it can overlap or conflict with other public discourses – legal, religious or moral in the case of debates about abortion or about criminal responsibility, for example – or with discourses identified with the private sphere – for example, those of gender, sexuality or pleasure in debates about sexual practices.

Discourse, then, allows us to think about the popular television drama text in a way which does not limit its meanings to a single unified 'dominant voice', recognising instead what Colin Mercer calls 'the existence and effect of . . . differently inflected voices which cannot be assumed to have unified meanings' (1986: 62). Discourses are not 'ideologically innocent'; through the stories they tell and the 'knowledges' they produce they will seek to organise and regulate relations of power in ways which serve the interests of dominant groups. But the axes of power on which they operate will not be identical or unified, and they may interact in ways which can be complex and sometimes contradictory.

This rethinking of the concept of ideology in terms of its operation through discourse also necessitates some rethinking of the relationship between ideology and genre. In many of the analyses we have looked at there is an assumption that the television genre format, with its structured fictional world and repetitive plots, acts in a directly ideological way to translate social reality into myth. Sometimes, indeed, as with Colin MacCabe's concept of the 'classic realist text', it seems that narrative itself must inevitably perform this function, so that only those dramas which in some way disrupt narrative conventions can be seen to question or oppose dominant ideology. If, however, we separate the concepts of narrative and genre from that of ideology by employing the idea of discourse, we can propose a rather less monolithic relationship between ideology and television drama. Christine Gledhill draws such a distinction in her work on melodrama, genre and popular film and television drama. Gledhill argues that popular genres draw on a melodramatic framework for their symbolic or 'mythical' structures, since 'the focus of melodrama is a moral order constructed out of the conflict of Manichean, polar opposites – a struggle of good and evil, personified in the conflicts of villain, heroine and hero' (1988: 75–6). Yet these figures, the stable fictional world which they inhabit, and the actions they perform, must be 'filled out' in popular drama by reference to contemporary social discourses if they are to be seen as 'realistic'. Thus, for example, the contemporary detective hero may be female; her outline will be 'filled in' with reference to contemporary discourses about social equality, the independent woman and femininity, some of them arising from feminism. This may well produce contradiction within the fictional world of the series, as it strives to incorporate the understandings produced within these discourses into a symbolic structure organised around quite different assumptions about the 'hero' and 'heroine'. In this case, as Gledhill writes, 'the intermeshing of symbolizing and referential modes constructs the female image as an object of contest, of negotiation, for the characters and for the audience' (ibid., 85).

Ideologies of 'Race' and National Culture: A Case Study

In the following case study we shall examine one particular ideological problematic, that of 'race' and national culture, in relation to two very different British television dramas. The first is the BBC drama, *A Man from the Sun*, a single play produced in the form of documentary-drama in 1956, the second a 1998 half-hour episode of the long-running ITV police series, *The Bill* (1984–), 'One Man, Two Faces'.

In *Formations of Modernity* (1992), Stuart Hall looks at the construction of this ideological problematic through what he calls the discourse of 'the West and the Rest'. He points out that the idea of 'the West' is 'a *historical*, not a geographical concept' (1992a: 277), arising with the emergence of modern industrialised, urbanised and secular societies. It depends for its meaning on a set of oppositions, in which the (positive) qualities of 'the West' are established in opposition to those negatively attributed to 'the East' (whether 'eastern Europe', 'the far east', or 'the middle east') or, more broadly, to 'non-Western' societies. These oppositions have the function of regulating and classifying our knowledge of these 'others' whilst affirming the 'natural superiority' of 'the West'. We can tabulate them as shown in Table 3.2.

Table 3.2 The West and the Rest

The West	*The Rest*
civilised	primitive
urbanised	rural
industrialised	'underdeveloped'
capitalist	pre-capitalist or communist
modern	'backward'
secular	superstitious/'fundamentalist'
free/democratic/liberal	rigid/undemocratic/despotic

Source: From Hall (1992a).

Hall identifies four 'discursive strategies' characteristic of Western representations of these 'non-Western' 'others', which have circulated from the fifteenth century onwards (ibid., 299–308). The first is *idealisation*: the representation of the 'non-Western' world as 'innocent', an earthly paradise whose people live the simple, innocent lives of children in a state of Nature. The second is its mirror image: *the projection of fantasies of desire and degradation*. Uncurbed by civilisation, 'innocent' desire can become bestiality and paradise turn into 'barbarism'. Together these two form the 'good' and 'bad' sides of a representational stereotype, that of the 'savage', noble or degraded, who haunts the pages of colonial literature. The third and fourth strategies also form a linked pair. These are *the failure to recognise and respect difference* and *the tendency to impose European categories and norms*. Here, difference only has meaning as difference from '*us*'; differences *between* other cultures are simply not recognised. 'Primitive' cultures must by definition be similar; they have not developed the refinements of 'civilised' societies. Hall's account of these discursive strategies concludes with the comment that 'the discourse of "the West and the Rest" is alive and well in the modern world' (ibid., 318), active in constructing 'knowledge' about the West's internal as well as its external 'others'.

Britain in the 1950s was very much concerned with the question of its 'internal others'. The postwar labour shortage, which led to workers from newly independent Commonwealth countries being invited to come to Britain, and the passing of the 1948 Nationality Act which gave them right of entry, had produced a wave of immigration, particularly from the Caribbean, which began with the landing of the SS *Empire Windrush* in June 1948. The resulting racially focused anxieties were evident in cabinet debates: despite official government policy of 'free entry into the Mother country of the Commonwealth', a Conservative cabinet in 1955 discussed the possibility of using 'Keep Britain White' as an electoral slogan (see Gilroy 1987: 46; Geraghty 2000: 116). They were even more evident in hostile press campaigns (see Gilroy 1987: 79–81), which focused on crime (particularly organised prostitution and drug trafficking), on housing (shortages, overcrowding, 'exploitation' by black landlords and the role of moneylenders in black house purchases), on 'immorality' (particularly reports of black men living on the 'immoral earnings' of white women), and on disease (especially sexually transmitted disease). The 1958 'riots' in Nottingham and Notting Hill – attacks by white youths on black people – were seen as further evidence of the 'colour problem', and in 1962 the

Commonwealth Immigrants Act, which restricted entry to those with employment vouchers, students and dependants, was passed.

A Man from the Sun was produced by the documentary section of the BBC's drama department[5] in 1956, one year after the establishment of independent television in Britain, at a time when, although it saw television as relatively unimportant compared to radio, the BBC very much still regarded itself as *the* national broadcaster, concerned to educate as well as entertain (Curran and Seaton 1985: 193–207). The 'documentary drama' or 'dramatised story documentary', scripted and acted but based on 'documentary research', was, as we have seen (Section 2.3) a way of addressing politically 'touchy' subjects (Elliott 1992: 88). Its claims to realism and impartiality,[6] its 'loose' format, its willingness to be controversial, all serve to align it with the greater ideological openness which has been attributed to the 'single play'.[7] This, then, was the first attempt by British television to deal with the arrival of the 1950s Caribbean immigrants, and it was to be the only one until 1996, when Channel 4 produced a two-part dramatisation of Caryl Phillips's *The Final Passage* (Bourne 1998: 210). It tells the story of Cleve Lawrence, a young carpenter from Jamaica, who arrives in Britain to find work. His journey, from helpless new arrival to mature adult who can accept Britain, in terms which echo the marriage service, as 'my home now, for better or for worse', is echoed by that of Ethlyn Roderick, a 19-year-old beauty queen from St Thomas with ambitions to become a nurse, who arrives on the same boat as Cleve and whose marriage to an already settled Caribbean immigrant closes the drama. Both have to resist temptation (in Cleve's case the offer of money for delivering drugs, and in Ethlyn's that of prostitution) and must be educated to accept the norms of British society and their place in it. Through their stories the drama tackles all the issues identified with black immigration in contemporary press reports and proposes its own answers to the 'problem' of 'race relations'.

The drama has been praised by its actors for giving 'a voice to black people who . . . had recently arrived in Britain' (Pauline Henriques, quoted in Bourne 1998: 211), and indeed it begins with Cleve's voice, in a direct-to-camera address from Jamaica. 'Want you do somethin' for me,' he says, 'Want you write a letter 'cos me don't write too good like an educated man. . . . Want you to send this letter to Mr. Alvin Jarvis of London, England. You write: Dear cousin Alvin . . .' His speech thus addresses or 'interpellates' us directly, but it functions to position him in relation to us. He is simple, innocent, 'a plain fella what does work with his hands'; he addresses us from his island paradise, surrounded by palm trees. We, the audience, are addressed as educated, able to play a supportive, parental role. White and British, we have, by implication, a broader and more complete perspective than has Cleve. In the drama's central expository scene, where arguments for and against racial segregation are presented in the traditional setting of the borough council chamber, this strategy is repeated. Visually positioned within the group around the council table, we listen to various expressions of white prejudice, from accusations that black immigrants 'drop down from the trees and expect us to fit them into the life of a modern city' to fears about 'swamping' and complaints of slum overcrowding and moral 'lowering of tone'. Brent, the representative of an educated black middle class, answers on behalf of the immigrants:

> My people, Mr. Chairman, are not straight out of the jungle. They come to England with glorious dreams of the mother country. Very often they get disillusioned. . . . When my people come to your country they look around for an example and a way to live.

Brent's speech confirms our role, the role of England/Britain, as responsible *parent*, but the central voice in the discussion is not his but that of Miss Prior. An elderly middle-class white community volunteer, Miss Prior speaks as the voice of British national identity (as 'mother England'), reminding us of our/Britain's history of tolerance and of racism's identification with fascism: '*Our* community must learn to adapt too. . . . If we don't face up to it we won't come through as a nation. . . . We must absorb these people, not force them into ghettoes.'

Despite its liberal intentions, we can see that the ideological problematic of *A Man from the Sun* is constructed through the representational strategies that Stuart Hall identifies with the discourse of 'the West and the Rest'. The Caribbean immigrants are childlike, superstitious (believing in magic spells) and in need of both education and moral guidance from 'us'. Without this, they are prey to the temptations of an immoral underworld which combines drug trafficking with prostitution. Their own culture is presented as simple and joyous, a matter of spontaneous music and dance, and they possess a sexuality not bound by marriage; it is also wholly undifferentiated, a single culture identical across the Caribbean and Africa. We can argue, too, that the documentary style which the drama adopts supports this process of regulation and classification. The 'documentary look', as John Caughie argues, is a look *at* its object, placing and objectifying it. Whilst the characters of drama 'exchange and reverse looks', inviting our identification, 'the figures of the documentary are looked at and look on', inviting our judgement (1980: 30).

Along with this discourse of 'the West and the Rest' we can see two others in operation, one aligned more or less comfortably with ideologies of national identity, the other much less so. The first is that of class. The journey of the working-class immigrants towards assimilation is also a journey of class mobility via education: both Ethlyn and Cleve have to learn the virtues of training and qualifications, and Cleve must also learn to read and write. But their lack of education is paralleled by that of an older white working class, who are shown to be ignorant of the anti-racist resolutions of their own Trade Union Congress, but whose children, better educated, are more willing to embrace change. Tolerance and understanding of the problems of race and national culture are thus identified with an educated white middle class, and it is the educated middle-class black character, Brent, played by the light-skinned Earl Cameron, who is seen to be most nearly 'like us', able to participate rationally in the council debate. Discourses of class and national identity are thus aligned through concepts of education and 'progress'.

The second discourse, that of sexuality, runs as a far less comfortable thread throughout the drama. Anxieties about sexuality are, as we have seen, a key component of ideologies of 'race' and national identity, and fears of black sexuality and its threat to the 'purity' of the nation through the 'invasion' and 'tainting' of the individual white family were a central component of the anxieties of the 1950s.[8] In a drama advocating assimilation as its solution to the 'problem' of black immigration, and using marriage as its key metaphor for such assimilation, this anxiety acts as a constant but unspoken threat. At a number of points it appears explicitly: 'benignly', in the comment from Alvin's 'woman' that he has 'so many cousins that they grow like bananas all over the place'; less so in the figure of the Americanised 'half-caste' pimp, symbol of miscegenation, who tempts Ethlyn towards prostitution and Cleve towards drug carrying. Most obviously, it appears in the relationship between newly qualified West Indian doctor Winston and white librarian Maggie, which elicits the direct-to-camera appeal from her working-class father: 'How'd you like *your* daughter carrying on with a black man?' Winston, the only politically radical black character we see, has his beliefs dismissed as 'immature' by the 'reasonable' Brent, and the relationship ends when Winston leaves for Africa and Maggie replaces her romantic relationship with him by the more acceptable role of teacher to Cleve. At the wedding service on which it closes Miss Prior makes explicit the drama's governing concept: the marriage relationship can be compared, she says, to that of 'two races who are going to live together'. But it is a metaphor whose sexual implications remain a powerful source of anxiety, so that at the wedding dance with which the drama concludes the camera slides away from Maggie and Cleve, to focus instead on the 'safe' black/white pairing of Brent and Miss Prior, both of whom are assumed to be 'beyond' sexuality, he by virtue of his education and presumed celibacy, and she as elderly and maternal representative of England itself.

A Man from the Sun, then, mobilises discourses of national identity and culture, of community and 'race', of class and sexuality, around a particular ideological problematic. But its ideological stance is neither as 'progressive' nor as coherent as it seems, undermined both by the discursive strategies on which it draws for its representational categories and by the anxieties about black sexuality which it constantly betrays and which cannot be resolved within its narrative. Our second case study emerges from a very different cultural moment and is structured according to very different conventions. *The Bill* (Thames TV, 1984–) is an ensemble-based police series, set in Sun Hill in the London borough of Canley, which over its 20 years has adopted a number of formats. The episode on which we shall focus, 'One Man, Two Faces' is a 25 minute episode screened in August 1998.

Looking first at the cultural context of this episode, we can trace a considerable shift in conceptions of 'race' and national identity since the wave of Caribbean immigration in the 1950s. The 'biological' conception of 'race' which underlies fears of sexual 'tainting', of 'miscegenation' and the degeneration of the British into a 'mongrel' race,[9] had given way to what Paul Gilroy has called 'cultural' definitions of 'race'. Manifest as early as Enoch Powell's speeches of the late 1960s, this view received its most powerful endorsement in Margaret Thatcher's rhetoric of 'one nation' in the 1980s, in speeches which make it clear, as Paul Gilroy argues (1987: 60), that 'cultural racism' is just as intractable as the notions of biological purity which preceded it. In this rhetoric it is the threat of 'being swamped by people with a different *culture*' which threatens British national identity (Margaret Thatcher, quoted in Webster 1990: 157, my emphasis). As Gilroy argues:

> We increasingly face a racism which avoids being recognized as such because it is able to link 'race' with nationhood, patriotism and nationalism, a racism

> which has taken a necessary distance from crude ideas of biological inferiority and superiority and now seeks to present an imaginary definition of the nation as a unified *cultural* community. (Gilroy 1992: 53)

Yet despite Thatcher's insistence throughout the 1980s that 'We British are as we have always been', these ideas became increasingly open to ideological contestation. 'Western nation-states', writes Stuart Hall, 'already "diaspora-ized" beyond repair, are becoming inextricably "multicultural" – "mixed" ethnically, religiously, culturally, linguistically' (1993: 356). In such a situation 'internal others' can not be so easily identified, as communities overlap, form and reform within the urban landscape, becoming increasingly hybrid and plural. Whilst ideologies of national identity might still be concerned to regulate boundaries, identifying, in Thatcher's words, 'the extremists' or 'the enemy within', the precise location of such boundaries, like the precise nature of the 'imagined community'[10] of the nation, becomes a more uncertain affair.

In *The Bill* we are presented with two communities. The first is that which lies outside the boundaries of the police station, the multi-ethnic inner-city Jasmine Allen estate, site of urban unrest and vulnerable to infiltration by extremists, those who want to politicise and use such unrest rather than subjecting it to regulation through law and order. It is here that we find the locus of disruption which drives many of the narratives. The second community is that of the police station itself, often besieged, existing in a complex relationship to the outer community, and containing its own mix across lines of culture, 'race', class and gender, its own hierarchies, its good and bad 'coppers', its traditional (uniformed) police and maverick detectives. It is this community, with its cast of 'known' characters, which stands in for 'us', displacing and resolving the tensions and conflicts of the contemporary inner city.

In 'One Man, Two Faces', PCs McCann (black) and Santini (white) investigate an attack on a 14-year-old black boy, Benjy Taiwo. Because the attack follows the establishment of a local office of the 'Nationalist Aligned Party', a racist motivation is urged by Vernon Johnson, a self-styled 'spokesman for the local black community', an interpretation supported by McCann but not by Santini. The two find the white attacker but, though the 'nationalist organisation' is found to be distributing racist leaflets, the attacker cannot be linked to it. Under interrogation he confesses that he was paid to carry out the attack by Johnson, in order to stir up anger against the 'nationalist organisation'. The charge cannot be proved, however, and

Johnson leaves the police station, only to receive violent retribution from a group of local black youths, including Benjy's brother.

The episode, with its 'closed' structure of disruption/investigation/resolution, supports many of the arguments of Schlesinger et al. about the ideological function of such series. It is the police, familiar to us across episodes, who truly represent the community, maintaining order by rejecting and expelling extremists of all kinds. When the representative of the white supremacist organisation (a Scot, not a local man) protests to Chief Inspector Conway that 'We're on the same side', Conway responds, 'Same side! We're not even on the same planet!', but he is equally unwilling to support Johnson, another outsider and politician. The central police figure in the episode is PC Gary McCann, who must choose between his identity as representative of law and advocate of 'correct' procedures, and his loyalty to the 'black community'. Set against him is Santini, the 'intuitive' but less ethical cop. In the end both are revealed to be half-right: the attack is a criminal not a political matter, but McCann's methods, which insist on the distinction between legal procedures and the vigilante actions to be found 'out there', are vindicated. More importantly, however, the notion of a 'black community' is seen to be as much a political fiction as the slogan 'Keep Britain white', and as dangerous. As Benjy's brother tells Johnson, 'I don't give a *damn* about the local black community. My brother's in there looking like he's done ten rounds with Mike Tyson . . . This ain't about politics. It's about *my* little brother'. It is the community of *families*, white or black, which the police must protect, and in this process the wider view is held not by McCann, who must learn, like Cleve, to broaden his loyalties, but by the white figure of authority, Conway.

We can see, then, that the episode employs a number of strategies in relation to ideologies of 'race' and national culture. The distinction drawn between 'ordinary' black families, who can now be included within an inclusive notion of 'the nation', and a politicised concept of 'the black community', which threatens it, serves a clear ideological function. In the representation of McCann's innocence and Johnson's corrupt brutality, too (he is often shown in extreme close-up, sweating), we can find traces of the discursive strategies which Stuart Hall describes as characteristic of representations of the non-Western 'other'. Finally, we can trace the ideological displacement of the actual conflicts of the 1980s and 1990s between a largely white (and racist) police force and a disenfranchised black population (Gilroy 1987: 98–104) onto a representation of conflicts *within* both the police force and the community, conflicts which can be narratively resolved. Yet this is not a text without ideological complexity. The various discourses of identity which confront McCann cannot be resolved: his identity is *multiply* constructed and subject to contradiction, as we see throughout the series. The community 'outside' is multiple and overlapping, too, and whilst we can read the episode's rejection of a 'black community' as an attempt to deny the political realities of racism, in the complex and multi-ethnic community which replaces it we can also see an extension of the concept of national identity and citizenship to include groups previously excluded. If, as Stuart Hall argues (1996: 31), ideological struggle often consists of 'attempting to win some new set of meanings for an existing term or category', then the episode becomes a site of struggle over the meaning of the term 'community'. Even the 'closed' format of the police series can present us with ideological contradiction.

Conclusions

Ideological analysis has proved a useful tool in the analysis of television drama because it concerns, in Terry Eagleton's words, 'the way power struggles are fought out at the level of signification' (1991: 113), through the narratives, images and forms through which television drama renders the world meaningful for us and through which we construct our sense of identity. Often, however, it has been used to draw distinctions within television drama, between the 'single play', 'open', experimental and ideologically oppositional, and the popular series whose 'closed' format can only perpetuate the 'dominant' ideology. In the case studies above we have tried to show something of the 'power struggles' which it can reveal, as each drama both pulls us towards an ideological consensus which serves the needs of the cultural formation that produced it and becomes a site on which the contradictions and tensions within that formation are played out.

3.2 Uses of Psychoanalysis

Psychoanalysis and Television

Psychoanalysis is the discipline founded by Freud which takes as its object of study the concept of the human unconscious and its desires. It is above all a theory of human subjectivity: of how we as human beings acquire a sense of self and sexual identity within a social and cultural order which at once assigns us a place and channels, disciplines and represses our most fundamental pleasures and desires. Psychoanalysis investigates these pleasures and desires, their unconscious structures, and the mechanisms through which they are channelled, repressed and find expression, often in displaced or fantasised form. Whilst ideological analysis emphasises the ways in which meanings and values are related to social structures and caught up in relations of social power, even if they are experienced at the level of the individual, it is the individual psyche and its desires, anxieties and repressions which is the focus of psychoanalytic enquiry. In both approaches *representations* play a key role, but whereas ideological analysis emphasises their importance as stories, images and forms which render the world *meaningful*, psychoanalysis stresses their function as embodiments of *desire*. Thus Elizabeth Cowie, arguing for the importance of a psychoanalytic approach, insists that the 'pleasure of representation lies not only in what is signified – a meaning'; it also lies in 'the scenario of desire which I come to participate in as I watch a film, view an image, or read a text' (1997: 4). The fact that our investment in such scenarios operates at an unconscious level also points to another key difference between psychoanalytic and ideological analysis. The viewer envisaged within ideological analysis is ideologically positioned by the text, but engaged in a struggle or negotiation over meaning, however much the text itself seeks to present that meaning as 'self-evident' or 'natural'. The viewer envisaged by psychoanalytic theory, on the other hand, is split, caught up in desiring fantasies which must by their very nature evade and subvert conscious meaning. The first suggests that representations provide the material through which we construct and negotiate our identities; the second that representations reveal again and again the irrevocably split nature of those identities – what Elizabeth Cowie calls the irredeemable 'otherness of ourselves' (ibid.).

Cowie's comments were made in the context of a framework for understanding *cinema*, however, and it is notable that whereas ideological approaches have been used consistently in the analysis of television, and specifically of television drama, psychoanalytic approaches, despite their emphasis on representation, on narrative and on images, have been much more infrequently applied. Critics, indeed, have often insisted that psychoanalytic approaches *cannot* be applied to the analysis of television drama – or at least not in the same way as they can be used in the analysis of cinema. Both Sandy Flitterman-Lewis (1992) and John Caughie (2000), in their discussions of this issue, move from an initial statement that psychoanalytic approaches have been 'mysteriously lacking' in the analysis of television drama (Caughie 2000: 137) to an argument that such approaches, developed as they have been in relation to cinema, are actually inapplicable to television. The reasons for this lie in the history of television analysis as it has developed since the 1970s. As we saw in Chapter 1, early analyses of television were concerned to insist on its *differences* from cinema. These differences were seen to lie in two essential aspects: the *social* nature of television as a medium, and its *undifferentiated* quality. The first of these places emphasis on television as an industrial medium whose programmes are *produced* centrally but *received* in the dispersed domestic setting of the family home. It can thus be seen as a very powerful transmitter of ideological meanings, particularly since its self-promotion as a live and immediate 'window on the world' suggests a transparency and neutrality about its images which serve effectively to mask their constructed nature. The second has its origins in the concepts of 'flow' and 'segmentation' introduced by Raymond Williams and John Ellis. If, as these writers suggest, television and its different genres offer us, not distinctive experiences but rather 'a single . . . flow of images and feelings' (Williams 1990: 92), then it is this 'flow' and its elements, rather than specific narrative or representational structures and images, which will be the focus of our analysis.

For both Flitterman-Lewis and Caughie, these differences produce fundamental difficulties for the application of a psychoanalytic approach to television. Flitterman-Lewis, arguing that we simply do not watch television in the same way as cinema, suggests that it cannot therefore engage our unconscious desires and fantasies in the same way:

> A film is always distanced from us spatially (we sit 'away' from it in the theater), making the screen image seem inaccessible, beyond our reach. The television set occupies a space that is nearby – just across the room, at the end of the bed, in the palm of our hand, or elsewhere. The television screen thus takes up a much-reduced, and more intimate, part of the spectator's visual field and seems available . . . at a moment's notice. It does not fascinate in quite the same way. (1992: 218)

She concludes that television produces a quite different kind of pleasure, one which positions us outside rather than within its fictional worlds, which offers us a multiplicity of identifications and sympathies rather than an intense absorption, and which 'embed[s] distraction in its very core' (ibid., 238). For Caughie, too, the combination of television's 'promise of endless flow' and its actual interruptibility (interrupted by ads, by channel switching, by domestic conversation, activities and comings and goings) means that it cannot engage our desires and fantasies in the same way as cinema. Instead, he argues, 'serious drama' plays on this greater detachment, offering modes of engagement which invite a sort of 'absent-minded' or 'distracted' but nevertheless critical attention, invoking distance and irony rather than involvement and fantasy (2000: 138–40).

Yet these accounts can be seen as limited in a number of ways. Caughie is concerned exclusively with 'serious drama', whilst Flitterman-Lewis takes as her case study the American daytime soap opera. Neither, then, discuss the popular television drama series, with its structured and repetitive narratives, its preoccupation with questions of identity, its constant restaging of threats to order and the self, and its persistent reworkings of familial, or pseudo-familial, relationships – all themes central to psychoanalytic theory. More important, however, are the limitations inherent in their model of 'television itself', rooted as it is in analyses of television produced in the 1970s and early 1980s. More recent accounts of television offer a number of challenges to this model.

In his 1995 book, *Televisuality*, John Caldwell attacks what he calls the 'distracted surrender gaze theory' (1995: 25): the notion that television both invites and is accorded not an intense and involved 'gaze', but a distracted 'glance'. This, argues Caldwell, is simply not true of contemporary television, which both invites and rewards an intense and discriminating involvement. The intensely involved 'cinephile' cited by John Ellis is today more than matched by the fan of *The X-Files* (1993–2002) or *Buffy the Vampire Slayer* (1997–), whose involvement in the series is furthered intertextually by books, CDs, magazines and websites.[11] Watching television may indeed involve 'wading through' its 'morasslike flow', but, argues Caldwell, this can be more than counteracted within the viewing experience itself. This can in fact be *more* intense than cinematic spectatorship, since, whereas 'viewership for film is a one-shot experience that comes and goes, spectatorship in television can be quite intense and ingrained over time' (1995: 26).

Some television viewers *are* deeply engaged in television's fantasies, then, and do 'find pleasure in entranced isolation whilst watching' (ibid., 27). Indeed, shifting patterns of both production and spectatorship can be cited in support of the notion of a convergence of viewing modes in relation to film and television. Caldwell describes the increasing crossover of directors and modes of production between the two which began in the 1980s, as well as a growing emphasis on high production values, stylistic exhibition and visual excess in the television drama series of the 1980s and

1990s. As spectators, too, we may now choose to replicate in some of our television viewing modes of spectatorship more commonly identified with film. With the aid of high-definition video or DVD recordings we may watch in uninterrupted fashion in a darkened room, transforming our domestic space into a space of fantasy, and electing to watch both films and TV dramas in this fashion. As Caldwell comments, 'Theorists should not jump to theoretical conclusions just because there is an ironing board in the room' (ibid.).

A more useful way of thinking about the *investments*[12] we make in the fictional narratives of TV drama might perhaps be to insist that they are *both* social – to do with meanings – *and* psychic – to do with desires, anxieties and pleasures. Linda Williams has argued of popular genres that they operate as a sort of 'cultural problem-solving. Genres thrive . . . on the persistence of the problems they address; but genres thrive also in their ability to recast the nature of these problems' (1999: 280). Popular narratives, then, are always historically specific: they deal with the issues and anxieties of the moment (issues, perhaps, to do with crime, social change, corruption or terrorism). But they also reach back to much more 'persistent' anxieties: anxieties to do with our sense of self or our sexual identities. In a similar way, James Donald has described popular TV dramas as creating not so much 'maps of meaning', as an ideological analysis would suggest, but 'mapping fantasies': 'mapping' because they refer always to the historical moment in which they are produced; but *fantasies* because they also 'give shape to unconscious wishes and anxieties' (1985: 125). It is psychoanalytic theory, these critics argue, that gives us insight into the ways in which such fantasies are structured and the ways in which we come to participate in them.

Psychoanalytic Theory

Psychoanalysis, as we have seen, is founded on the concept of the unconscious. The unconscious, according to Freud, is both the source and repository of our most fundamental drives, drives for (sexual) fulfilment and pleasure. It comes into being at the point when the human infant must learn to repress or modify those desires in order to become a social being. This is the point at which the infant enters culture and language, with all the structures and rules that these orders imply, and in so doing acquires an identity and sense of self (a *subjectivity*). It is an identity, however, which is always *subject to* the regulatory structures of culture. For Freud, the human psyche comprises the unconscious, which remains the source of our individual desires but becomes also the repository of our anxieties, and consciousness, through which we operate rationally and socially in the world. Later, Freud named the unconscious the *id* (or 'it') and consciousness the *ego* (or 'I'), and added to them the concept of the *super-ego*, the internalised voice of authority or society's rules which we all acquire. In such a scenario identity is always precarious, always in some sense at odds with itself, and always – in that the word 'identity' implies 'oneness' or 'sameness' – illusory. The ego is caught between powerful desires and anxieties and the forces of social regulation, and both come from outside itself; identity is always split, and we can never know ourselves.

There are a number of key elements of psychoanalytic theory, as it was elaborated first by Freud and then by the French psychoanalyst Jacques Lacan, which were taken up by theorists of cinema. I shall focus here upon three – the child's *acquisition of identity*, *dreams*, and *fantasy* – before turning to the ways in which these ideas have been used in the analysis of film and television drama. The first element centres upon Freud's concept of the Oedipus complex and its later reworking by Lacan. The child's early relationship with the mother is mutual and exclusive: the child both desires and identifies with the mother, and the gratification of its demands is constant and immediate. This unity must be broken if the child is to acquire a separate identity and a place in the social order. For Freud, it is the father who intervenes to effect this (for Lacan it is what the father represents: the social and cultural, or 'symbolic', order), by barring the child's exclusive access to the mother. The male child, in the words of Elizabeth Grosz, construes these prohibitions as castration threats, and these eventually lead him to renounce his desire of the mother because of his fear of the organ's loss, that is, because of the father's authority and power as 'possessor' of the phallus (1990: 68). The female child (who receives much less attention from both Freud and Lacan) must also renounce her desire for the mother; instead she must learn to identify with her and, since she does not 'possess the phallus', learn to relinquish her role as active desirer and become instead the object of masculine desire.

Importantly, this moment when the child moves from the pleasurable, symbiotic, and sexually undifferentiated relationship with the mother into a mature identity within culture, the moment in which the unconscious is formed, is, in Freud's account, one in which *the visual* is central. The boy, writes Freud, begins by believing that all human beings possess a penis; it is the sight of the woman's difference which precipitates the Oedipus complex. For the girl, too, knowledge of sexual difference is precipitated by an act of vision, though for her the outcome is rather different: 'She has seen it and knows that she is without it and wants to have it', writes Freud (1977: 336). Thus, at the moment when a sense of identity is being formed, the act of vision is identified for the male child both with erotic pleasure in looking (what Freud called scopophilia) and with anxiety about sexual difference. This last leads to what Freud calls 'disavowal', in which the boy simultaneously *knows* that the woman is different and 'covers over' this difference, by investing her with a substitute phallus in the form of a fetishised object or body part.

An act of vision is also central to Lacan's account of the child's separation from the mother. His description of the 'mirror stage' identifies an intermediate stage between the child's total absorption in the mother and its entry into the social and symbolic order, a stage which is dominated by the child's identification with an *image*, the image of itself. It is this recognition of the image of the self which begins the process by which we see ourselves as having an identity separate from the rest of the world. We assume our *identities* through a process of *identification*.[13]

In addition to the importance of identification with a visual image, in this account of how we acquire a sense of identity, there are three further points which we should note. One is that this first recognition of itself as a discrete individual is in fact a *mis*recognition. The mirror-image with which the child identifies is more co-ordinated, more unified and in control, than is the child itself. Nevertheless, it is this imaginary wholeness which the child internalises as an 'ideal ego'. The mirror phase is, in Sarup's words, 'a moment of self-delusion, of captivation by an *illusory* image' (1992: 83, my emphasis). The second point to note is that, as in its earlier relationship with the mother, the child both identifies with and *desires* this image of itself. Thirdly, Lacan emphasises that this moment of self-recognition is also a moment of self-alienation, of splitting. The child identifies with an image of itself that is always – like the images on the cinema or TV screen – *elsewhere*, and always in some sense the image of another. We cannot close the gap between the self which looks and the image-of-self which is looked at, though we constantly seek to do so.

All of these ideas were to prove highly suggestive for later accounts of how and why we find ourselves so caught up in the images produced on the cinema screen. But films and TV dramas are not just a matter of images; they are also stories, a product of culture and the 'symbolic order' as well as the Imaginary. In Lacan's account of the child's entry into language, or the Symbolic, he rewrites Freud's Oedipal process as an account of the child's entry into culture. If it is the sense of identity and separation experienced through the mirror stage that creates the *possibility* of a sense of self, of being able to say 'I', the language which we learn to use is a structure which is always there before us. In entering it we learn to say 'I', and so construct a sense of self, but that sense of self is precarious. Others can be 'I' too, and in language we are positioned also as 'he' or 'she', 'him' or 'her'; language, in other words, constructs *us* even as we assert ourselves as subjects within it. Language is, moreover, the realm of the Symbolic, substituting linguistic and cultural symbols for a reality which is always absent, at one remove; and promising *meaning* in exchange for the immediacy of being. It is this linguistic and cultural system which for Lacan constitutes that 'father' which represses the child's desires (Lacan calls it the 'name-of-the-father' or the 'Law of the Father'), not, as with Freud, the real, flesh-and-blood parent.

This means that when we use language, when we tell and are told stories, desire is operating in two ways. The first concerns the way in which we become caught up in the chain of meanings which constitute a story, desiring the moment of completion – the end of the story when meaning is established and identity (our own and that of the characters in the story) is confirmed. This is a moment, however, which is always fleeting and always disappointing, because after all this is *only* a story, and the desires it enacts remain unfulfilled. So we turn to the next story, whose structures and processes repeat those of the one we have just finished. The second way in which desire operates concerns repression. If the stories we tell and are told are always the stories which the social and cultural order permits us to tell, then they are always simultaneously repressions or distortions of those desires and fears which *can not* be expressed. Words or images which express some (permitted) meanings simultaneously repress others which are literally unspeakable. Yet these repressed desires continue to shadow the story, producing those shivers of fear and delight when the unconscious and its desires and fears come too close to the surface.

This *doubleness* of narrative, particularly a narrative told in visual terms, in which desire is simultaneously expressed and repressed, is also a key feature of the two other elements of psychoanalytic theory which we shall emphasise here: *dream theory* and *fantasy theory*. In Freud's model of the human psyche, those impulses which in the post-Oedipal subject are repressed strive constantly for access to consciousness. In sleep, when impulses are denied access to active expression, the psychic sensor can afford to relax. Unconscious wishes can therefore achieve limited expression, by attaching themselves to fragments of visual memory in the form of an hallucination. Thus the dream is a disguised and hallucinatory fulfilment of a repressed wish. The disguise is the result of the 'dream-work', which, in Madan Sarup's words, 'transforms the "latent" content of the dream, the forbidden dream-thoughts, into the "manifest" dream-stories – what the dreamer remembers' (1992: 6). This 'dream-work' has four aspects. The first is the transformation of desires or fears into *visual images*. Dreams must be able to represent logical or causal relations and abstract thoughts in visual form. The second is *condensation*, in which two or more ideas are compressed, to become a composite image which carries a number of repressed desires or anxieties. The third aspect of the dream-work is *displacement*. Here the unconscious wish or fear is disguised by being displaced on to a figure or image with which it is associated in some way, but which does not itself attract repression.

All of these processes help to explain why the emotions we experience in relation to a dream often seem out of proportion to the dream's content. If the same processes are at work in relation to *screen* images, they might explain the intensity of our responses to these too. Finally, there is *secondary revision*. In this process, the dream is reorganised so as to form a relatively coherent and comprehensible story; when we recount our dreams, we are engaged in this process, smoothing out gaps and contradictions to produce a consistent narrative. Freud's account makes no firm distinction between the unconscious fantasies of dreaming, the more conscious fantasies represented by daydreams, and the public fantasies constructed within popular narratives. This broader concept of fantasy is one which has also proved productive for film and TV drama, as seen in James Donald's description of popular drama series as creating 'mapping fantasies'.[14]

Psychoanalysis, Film and Television Drama

Most of the applications of psychoanalytic theory to the analysis of visual narratives have concerned cinema. Cinema, with its darkened auditorium, its immobile spectator and its huge screen, seems to replicate the situation of dreaming and so give us access in the same way to fantasy and desire. Moreover, it not only provides 'condensed' and spectacular images of fear and desire; it also provides us, through the figures of its stars, with 'ideal ego' images with which to identify. Like Lacan's mirror-image, the star is more powerful, more in control than the spectating self, and the star's ultimate triumph acts as reinforcement to the spectator's sense of identity. Like the male child, too, the spectator of popular cinema is offered eroticised images of sexual difference through the figures of the women whom the hero possesses; but as with the child, he may find them not only erotic but disturbing and threatening in their difference, as, for instance, with the figure of the *femme fatale*. Two final points of comparison can be made. First, as in the psychoanalytic account of fantasy, the spectator is offered '*scenarios* of desire', often – through camera angles and movement, and point-of-view shots – with multiple and shifting points of identification. Second, these scenarios offer not only visual images but *stories*; like the dream narrative, they seek to smooth out gaps and contradictions and, as with any story, they simultaneously speak to and repress our desires.

Psychoanalytic theory has been applied, then, in two ways. First, it has considered the *text* as a repository of cultural anxieties and repressions, fears and anxieties about difference. Such an approach, in Annette Kuhn's words, 'implies that cultural productions, such as films, may be regarded as sites of unconscious meanings – unconscious because repressed, and therefore inexpressible in direct form'. Such meanings, she continues, 'are there in the text, but appear in disguise – betraying themselves only in certain cues or clues, which have to be interpreted' (1990: 92). These public forms of fantasy, then, replay their stories 'before the cameras, always the same but differently' (Cowie 1997: 138), drawing us in to their structures of desire and fear which are also our own. Attention to them can reveal culture's repressions, taboos and obsessions, as they play on unconscious processes whilst working them through in the form of cultural productions.

The second, but clearly related, application of psychoanalytic theory has been to the *spectator–text relationship*. This has included ways of understanding the processes of *identification* that operate, as the spectator identifies first with the camera, whose gaze we must share and which is, in Christian Metz's words, '*all-perceiving*'(1975: 51), and second with the central figure of the hero, whose point of view the camera often takes. It has also sought to account for the *pleasures* experienced by the spectator: cinema's pleasures, argues Metz, are those of Freud's 'perceptual passions', and particularly 'the desire to see' or 'voyeurism' (ibid., 59). As used by feminist critics, it has also been used to account for the *sexual imbalance* in the structures of visual pleasure the screen offers. In mainstream film, argues Laura Mulvey (1989), it is the figure of the *male* star which offers the image of an 'ideal ego'; the image of woman in cinema is more often coded for her 'to-be-looked-at-ness', remaining as object – both erotic and disturbing – for the male gaze.

Finally, and more recently, psychoanalytic *fantasy* theory has been used to suggest a conception of spectatorship which, whilst still emphasising what John Caldwell calls the 'entranced isolation' of the viewing process, offers a rather more fluid and mobile model of how this operates than one which fixes us in a position of gendered identification. Fantasy theory, because it suggests that the public fantasies of cinema or television are *both* historically and culturally specific *and* responsive to unconscious drives, also provides a way out of thinking of them as *either* social and public *or* psychic and individual, and of the argument that so often follows, that it is *television* which deals with the former, whilst *film* is concerned with the latter. Indeed, in its greater reliance on generic patterns of repetition through the series form, its tendency to privilege the group or pair (often with a mix of genders and 'races') rather than the single hero, and its use of multiple and shifting patterns of identification within its 'scenarios of desire', popular television drama might be said to offer *more* correspondence to the concept of fantasy as developed within psychoanalytic theory than do the more differentiated narratives of film.

Not surprisingly, the two genres of television drama which have received most attention from this approach have been the *detective* or *crime series*, with its play on concealment and investigation, the unlawful and the permitted; and the *science fiction series*, with its creation of fantasy figures of desire and horror, and the 'other worlds' which they inhabit. In Section 3.1 we saw how the police series has been analysed in relation to theories of ideology, so that its characteristic structure of disruption/investigation/resolution is seen to restore the ideological status quo by expelling disruptive or threatening elements. Steve Neale, however, argues that this structure also serves a rather different function. Popular genres, he argues, operate as ways of regulating difference, anxiety and desire. The threat of disruption is a threat to order, coherence and identity; its restoration confirms the coherence of our sense of self (1980: 26). But if the restoration of order offers us obvious pleasures, its disruption creates pleasure of a different kind, through the release, however temporary, of unconscious desires and fears. In the case of the detective genre, these processes are particularly prominent. Its stories are explicitly concerned with the Law and its symbolic structures. The detective, usually male, must deal with threats to these structures, and he must do this through a process of visual investigation, a voyeuristic uncovering of clues leading to knowledge. Thus the detective hero constantly repeats the processes through which, in the psychoanalytic account, masculine identity is established. Popular genres, writes Neale, are engaged constantly in 'an ongoing process of construction of sexual difference and sexual identity' (ibid., 56).

James Donald draws on this approach in his analysis of the 1970s series, *The Sweeney*. Its central character, the rebellious and anti-authoritarian detective, Regan, functions, he argues, as 'the Oedipal son, bridling against the phallic authority of the law, yet desiring to embody that authority himself, to *be* the law' (1985: 129). In this sense the series, though still very much of its cultural moment, is concerned less about threats to law and order than with anxieties about masculine identity. Female sexuality in the world of *The Sweeney* is 'mysterious and troubling'; women in the series are either symbols of a threatened purity – innocent princesses who must be rescued by the hero – or sexualised and 'deviant' figures who represent a threat to his authority. Thus the order which Regan seeks to restore is as much an imaginary order of 'wholeness' – 'an infantile, pre-cultural world devoid of anxiety and threat' (ibid., 131) – as it is the ideological status quo. What popular series like *The Sweeney* offer, argues Donald, is above all 'the fantasy experience of fear – precisely the playing out of repressed anxieties' (ibid., 134).

In the case of science fiction, these anxieties can be embodied directly, in the form of the alien worlds and their fantastic, often monstrous inhabitants, which characterise it as a genre. In their analysis of the long-running BBC series *Doctor Who* (1963–96), John Tulloch and Manuel Alvarado make explicit many of these ideas. Drawing on Tzvetan Todorov's work on *The Fantastic* (1975), they argue that we can find two kinds of identity myth in operation in such narratives. The first concerns 'themes of the self' (Todorov 1975: 146) and we can see it exemplified in stories like Mary Shelley's *Frankenstein* (1818) or Robert Louis Stevenson's *The Strange Case of Dr. Jekyll and Mr. Hyde* (1886). Here the threat to the self is internal, in the form of self-alienation or splitting of identity, caused by the excessive desire for knowledge, reason or control. The second concerns 'themes of the other' (ibid., 147) and we can see it in Bram Stoker's *Dracula* (1897) and tales of vampirism. Here the threat to the self is external, the threat of bodily invasion, metamorphosis and fusion (Tulloch and Alvadaro 1983: 127). In fact, of course, the two are intertwined: the monstrous 'other' is no less a 'monster from the Id' than the split-off self: both embody fears about the body and its (alien) desires, about sexuality and about sexual difference; both are preoccupied with the fragility of identity. Thus Freud's 'primal fantasies' figure prominently in these stories, as does the figure of the double, or 'deviant' self (in the case of *Doctor Who*, the Doctor's fellow Time Lord, the Master), and the dark and underground caves and tunnels (the unconscious) through which this figure frequently roams. Freud's notion of 'the uncanny' (*das Unheimlich*) is a common theme, in which that which is most familiar (*heimlich* or homely) is also that which is most hidden, most secret and obscured, so that the familiar and the unfamiliar become disturbingly identical.

Science fiction, of course, is not the same as 'the fantastic', and writers of science fiction have sought to distinguish the two. Science fiction has been identified with 'scientific realism': its alternative worlds are described with technical precision and presented as internally coherent, *possible* worlds, unlike the 'irrational' transformations of the fantastic (ibid., 99–127). For Tulloch and Alvarado, however, this is too simplistic a division. *Doctor Who*, like other science fiction, is, they write, concerned *both* with 'the drive towards the coherent' – towards naming, defining, making explicable – *and* with 'the recognition of the incoherent' (ibid., 141) – the monsters and doubles who can be neither explained nor repressed, and who constantly, insistently *return*.

Psychoanalysis and Television Drama: Two Case Studies

In the following case studies we shall examine an example of each of the two popular genres mentioned here, the *science fiction series* and the *detective or crime series*. The first is an episode from the first series of that most enduring of science fiction series, *Star Trek*. Screened first in the USA on 20 October1966, 'What Are Little Girls Made Of?' was the sixth episode shown after the series pilot, and the title makes clear its concerns with questions of identity and sexual difference. In it the Starship Enterprise arrives at planet Exo III in search of the man 'often called the Pasteur of archaeological medicine', Dr Roger Korby, who disappeared there five years earlier. Korby makes contact, and Captain Kirk and Korby's fiancée, Christine, beam down to the planet, where Korby and his team are living in underground caverns beneath the planet's frozen surface. Korby, with the aid of Roc, a giant android left behind by the planet's lost civilisation, has learnt how to create androids through which he intends to inaugurate 'a new paradise'. Holding Kirk prisoner, he demonstrates his powers by creating an android double for the captain, but Kirk escapes into the underground tunnels. He is caught and returned by Roc but, by introducing the androids to emotion (desire), causes them to destroy each other. Finally, we discover that Korby too has an android body, into which he has transposed his own mind, but in the fusion has become alienated from his human identity. Realising this, he annihilates himself and his 'mechanical geisha', the female android Andrea, with a single ray from his phaser gun, as she tries to kiss him. Questioned about the doctor's disappearance by Spock, Kirk replies that Dr Korby 'was never here'.

It is an episode which displays many of the characteristics of Freudian dream and fantasy theory. Most obviously, in this underground world with its tunnels and chambers we find enacted Freud's three 'primal fantasies'. There is the fantasy of (self) conception and birth, as Korby as father and Kirk as son together produce a cloned Kirk, split off in pain from the original, and created naked in the mechanical womb of Korby's cavern, aided by the male and female androids, Roc and Andrea. In Andrea, the android child-woman, we see enacted the Freudian 'upsurge of sexuality' through seduction, as Andrea's own access to desire is created through Kirk's seduction of her (access to desire for the male android Roc is through his discovery of *aggression* towards the father, Korby). Finally, we can trace fantasies of 'castration', most obviously in the huge phallic 'rock' which Kirk wields as a weapon against his rival, Roc, but also in the visual revelation that these men of authority, *Dr* Korby and his assistant *Dr* Brown, are not in fact men at all, a revelation that strips them of their power.

Above all, this is an episode preoccupied with anxieties about masculine identity and authority, and with fears of racial and sexual difference. For Kirk, the idealised hero-figure (or ideal ego), Korby is a lost father, an authority figure (Kirk calls him 'sir') whom Kirk, like Oedipus, must displace if he is to affirm his own authority. Christine, Korby's fiancée, is ambivalently positioned, alternately maternal and jealous towards the child-woman, Andrea, and torn between the two figures of masculine authority, Korby and Kirk. Korby himself is the corrupt father, object (and perhaps subject) of incestuous desire in relation to his 'daughter' Andrea, and usurping, like Dr Frankenstein, the functions of both conception and birth through his use of technology. His ultimate arrogance is to seek to create/give birth to *himself*, a crime punished by his loss of self: 'I *am* Roger Korby!' he cries at the end, before realising that he can in fact claim no such unified identity. A parallel splitting also threatens Kirk, whose android double shares his tastes and memories, but not his capacity for ego-control: it is when, programmed by the real Kirk, the android calls Mr. Spock a 'half-breed' that Spock understands that this is not in fact the real captain. Yet anxieties about miscegenation are in part what the episode expresses – and represses. Korby, Brown, Andrea and Roc are all 'half-breeds', as is the split-off 'copy' of Kirk. By far the most disturbing figure in the episode, however, is Roc, who combines this racial indeterminacy with sexual ambiguity. Inhabitant of the underground tunnels, given 'ancient' clothing and 'primitive' speech, Roc embodies the barely controlled impulses (sexual and aggressive) of the unconscious or Id. Yet his desire – and contempt – for the two female characters takes the form of *identification*: Roc can produce perfect copies of their voices, seductive and gently reassuring in turn, and in so doing he enacts a performance of femininity which both parodies and disturbs gender boundaries.

At the end of the episode the identity and authority of Kirk's perfect (white American) masculinity is reaffirmed. In this narrative of its temporary disturbance, however, we can trace both historically specific anxieties, and fears about identity which are more deeply rooted. America in the 1960s saw the civil rights, anti-Vietnam war and student movements, and the beginnings of what was to become the Women's Liberation Movement. Against these threats to the established order, *Star Trek*'s constant reassertion of the *rightness* of the USS Enterprise's civilising mission, 'to boldly go where no man has gone before', bringing scientific rationalism and American values, and organising its multicultural crew under white American leadership, clearly served an ideological purpose. At the same time, however, in the series' preoccupation with the fragility of identity, with threats of bodily dissolution and alien invasion, with forbidden desires and fears of otherness, it played out anxieties which, in the words of Annette Kuhn, work through 'under seemingly innocent cover, . . . cultural taboos and obsessions which cannot be expressed openly' (1990: 92–3).

Waking the Dead is a British crime series first aired in September 2000, in which a group of detectives, the 'Cold Case Squad', investigate serious crimes which have gone unsolved. As with many such series, its 'squad' forms a pseudo-familial grouping offering multiple points of identification: the paternal – but still rebellious – leader, Detective Superintendent Peter Boyd, a maternal figure in psychological profiler Dr Grace Foley, and three younger characters: female forensic pathologist Dr Frankie Wharton, black detective Spencer (Spence) Jordan, and the young female detective Mel Silver. As in many other such series, too, it is the investigation of the family and familial relationships which is at its centre, a centrality strengthened in this case by the basic problematic of the series: its investigation of the hidden secrets of the past. Like the psychoanalytic investigation,[15] it offers itself as an archaeological exploration of that which is hidden at the heart of the most familiar (Freud's *heimlich/unheimlich*).

The episode 'Thin Air', thc last of the second series, was screened on 3 and 4 November 2002. Joanna Gold, 18-year-old daughter of a wealthy publisher, disappeared 12 years earlier on Hampstead Heath, near her home. The red dress which she was wearing has been found in a rented underground lock-up, displayed on a shop mannequin and accompanied by a scrapbook about her disappearance. The renter of the lock-up, Alec Garvey, is traced and, after pressure for an early arrest from the Police Commissioner, who is chairman of the Joanna Gold Trust, he is charged with Joanna's murder. After Garvey attempts suicide, however, Boyd reopens the investigation. He discovers that Joanna, unknown to her parents, had a black boyfriend whom she met in a ruined church at the centre of the heath on the day of her disappearance, watched by Garvey. The family's former nanny, who knew the identity of the boyfriend, is murdered. Urged on by Joanna's younger sister Clara, who is now the same age as her sister at the time of Joanna's disappearance (she is played by the same actor), and who feels that she too is being followed and watched, Boyd permits Clara to return to the ruined church at night, wearing Joanna's dress. Once there, Clara embraces Boyd and they hear the click of a camera, but the watcher eludes Boyd. Joanna's brother David, an emotionally dysfunctional young man, who was 13 at the time of her disappearance, confesses to killing both Joanna and the nanny and reveals that Joanna's body is buried in the Golds' garden. However, Boyd discovers that David only watched the murder and burial; the murderer is Joanna's father, whose possessive desire for his daughter (now repeated with his younger daughter) caused him to kill her when she returned to the house on the evening of her disappearance and declared her intention of leaving with her black boyfriend.

That this is an episode which will be concerned with the loss of girlhood innocence and the transgressive desires of a paternal figure is indicated from the start by the recurring references to Lewis Carroll's *Alice in Wonderland*. Like Alice, Joanna disappeared 'down a hole', the assumed name under which Garvey rents the lock-up is Mr White of Alice Street, and Garvey's mother made dolls' houses. But Carroll's stories are themselves reworkings of earlier fairytales, as Marina Warner (1998) has shown. The girl whose white clothing is overlain by red and spotted with blood, who enters the dangerous tunnels of the forest where she meets the ambiguous figure(s) of the huntsman/wolf, and who is punished for her emerging sexuality, is a central figure of fairytale. Her journey into the forest is the Freudian story of the awakening of desire through seduction, and she is always an ambiguous figure. Jack Zipes's analysis of the Red Riding Hood story and its successive illustrators reveals both the persistent eroticism of the forest meeting and its disturbing nature, for the forest, a place outside the conventions of society, is both 'the natural setting for the fulfilment of desire', and also 'a meeting place of witches and the haunting place of werewolves' (Zipes 1989: 243). Wolf and girl, he suggests, are mirrored figures: 'for the little girl is a potential witch figure in her red hat . . . and the wolf, whose ancestor was the werewolf, was an accomplice of the devil' (ibid., 244). Both are 'other' to the male ego. Alice, too, is both innocent investigator and monstrous shape-shifter, as Marina Warner – who also points out the 'patent erotic character of [Carroll's] fantasy' (1998: 90) – has suggested. In 'Thin Air', this ambiguity in the figure of the lost girl is indicated by the linked images which recur throughout the story: those of the red kite which is flown by the still intact family as they run, laughing, across the heath, and of its 'other', the red dress worn by the daughter(s), which signals the breakup of the family through the intrusion of sexuality.

In 'Thin Air' it is the second sister, Clara, who is investigator, and her older double, Joanna, who is overtly sexualised. Clara's investigation of her double thus becomes a journey 'through the looking glass'. Joanna's meeting with the black boyfriend signals her loss of innocence: 'I don't think she was a virgin anymore', comments her former (white) boyfriend. But the daughter's story is repeated and archetypal, as Boyd makes clear. Provoking the father, Gold, into a confession, he caresses Clara's face, murmuring, 'They're so beautiful at this age – just before they leave you. Not yet women, but no longer girls.' Both daughters find their way into the ruined church at the centre of the heath, both have an erotic encounter there and become spotted with blood (Clara cuts her hand; Joanna's nose bleeds after she is hit by her black boyfriend), and both are secretly watched. The fantasy nature of these scenes is emphasised by the dreamlike quality of the camera work, which intercuts present and flashback sequences, follows the characters through tunnels of branches, and dissolves the edges of the frames.

There are other doubles, too. Most obviously, Boyd, the paternal investigator,[16] is paralleled with the guilty father, Gold. Clara's relationship with both is seductive; both respond with guilty desire. Both are challenged by younger men whose threatening 'otherness' is signalled by their blackness: 'It's a young man's game, sir', comments Spence as he beats Boyd at squash, thus threatening to displace the older man. To these dangerous younger men are contrasted the 'castrated' Oedipal sons, David and Garvey. Both are unable to form relationships with women: Garvey has Asperger's syndrome and David, the child of his mother's affair with Joanna's headmaster, is paralysed by his stepfather's coldness. Both sons can merely watch as versions of Freud's 'primal scene', in which the erotic and the violent are fused, are played out. In both 'families', the mother is a helpless, discarded figure: Grace Foley can merely watch as Boyd pursues a secret relationship with Clara, and Leah Gold accepts her secondary status ('It seemed that the more [Gold] wondered at Joanna, the less he thought of me') in exchange for being allowed to keep her son.

Here, then, is an investigation of the family which reveals the secrets (literally) buried in its past. It is a story whose origins, on the one hand, lie very much in contemporary concerns and anxieties: at the time of its production and screening there were two cases of the disappearance and murder of young girls, which received intense national publicity, and the episode's screening was delayed by six weeks because of that – and perhaps also because of the disturbing nature of its denouement. Yet it is a story whose power lies in its capacity to evoke far more persistent anxieties centring on the nature of sexuality and desire and the precariousness of identity. Through its doublings and repetitions, and its evocations of fairy-tale and myth, it returns us to the scenarios of desire familiar from psychoanalytic theory. Like the *Star Trek* episode we looked at, it is a story concerned with masculine fantasies about female sexuality and its ambiguous and threatening nature, and with the fragility of male identity and power. But – particularly through its troubled central figure, Boyd – it is far more willing than the earlier series to acknowledge the disturbing nature of *male* desire and power. Freud's 'archaeological' explorations of the memories, dreams and fantasies of his patients led him to conclude that the stories of paternal desire which so often emerged were evidence of *female* fantasies of seduction. *Waking the Dead* seems willing to expose the guilty passions of the Father.

Watching an episode like 'Thin Air' it is difficult not to be drawn into its 'scenarios of desire' – particularly as it is screened in uninterrupted fashion on British television. As a 'mapping fantasy', its co-ordinates are the very real anxieties about the safety of our daughters, which are the stuff of news. But in exploring these it moves into other territory: into anxieties about identity and sexuality, about male power and female difference, and about the repressed desires at the heart of the family. In so doing it enters the territory which has been explored by psychoanalytic theory, to whose insights – if not always its conclusions – we can usefully turn in our analysis.

Chapter 4

Gender and Sexuality

4.1 Feminist Approaches

Feminism and Media Theory

In 1990 Jane Miller introduced her study of the relationship of women to cultural theory with this definition of feminism:

> The purpose of feminism as I see it is to disturb, irrevocably, the steady male gaze and the unquestioning male possession of the structures of economic and cultural power. (Miller 1990: 10)

Miller's definition is useful here because it highlights the interconnectedness of three concepts that have been central to feminist media theory and criticism. First, feminism is *political*: it is concerned both to analyse and to change – 'to disturb, irrevocably' – existing power structures in society. These power structures, whilst they may also be analysed in other terms, for example those of class or 'race', are fundamentally *patriarchal*: that is, they subordinate the interests of women, which they identify with the domestic or 'private sphere', to those of men, which are identified with the wider 'public sphere'. Gender, then, is a structuring principle of our material – our economic, social and political – existence. Second, this power, Miller insists, is also 'cultural' and 'unquestioning'. Patriarchal power, in other words, is also *ideological*: it structures the symbolic forms through which our material existence is represented. Finally, in linking this power with 'the steady male gaze', Miller draws attention to the centrality of *representational systems* – of images, visual representations and structures of looking

– in maintaining both that ideological structure and our sense of our own identities as gendered and sexualised individuals within it.

Analysis of media representations has thus been central within the development of feminist theory and criticism as a whole. As Annette Kuhn writes, 'From its beginnings, feminism has regarded ideas, language and images as crucial in shaping women's (and men's) lives' (1985: 2). Media images of women were a central concern of the 'second wave' feminism of the 1960s and 1970s. Betty Friedan's *The Feminine Mystique* (1965) traced the postwar construction of the American ideal image of femininity (what Friedan called the 'happy housewife heroine') through media representations she found in women's magazines and advertising images. Demonstrations were organised against the 1968 Miss America contest and the Miss World competition in London the following year. And when the feminist journal *Women and Film* was launched in 1972, it saw its political task as that of 'taking up the struggle with women's image in film and women's roles in the film industry' (1972: 5), thereby signalling its sense of the interrelationship of social and representational structures.

The questions raised by such concerns, however, constituted a major challenge to existing work in media, film and television studies. The focus on gender as a structuring principle of our social and symbolic worlds, combined with 'second wave' feminism's insistence that 'the personal is political', produce a very different set of research questions to those which had hitherto preoccupied those fields. Annette Kuhn suggests some of these questions:

> What does looking have to do with sexuality? With masculinity and femininity? With power? With knowledge? How do images of women, in particular, 'speak to' the spectator? Is the spectator addressed as male/female, masculine/feminine? Is femininity constructed in specific ways through representation? Why are images of women's bodies so prevalent in our society? (1985: 2; 6)

These are questions which bring together issues of social power and knowledge – often seen as concerns of the 'public' world – with issues of gender and sexuality – matters of individual identity and 'the personal'. To explore them feminist media theory and criticism drew both on existing theories of ideology and discourse, and on psychoanalytic theory. In doing so, it forced these two often antagonistic theoretical traditions into relationship, and it challenged, and ultimately transformed, existing theoretical paradigms.

Describing this intervention as it affected cultural studies, Stuart Hall wrote in 1992 that 'the intervention of feminism was specific and decisive. It was ruptural. It reorganised the field in quite specific ways' (1992b: 282). The 'reorganisations' he describes fall into two related groups. The first concerns the impact of feminism on theories of power and ideology. Feminism insisted that 'the personal is political', that not only is male power exercised and naturalised through 'personal' institutions such as marriage, child-rearing and sexual practices, but that the very concept of a separate realm of 'the personal' which is *outside* politics is one which serves political and ideological purposes. This meant that the concept of power had to be rethought, and with it the theoretical concepts of ideology and hegemony. Questions of gender and sexuality became central to the understanding of power. But – and this constitutes Hall's second group of 'reorganisations' – in subjecting the area of 'the personal' to analysis in this way, feminism also opened up questions of subjectivity and individual identity, and it used psychoanalytic theory to do this. It therefore linked psychoanalysis with theories of ideology through its concern with individual gendered identity, and in so doing it politicised psychoanalytic theory.

Ideology

If ideology is the process of making the world *mean*, so that we live our lives and construct our identities within the frameworks it provides, and if those frameworks operate through representations, then it is clear that a key concern for feminist criticism must be with ideologies of femininity and the representations through which they circulate. Feminist criticism of the 1970s therefore moved away from the criticism of media representations as stereotypes or *distortions* of reality, which had characterised it in the late 1960s and early 1970s, and towards an exploration of the ways in which representations *construct* that reality for us. Much of this early work focused on film. In the early 1970s Claire Johnston adopted Louis Althusser's definition of ideology as a system of representations whose meanings *seem* transparent or 'natural' to us (Johnston 1988: 38) but actually serve dominant power structures. Johnston, however, employed this concept in the analysis of *patriarchal* ideology. 'Within a sexist ideology and a male-dominated cinema', she writes, 'woman is presented as what she represents for man'. Despite the 'enormous emphasis placed on woman as spectacle in the cinema', therefore, 'woman as woman is largely absent' (1973: 26). Instead, the image of woman operates in film as a *sign*, but one which refers not to the 'reality' of women's lives, but to the desires and fantasies of men. Referring to Roland Barthes's concept of 'myth' as the affixing of ideological values to signs, Johnston argues that 'myth transmits and transforms the ideology of sexism and renders it invisible' (ibid., 25). Patriarchal myth, or ideology, empties the sign 'woman' of its meaning in relation to real women and replaces it with male fantasy. Johnston's analyses drew attention to the way in which apparently strong female central characters in film are constantly reduced to erotic spectacles or are 'punished' within the narrative for their rebellions, but also to the way in which these figures remain sites of anxiety within the film text, threatening always to disrupt its narrative and ideological coherence.

Other feminist critics appropriated Antonio Gramsci's concept of *hegemony*, which Stuart Hall had used to argue that ideological 'maps of meaning' are never simply imposed but always contested, with every sign or representation a potential point of struggle over meaning. Christine Gledhill argues that popular film and television genres like the detective genre or the 'woman's film' may indeed reproduce gendered ideologies as Claire Johnston suggests, reaffirming the centrality and strength of the male hero and marginalising or punishing the active or rebellious woman within their familiar patterns of plot and character. But she adds that such texts are also sites of discursive struggle. If mainstream texts are to command a popular audience, they must, on the one hand, draw on a familiar generic and moral order, reproducing well-worn archetypes of good and evil, hero, villain and victim. On the other hand, however, they must refer outwards to a recognisable contemporary social world, with its historically specific cultural anxieties, debates and discourses. In such conditions, the figure of woman will always function as more than simply a patriarchal symbol: if female characters are to be seen as 'realistic' by their audience they must draw on the experiences, roles and positions of contemporary women, and speak with their voices. For Gledhill, then, the 'figure of woman' within the popular film or television drama text is always a figure whose meanings are contested or negotiated, so that the text offers a range of positions for interpretation and identification. What we find is a 'struggle between male and female voices' (Gledhill 1987: 37), or, as Teresa de Lauretis puts it, between 'woman' – the 'fictional construct' which is produced by hegemonic discourses – and *women* – the 'real historical beings' who cannot escape these discourses but who *can* contest them (de Lauretis 1984: 5).

Cagney and Lacey, the 1980s female-centred US police series,[1] is the television text which Gledhill uses for her examples of 'cultural negotiation' within popular television drama.[2] The decision to use a *female* buddy pair in the series, she writes, produces 'conflicting codes of recognition'. Some of these conflicts are inter-generic: between the expectations we bring to the cop show or the buddy series on the one hand, and to the figure of the 'independent heroine' – a character more frequently found in the 'woman's film' or soap opera – on the other. But our 'recognition' of these characters and their situation, writes Gledhill, also goes beyond genre:

> [T]he female 'buddy' relationship can be 'realistically' constructed only by drawing on the sub-cultural codes of women's social intercourse and culture. Inside a soap opera, such codes are taken for granted. Inside a police series, however, they have a range of consequences for both genre and ideology. (1988: 70)

The result is a text woven from a 'series of negotiations, around definitions of gender roles and sexuality, definitions of heterosexual relations and female friendships, as well as around the nature of the law and policing' (ibid.) Danae Clark in her essay on *Cagney and Lacey* (Clark, 1990), elaborates these points further. The series, she writes, disrupts the ideological assumptions of the male-centred police series in a number of ways. One is through its narrative structure: the series combines the 'closed' structure of the police series, in which each episode closes with the resolution of a case, with the open-ended structure of soap opera, in which the personal lives of the protagonists are foregrounded and discussion is more important than action. Moreover, the police-centred stories of the characters' professional lives parallel and interact with the issues confronting their private selves, disturbing the public–private hierarchy which underpins the police series. Second, in featuring *two* women rather than a single 'heroine', *Cagney and Lacey* both places the relationship *between* women at its centre and enables the series to explore, in de Lauretis's words, the differences between 'woman' and *women*. The two women, and those they encounter in their professional lives, are constructed across differences – of class, ethnicity, marriage and motherhood – as well as similarity, and these differences must be negotiated. Third, in foregrounding women as active decision makers and uncoverers of 'truth', the series makes the voices of women, not men, the bearers of discursive authority. Finally, argues Clark, the series challenges patriarchal discourse through its 'economy of vision'. These women are subjects, not objects of the gaze. Traditional gendered relations of voyeurism and fetishism are subverted in a number of ways: by suggesting that traditional 'femininity' is not a 'natural' identity but rather a constructed performance or 'masquerade' (the detectives must frequently work undercover 'as women dressed up as women'); by giving the investigating gaze and point of view to women; and by refusing the sexual objectification of female characters (Clark 1990: 128–32).

Psychoanalysis

This last argument takes us into rather different theoretical territory from that which underpins Gledhill's analysis of popular film and television drama. The question of how gendered subjects are constructed as sexed objects and positioned by representations takes us into territory which was opened up in the 1970s by feminist psychoanalytic film theory, a theoretical tradition which Elspeth Probyn has described more recently as 'a condition of possibility for any present theorizing' of television drama (1990: 154), however much we might now want to modify it. Laura Mulvey's 1975 article, 'Visual Pleasure and Narrative Cinema', set the terms for this analysis.

Like Claire Johnston, Mulvey argues that the image of woman in film is one constructed by and for a patriarchal culture, enabling man to 'live out his fantasies and obsessions . . . by imposing them on the silent image of woman still tied to her place as bearer, not maker, of meaning' (Mulvey 1989: 15). Cinema's pleasures include erotic pleasure in looking, the fulfilment of desire through fantasy, and a return to the pleasures of infancy's 'mirror phase',[3] when the child's sense of identity was formed through identification with its own idealised mirror image – an image provided in film by the male star. But these are pleasures provided only for the *male* spectator. Women are objects, not subjects, of the gaze, their bodies eroticised and often fragmented for the spectator's pleasure. Visual pleasure, however, has two aspects. The first is voyeuristic, the active (and often aggressive) gaze at the eroticised image of woman. The second is narcissistic, the pleasure of identification with one's own 'ideal ego', that more perfect, more complete, more powerful figure first glimpsed by the infant in its idealised mirror image and now rediscovered in the figure of the male movie star. The division between active/male and passive/female, argues Mulvey, also structures film narrative. It is the film's hero who advances the story, controlling events, the woman and the erotic gaze. 'Woman', in contrast, functions as erotic spectacle, interrupting rather than advancing the forward movement of the narrative as the camera slowly sweeps over her body.

Cinematic codes, then, construct meaning not only through visual images but also via film's ability to control the dimensions of time and space: through choice of shots, framing, editing and narrative pace. Its power and its pleasures come from the alignment of what Mulvey calls the 'three different looks' of cinema. What *we* see, as spectators, is determined by the gaze of the camera, and that in turn is aligned, through point-of-view shots, with the gaze of the film's characters at each other. In the latter, it is the look of the central male character which is privileged, so that we see events largely through his eyes and identify with his gaze. Thus 'the power of the male protagonist as he controls events coincides with the active power of the erotic look', the combination providing for the male spectator 'a satisfying sense of omnipotence' (ibid., 20).

These codes, of course, operate not only in mainstream cinema but in the popular drama series which are its successors. John Fiske's analysis of the 1980s US action series *The A-Team* describes its preoccupation with the constant reassertion of a unified notion of masculine identity premised on notions of power and independence. In *The A-Team*, he writes, as in other similar series, women are represented 'solely as threats to masculinity' (1987: 204). They are eroticised and victimised, used to guarantee the heterosexuality of the male group who are the series' protagonists but ultimately excluded from the narrative. Through a process of what Fiske calls 'exscription' – the process through which that which disturbs is 'written out' of a discourse – traces of the feminine are removed from the masculine discourse of *The A-Team* 'just as women are written out of the narrative'. (ibid.) Lorraine Gamman, too, draws on the terms of Mulvey's analysis in arguing that women in the police/detective series 'are all too often represented for the sake of glamorous spectacle', even in instances where they are the protagonists, as, for example, in the 1980s US series *Police Woman* or *Charlie's Angels* (1988: 9) Glamorised and fetishised, these figures are, she suggests, constructed as objects for male fantasy rather than as the focus of 'significantly women-centred entertainment' (ibid., 9–10).[4]

To Mulvey's arguments about the 'male gaze', E. Ann Kaplan adds two further points, which have proved influential within film criticism and in the analysis of television drama. The first concerns the question of what happens to these structures in genres which are aimed at women and feature female central characters – the 'woman's film' or the soap opera, for example. Both of these focus on the personal and intimate world of family and sexual relationships, and are associated with the high intensity and emotional excess of melodrama. Drawing on Mary Ann Doane's work on the 'woman's film' of the 1940s, Kaplan argues that in these genres the fantasies offered are *masochistic*: they invite from their female spectator not a distanced and powerful erotic gaze, as with male-centred drama, but rather a suffocating identification with the powerlessness and suffering of their female characters (Kaplan 1983: 28).

Kaplan's second point concerns a more recent figure in popular film and television drama: the woman who takes on a 'male' action role. If the women of TV's *Charlie's Angels* remained fetishised figures of male fantasy, the more active figures who have succeeded them have stepped more fully into the 'male' role. In such instances, writes Kaplan, the female protagonist 'nearly always loses her traditionally feminine characteristics in so doing – not those of attractiveness, but rather of kindness, humaneness, motherliness. She is now often cold, driving, ambitious, manipulating, just like the men whose position she has usurped' (ibid., 29). In appropriating the 'male gaze', she has stepped into the 'masculine' position, and for this she will be punished, both within the narrative and by the loss of 'feminine' characteristics. Critics have pointed, for example, to the descent into alcoholism and loneliness of the ambitious and unmarried Christine Cagney in the later series of *Cagney and Lacey*, or the childlessness, family alienation and loss of partner of Jane Tennison in the ITV series *Prime Suspect* (1991).[5]

Television Drama and Feminism

Early feminist analyses of television drama focused on soap opera and took as their starting point work done on melodrama and the 'woman's film'. By the late 1980s we can trace two interrelated shifts of emphasis. The first is a widening of analytic focus to embrace other television genres, most notably sitcom and the detective genre. The second is an increasing concern within those genres themselves with issues originating in feminism, and more specifically with the problems of reconciling 'the feminine' and 'the feminist'.

As Patricia Mellencamp (1986) has demonstrated, even early situation comedy constituted a space in which women's rebellion against the stereotype of the 'happy housewife heroine' (Friedan) could be explored. In her analysis of the US sitcoms *The George Burns and Gracie Allen Show* (1950–8) and *I Love Lucy* (1951–7), Mellencamp demonstrates how they gave space to their female stars' 'unruliness' and desire for independence and escape from domesticity. At the same time the shows returned them each week to domestic subordination, via the repetitive structures of the sitcom form. In these series humour became the means by which conventional 'meanings' of femininity could be 'unmade' and patriarchal assumptions overturned by female leads who were the physical and verbal centres of their shows. Yet humour – together with the sitcom form which returns each episode to the point at which it began – is simultaneously the means through which these reversals can be rendered 'unserious', and hence both pleasurable and contained.

Sitcoms of the 1970s, like *The Mary Tyler Moore Show* (1970–7), and its spin-off *Rhoda* (1974–8), moved their divorced central characters into the public sphere (Mary works in a newsroom), in a context where, as one of the show's producers stated, 'women's rights were being talked about and . . . having an impact' (Bathrick 1984: 103–4). Here again, however, the sitcom form becomes a structure through which women's dissent can be contained as well as explored. As Serafina Bathrick writes, these series featured single working women who provided mutual support, but they also reconstructed the working environment as a patriarchally structured pseudo-family in which women embodied not the power and independence which characterise masculine groups but familiar 'feminine' competences of familial trust and co-operation.

More recent feminist critics, writing about sitcoms of the 1980s and 1990s, have tended to focus more on the disruptive potential of these post 'second wave' sitcoms than on the strategies of containment[6] mobilised by the sitcom form. Kathleen Rowe, writing about the US series *Roseanne* (1988–97), emphasises Roseanne's inheritance of the role of 'unruly' domestic woman from earlier figures like Gracie Allen and Lucille Ball. But she argues that in *Roseanne* this 'semiotics of the unruly' is employed to 'expose the gap . . . between the ideals of the New Left and the Women's Movement of the late 60s and early 70s on the one hand, and the realities of working-class family life two decades later on the other' (Rowe 1990: 409). *Roseanne* is a domestic sitcom, but one whose star's unruly and *spectacular* excesses violate all the norms of domestic and erotic femininity, drawing attention to the impossibility – and absurdity – of such norms. Referring back to the arguments of Laura Mulvey, Rowe argues that such '*making visible* and *laughable*' of the norms of femininity disrupts conventional gendered power relations and begins to construct another possible position for the female subject, one which can lay claim to desire – however 'excessive' – rather than represent desirability. To be looked at, she argues, is not necessarily to be powerless; after all, visibility is a precondition for action in the public sphere. Roseanne's indifference to the objectifying gaze can be a source of empowerment for her viewers: 'By returning the male gaze, we might expose (make a spectacle of) the gazer. And by utilizing the power already invested in us as image, we might begin to negate our own "invisibility" in the public sphere' (ibid., 412).

The power of the 'unruly' or 'excessive' woman to disrupt assumptions about the 'naturalness' of feminine norms is an argument which has also been used about the British sitcom *Absolutely Fabulous* (1992–6 and 2001). Like *Roseanne*, *Absolutely Fabulous* is the product of a post 'second wave' questioning of assumptions about appropriate feminine conduct and its associated ideal image. With its reversal of 'normality' in the mother–daughter relationship, its refusal to grant the kind of ideological 'closure' with which most sitcom episodes end, and above all the parodic visual and social excesses of its central characters, Patsy and Edina, *Absolutely Fabulous* draws attention to both the absurdities of the feminine ideal and its function as regulator of women's conduct and bodies. Pat Kirkham and Beverley Skeggs argue that the 'feminine masquerades of Patsy and Edina are a humorous exposé of the impossibility of femininity. . . . [Their] spectacular displays challenge propriety, care of the self, female responsibility and respectability by parading femininity as a mode to be put on and off rather than something which comes naturally' (1998: 295). Like *Roseanne*, *Absolutely Fabulous* exposes the *regulatory* function of the feminine ideal. But Kirkham and Skeggs, like other writers on sitcom, also emphasise its ambivalent nature. If Edina and Patsy's unruly excess offers potentially empowering transgressive pleasures for its female viewers, it is also confined to a world of wealth and hedonistic consumption beyond the reach of most of us. Patsy in particular – as played by the beautiful and aristocratic Joanna Lumley – continues to function as a symbol of white, upper-class femininity even as she exposes this ideal to parodic excess. To those of us who, whether by class, race or other cultural barrier, are excluded from this ideal, its reduction to comic masquerade may not reduce its desirability.

Feminism and the Detective Series: A Case Study

The exploration of feminist concerns within the television detective or crime series began in the 1980s, as we saw with *Cagney and Lacey*. The crime genre is concerned with issues of the public social world, its central characters both confident actors in that world and uncoverers of truth, empowered with the investigative and surveillant (and conventionally also the erotic) gaze. Traditionally these investigators are men, often in a buddy or father–son relationship, and the investigation first threatens their integrity and even identity, and then reaffirms it through the linked modes of action and knowledge. Women are marginal figures, either symbolic of the domestic world from which the detective's mission excludes him but which it is his task to preserve, or – as 'bad woman' – duplicitous, tempting the detective away from his investigative path. Finally, unlike the traditionally 'feminine' genres of soap opera or sitcom, the concern of the crime series with the public world of action rather than emotion has identified it with a 'realism' which is an added form of prestige.

The *female* detective – or indeed her counterpart the female criminal – is thus potentially a highly transgressive figure. She emerges at a time of social change itself influenced by feminism, often speaking directly to and about those changes, and she challenges both traditional gendered representations and traditional generic and visual structures. *Cagney and Lacey* was one such landmark series, as we have seen; another was the 1991 British series *Prime Suspect*. A two-part police drama, scripted by Lynda La Plante and starring Helen Mirren, *Prime Suspect* was first shown on ITV in April 1991, attracting an audience of 14 million viewers. Its narrative concerns DCI Jane Tennison, who is given leadership of her first murder investigation after the sudden death of the investigating officer, DCI John Shefford. She identifies the murder as the work of a serial killer and, despite hostility from male colleagues and lack of support from her superiors, succeeds in obtaining a confession from the prime suspect, George Marlow.

For the institution of television, this introduction of a female central figure into a traditionally male-centred genre responded to social change – Tennison was officially based on DCI Jackie Malton, one of only two female DCIs in the country, but the character also became linked with the story of Alison Halford, the Merseyside assistant chief constable whose case alleging sexual discrimination in the police force began in May 1990 and continued until 1992. At the same time, however, it offered refreshment of a generic form which, in the words of one reviewer, had 'become drama's equivalent of televised snooker: male dominated, highly predictable, and . . . not as much fun as they used to be.' (Robert Chalmers, *Independent*, 7 April 1991). Like La Plante's earlier series, *Widows* (1983), however, *Prime Suspect* also represents a conscious feminist intervention into a masculine genre. As Gillian Skirrow commented on the earlier series: 'The contribution of *Widows* was to try to engage with these conventions, using them and questioning them at the same time; a constant process of negotiation with the expectations of both the audience and the institution of television' (1985: 174). The women of the 1983 series could become active only by being *widowed*. By 1991, however, at the end of the 'Thatcher decade', *Prime Suspect* could draw on a changed social situation and a different set of discourses around the position of women. Jane Tennison is the apparently successful woman of the post-1970s workplace, superficially accepted into the structures of male power but more subtly marginalised by them – she has been promoted but confined to desk work – and inevitably disruptive when she seeks to appropriate them. This ambivalence in her institutional positioning is paralleled by the impact on the generic and visual structures of the police series once a woman is placed at their centre. For a female character to become the *hero* she must appropriate agency, action, command, the occupation of public space, discursive authority and the control of the investigative gaze. All of these, of course, run counter to the norms of femininity.

Prime Suspect at once operates within and draws attention to both of these sets of structures: the social and institutional, and the generic and representational. As we have seen, popular television drama series must refer outwards to contemporary social discourses if they are to be recognised as 'realistic', and *Prime Suspect* is very pointed in its references. Tennison's treatment by the all-male police establishment draws on the Alison Halford case, as we have seen, but the series also makes explicit reference to the social and media discourses around the 'professional woman' which were evoked in the reporting of that case. Tennison, like Halford, is the victim of a tabloid spread about an 'obsessive' and isolated professional woman.[7] Second, the serial murders which Tennison investigates echo those carried out between 1975 and 1981 by the 'Yorkshire Ripper', Peter Sutcliffe, both in their targets – women who in some way 'perform' femininity – and their method – the serial killer attacks those parts of the female body which 'signal gender', stabbing and mutilating them with a sharpened screwdriver. In Joan Smith's feminist analysis of the Yorkshire Ripper case, published two years before *Prime Suspect*, it is Sutcliffe's very ordinariness which delayed his capture. In particular, the misogyny which motivates the killer is shared by the police. In *Prime Suspect*, this misogyny is directed at both the victims ('Slags isn't the word for it . . . like rodents', according to one police officer) and at Tennison herself (a 'tart', a 'dyke', a 'tight-arsed bitch', according to another). As Tennison investigates, the only suspect in the case other than George Marlow becomes Shefford himself, who was both the investigating officer in two of the murders and a client of the prostitute victims. The series persistently points up the parallels between police and killer, so that the object of investigation at times becomes masculinity itself.

In a similar way, the series both employs and opens up to critical exposure the conventions of the crime series. The precipitation into an investigation of an 'outsider' cop is a familiar generic device in the police drama: it introduces a double plot structure which involves both the solving of the murder(s) and the initiation and acceptance of the untried and 'different' hero. But placing a woman in the central role disturbs and questions this familiar structure. The fact that Tennison 's final acceptance is marked by a *masculine* ritual (complete with rugby song and champagne), and reinforced, as so often in this drama, by a circling camera which draws attention to the sheer physical presence of some forty police*men*, signals its problematic and even impossible nature. As a woman, Tennison's 'difference' cannot be resolved. The usual structuring oppositions of the police series – between the 'instinctive' policing of the 'maverick' cop and police bureaucracy, and between cop and villain – are displaced. Both the 'intuitive' cop Shefford and the police camaraderie which supports him have disturbing parallels with the killer, Marlow. The masculinity of both, as we see in the scene of the boxing match organised to raise money for Shefford's widow, is founded on ritual violence, on the exclusion and denigration of women, and on concealed homoeroticism.

Prime Suspect is most adventurous in its use of the visual conventions of the police drama. Identification, detection and visual clues are all linked with a specifically masculine 'seeing'. Detection, as Beatrix Campbell has written (1988: 71), is above all about what is *evident* and what is *evidence*, and these decisions are not ideologically neutral. Shefford wrongly identifies the body of the first victim because he sees *only* the body; it is Tennison who insists on looking at the victim's *face*, and at the markers of her individual identity. Glances between women across boundaries of rank and class contrast repeatedly with the institutionalised looking – surveillance, autopsy, photographic evidence – of the masculine world. In *Prime Suspect* both we and the police are positioned repeatedly as viewers of evidential photographs of fragmented and mutilated female bodies. In Tennison's final briefing session, these images – photographs of mutilated sections of the female body, intercut with snapshots, school photographs, home videos – work to divide viewers along gender lines. Tennison herself, standing in front of the photographs, seems at times to dissolve into them. But evidence is verbal as well as visual, and a contrast is also drawn between public (masculine) discourse and the informal, often snatched exchanges which characterise the women's interactions. It is Tennison's empathy (across evident class boundaries) with the prostitute's two friends that elicits vital information. And it is the marginalised and largely (to the men) invisible WPC Maureen Havers whose suggestions – offered informally, tentatively, and only to Tennison herself – twice enable Tennison to make crucial progress.

At the heart of the police series lie questions – and anxieties – about gendered identity. But whilst most series are concerned to confirm conventional notions of these identities, *Prime Suspect*'s play with gendered conventions opens them up to question. It is *performance* which is seen as central to both masculine and feminine sexual identities, whether in the ritual performance of the police boxing match or the rituals of makeup, clothes and hair in which the female victims are engaged. At the heart of Marlow's hatred of women lies his horror/fear of what their rituals of adornment conceal: sexual difference. But this preoccupation is also found in the version of the Red Riding Hood story told at the police boxing match, where once again the theme is female concealment and disguise, and sexual difference is both exposed and punished.

Women do adopt disguises in this drama, but these are not seen, as so often (and as Marlow sees them), as intrinsic to femininity, but as strategies for economic survival. The strongest disguise, however, is adopted by Jane Tennison herself, as in manner and speech as well as in clothing she adopts 'male uniform' to become, as Charlotte Brunsdon writes, 'one of the lads' (1998: 231). As she is increasingly accepted by the men under her command, so she becomes the conventional 'boss' – and so the programme itself, like Tennison, loses its more 'feminine' aspects – the portrayal of her domestic life – and sticks more closely to generic conventions: the chase, arrest and confession. The moment of her 'acceptance' into the all-male group is thus one poised between triumph and loss.

'Postfeminism' and Television Drama

The generic shift established by *Prime Suspect* has been continued in other British drama series, most notably perhaps in *Silent Witness* (1996– , see Thornham 2003) where the role of woman as investigator of embodied performance and 'truth' is heightened by her position as forensic pathologist. But alongside this, and in some ways contrasting with it, we can note another shift: that from an – often troubled – engagement with the relationship between the 'feminine' and the 'feminist' to a celebration of the 'resolution' of this issue through an embrace of the 'postfeminist'.

The term 'postfeminist' (or 'post-feminist') emerged in both academic and popular discourse in the 1980s. To Susan Faludi, its emergence within popular discourse is unambiguously a product of a backlash against feminism: 'Just when record numbers of younger women were supporting feminist goals in the mid-1980s . . . and a majority of all women were calling themselves feminists, the media declared that feminism was the flavour of the seventies and that "post-feminism" was the new story – complete with a younger generation who supposedly reviled the women's movement' (1992: 14). The academic definition offered by Deborah Rosenfelt and Judith Stacey is rather more complex but in the end just as critical. Postfeminism, they write, demarcates 'an emerging culture and ideology that simultaneously incorporates, revises, and depoliticizes many of the fundamental issues advanced by second-wave feminism' (1990: 549). The key word here is of course 'depoliticizes', and it is this debate about the precise political or ideological charge of the prefix 'post' which has dominated feminist discussions of the meaning and usefulness of the term.

For writers like Susan Faludi (1992) and Tania Modleski (1991), addressing, respectively, the popular and the academic uses of the term, the periodisation it claims (feminism, it suggests, is over by the mid-1980s) is inevitably reactionary, asserting on the one hand that the project of feminism is somehow completed and on the other that it has failed, and can now be replaced. Such claims, argues Modleski, 'are actually engaged in negating the critiques and undermining the goals of feminism' (1991: 3). Other critics, however, have sought to appropriate the term, aligning it with a related term, 'postmodern feminism'.[8] In this view, postfeminism is both a continuation and a critique of 'second-wave' feminism, incorporating its goals of equality whilst adopting poststructuralist definitions of the subject. In such definitions, gender is not the only site of difference and oppression but is complicated by multiple positionings across class, ethnicity, sexuality, age and cultural differences; identity is not fixed but in process, established through performance not 'essential nature'; and power is experienced differently by women according to the range of subject positions which they occupy. For such writers, the identity 'woman' is highly problematic, and that of 'feminist' perhaps less useful as a self-description than one which embraces difference, diversity and a blurring of boundaries.

What is clear, however, is that as a description of a range of contemporary popular cultural texts featuring and aimed at women, the term postfeminist – perhaps *because of* its political ambivalence – has proved useful. Within television drama, it is a range of popular US series which has most often been designated in this way,[9] series like *Buffy the Vampire Slayer* (1997–2003), *Ally McBeal* (1997–2002) and *Sex and the City* (1998–2004), though more recent British series like *Cutting It* (2002–) or *Footballers' Wives* (2002–) can also be included. All of these series are generic hybrids, merging elements of soap opera, series drama, comedy, fantasy and, in the case of *Buffy*, horror. All are aimed primarily at a female audience,[10] feature young, independent, usually single women in an urban environment, and engage with issues generated by 'second wave' feminism but in an ironic, playful and style-conscious manner which might be seen as antithetical to an earlier generation of feminists. The question with which Patricia Pender begins her article on *Buffy* can serve as a more general introduction to the issues they raise: is it, she asks, 'a groundbreaking, empowering, and transgressive text, or is its political potential compromised, commodity driven, and contained?' (2002: 35). The answer is not at all clear.

'Sex and the City': a Case Study

Sex and the City, which features the intertwined lives of four thirty- and forty-something friends in New York, can be said to be both emblematic of, and directly *about*, the dilemmas posed by postfeminism. Samantha's statement in the first episode – typically made at a gathering of the four friends in the public space of a restaurant – sets the tone: 'Sweetheart, this is the first time in the history of Manhattan that women have had as much money and power as men – *plus* the equal luxury of treating men as sex objects.' If the female detective of the 1990s exists within a world which remains firmly patriarchal – a world which she must negotiate as well as oppose – the women of *Sex and the City* live in a postpatriarchal world characterised by *choice*. Those choices are explicitly informed by feminism, as Charlotte paradoxically insists when she tries to justify her choice to give up work: 'The women's movement is supposed to be about choice. And if I choose to give up work, that's my choice. . . . I choose my choice' ('Time and Punishment', 4.7).[11] Women have choice over where to live, whether to live alone, whether to have relationships or 'sex like a man' (1.1), whether to have oral, anal, threesome or solitary sex, whether to sleep with men or/and women, whether to have abortions or children. Women also confidently occupy public space. Unlike their 1980s forerunners, Cagney and Lacey, whose lives were also set against the New York cityscape, these women do not have to retreat to the 'women's room' to discuss their lives; they appropriate public as well as private space for a women's discourse, the primacy of women's friendship, and a shared 'economy of vision'.[12] Indeed, as the title sequence makes clear, they appropriate New York itself. The sequence intercuts between shots of Carrie's face as she walks through the New York streets, clearly in love with the city itself, and speeded up shots of the skyscape and city streets. Though Carrie's daydream is broken, it is reinstated by the reiteration of her image, as it travels through the streets on a New York bus. 'No-one is more New York . . . than you', as 'fashion guru' Lynne Cameron says to Carrie ('The Real Me', 4.2).

These are also women who have taken control of their bodies, sometimes in a way which explicitly echoes 1970s feminism (as, for example, when Charlotte learns to examine her vagina with a speculum and a hand mirror[13]), but more often in a way which emphasises the *performativity* of femininity and sexual identity. More than once the series sets up an opposition between 'models' and 'real women' only to deconstruct it. Carrie, in particular, is 'both': she can both perform an idealised femininity ('Secret Sex', 1.6; 'The Real Me', 4.2) and explode it as myth; she can play the role of fetishised sexual object, but also play with owning not being the fetish.[14] As the title sequence shows us her sense of self, in Diane Negra's words, 'restabilized by her own idealized, eroticized image' after the temporary shattering of her daydream, we see the way the series plays on the notion of contemporary woman as both desiring and desirable but does so ironically and with some ambiguity. Carrie's ideal self is a commodified fantasy, her dreaming self a 'forlorn urban Cinderella' ('Negra', forthcoming: 17), complete with tulle skirt (not the 'naked dress' of the poster); she is her own fetishised object of desire.

This ironic visual play is a constant feature of the series' style, which frequently seems to make reference to the techniques of feminist cinema but in a playful, often ambiguous way. In the sex scenes the men are frequently made to look ridiculous, and we are invited to share a knowing exchange of glances with the women. Women's bodies, eroticised and fragmented by the camera, can apparently be offered for display, only for the camera to pull back and expose the image as constructed, controlled by the women in a way which invites our knowing complicity (through a look direct to camera, or a voice-over by Carrie), or to reverse the gaze so that it exposes the inadequacy and absurdity of the male photographers/spectators ('The Baby Shower', 1.10; 'The Real Me', 4.2).

But if all of these apects can work to make the series seem 'empowering and transgressive', in Patricia Pender's words, we can equally point to its 'containing' elements. The 'postpatriarchal' world of these women is highly specific, located in a wealthy, overwhelmingly white New York world[15] of style and celebrity. Their choices are choices of style and consumption, which makes them, despite the centrality of the all-female group to the series, easily co-optible to Western ideologies of individual success and freedom. Indeed, what seems to structure the serial narrative of *Sex and the City* is an ongoing dialogue with conventional Western narratives of femininity. The visual reference to Cinderella in the title sequence is only one of many references to fairytale romance (in 'I Heart New York', 4.18, for example, 'Big' is explicitly referred to as 'Prince Charming'), and romance, marriage, babies, family structures, life outside the city are all persistent counter-narratives in the ongoing text – encountered on the fringes of the women's lives, usually employed to validate their choices, but persistently *there* as alternative constructions of femininity. This is a world, then, in which the personal is the only form of politics,[16] and the encounters with the social – and with social and class difference – which characterised the New York of detectives Cagney and Lacey is replaced by encounters with dream, fantasy and image. Identities can be tried on and performed in ways not available to these women's 1980s predecessors, but at the expense of locating difference as a matter of style, not social and class positioning, and of constructing this postpatriarchal, feminised version of New York as a fantasy space which can leave reality – the reality glimpsed at the fringes of the women's world – untouched.

'Postfeminist' television drama, then, reminds us, as Charlotte Brunsdon writes, of 'the changed context of debate on feminist-related issues' (1997: 102). The relationship between 'feminism' and 'femininity' which has preoccupied both academic writing on popular television drama and, increasingly, television drama itself, is now inflected differently. Television drama's postfeminist protagonists incorporate and often explicitly reference the gains of 'second wave' feminism, but frequently, it would seem, at the expense of any political engagement beyond that of the narrowly personal. For feminist criticism, such 'transgressive play' offers texts which, as so often with popular television drama, can be analysed as 'sites of intense cultural negotiation' (Pender 2002: 42–3) as well as personal and popular pleasure.

4.2 Sexual Subjects

In the recent past the belief that lesbians and gays were identifiably or visibly different coexisted with the belief that these same people were invisible. Indeed, central to debates about the representation of homosexuality has been a concern over how homosexual identities and same-sex practices might be visualised in cultures which often made such identities invisible. Many texts from the recent past, for example, reveal varying degrees of trepidation and anxiety about the hidden world of lesbians and gays. Michel Foucault shows in his *The Archaeology of Knowledge* (1989 [1969]) how discourses, operating in and through institutions, establish the grounding terms upon which subjects understand the truth of self and world. His *The History of Sexuality*, volume I, (1978 [1976]) exposes how it has often been taken for granted that the heterosexual order, because dominant, is also natural, 'truthful' and easily visualised. Alternatively, the unnatural homosexual subject is figured as someone whose actions and performances will reveal something at odds with the way dominant social groups will read and visualise his/her sexed body. Equally, if society's legal and medical discourses have reflected ambivalent suppositions about the recognition and identification of homosexuals, then clearly how the (in)visible homosexual subject is represented will have been ambivalent and 'queer'. Like criminals in detective fiction, cultural texts have often recorded that the majority of homosexuals are *virtually* impossible to detect.

The cultural practices of lesbian and gay subjects are associated with secret knowledges and codes, or what Eve Sedgwick calls the 'epistemology of the closet' (1990: 1–63; 67–90).[17] But homosexuals, in popular representations, are also prone to let things slip, conscious of giving the game away. Inside but always outside, public but covertly closeted, homosexuals have traditionally been visualised in terms of secrecy, concealment and isolation. Central to the theoretical trajectories which inform lesbian and gay studies[18] is still the question of (a) the representation of *identity*, and (b) *how* identity is visualised in cultural texts and practices. What is it, then, that is captured when lesbians and gay men are visualised? What do audiences detect? Are lesbians, gays and bisexuals (in)visibly 'queer'? And who are these 'queers'? Are their dress codes, their ways of speaking or their erotic practices different from the lesbian and gay world of the past?

Sexuality, language and discourse

It is issues to do with identity and visualisation which inform some of Foucault's work on sexuality. His *The History of Sexuality*, volume I, documents how the version of sexual identity which came to dominate Western cultures at the end of the nineteenth century was grounded in the premise that *hetero*sexual object choice was both the normal and natural expression of sexual desire. Crudely, in all sexual relations, man is for woman and woman is for man. Of course there are many exceptions to this claim, and non-heterosexual expressions of desire persist despite the prohibitions and punishments of the nineteenth century. Nonetheless, far from being repressed in earlier periods, *The History of Sexuality* demonstrates how sexuality is inscribed in a multitude of discourses. Foucault famously describes how during the nineteenth century the homosexual 'became a personage . . . a type of life, a life form' possessing a special anatomy and 'a mysterious physiology' (1978: 43). Unlike heterosexuals, whose bodily markings are discreet and unremarkable, the sex of homosexuals is 'written immodestly' on the face and body, a 'secret that always gave itself away' (ibid., 43). Sexuality, no longer simply *one* aspect of identity, and no longer conceived in terms of sexual acts, is now viewed as the whole truth of the self, something which has to be brought into cultural visibility. Foucault's work is important because it proposes that sexuality is not simply the natural *expression* of some inner drive or desire. Sexuality is about the operation of power in all human relations as much as it is about the construction of a personal identity and truth. Foucault examines how the power and authority attached to some expressions of sexual desire are more legitimised than others. At the same time as opposite-sex relations became normative and valorised, so whole populations were categorised in terms of an identity which was either hetero- or homosexual. By the beginning of the twentieth century, religious, medical, scientific and legal discourses ensured that heterosexuality became the acceptable and public face of private sexual relations. Whilst *how* an *identity* is represented is important, Foucault's work establishes that (a) sexuality is only *one* aspect of identity; (b) identity – one's sense of self or subjectivity – is constituted in discourse; and (c) the operation of discourse is not only tied to power but to how the body is 'written' (visualised) in culture.

By stressing the ways in which sexuality is written in/on the body, and in showing how the homosexual is forced into cultural (in)visibility, Foucault begins to dismantle the notion that sexuality is a natural or transparent fact of life. If sexuality is inscribed in/on the body, then it is discourses (medical, legal, religious, for example) which make the sexual into something that is also *textual*. In an important essay written in 1981, Harold Beaver, utilising Roland Barthes's work on semiotics, expands Foucault's examination of sexuality. Beaver's 'Homosexual Signs (*In Memory of Roland Barthes*)' positions (homo)sexuality as textual (an arrangement of signs), but where the texts which signify sexuality are both multiple and problematic. ' "Homosexuality" is not a name for a preexistent "thing" ', writes Beaver, 'but part of a network of developing language' (1981: 103). To argue that sexuality and textuality are linked is to propose that the sexual is conceived in relation to words, sign-systems, discourses and representations. However, the multiplicity and plurality of signs which have served to structure how sexuality is conceived suggest that no one sign adequately appropriates or contains what sexuality is.

The signs of sexuality, Beaver suggests, are less reliable in terms of their *denotative* than in relation to their *connotative* power. Beaver's argument is twofold: lesbians and gays have been placed in a powerful relation to signs as: (a) readers-consumers, and (b) writers-producers. Beaver's position, which is ultimately deconstructive, offers useful insights into the links between sexuality and textuality:

> The homosexual is beset by signs, by the urge to interpret whatever transpires, or fails to transpire, between himself and every chance acquaintance. He is a prodigious consumer of signs – of hidden meanings, hidden systems, hidden potentiality. Exclusion from the common code impels the frenzied quest: in the momentary glimpse, the scrambled figure, the sporadic gesture, the chance encounter, the reverse image, the sudden slippage, the lowered guard. In a flash meanings may be disclosed; mysteries wrenched out and betrayed. (ibid., 105)

Although Beaver is proposing that the signs of homosexuality are constructed on the basis of arbitrary as opposed to essential relations, he makes clear that the connection between sexuality and sign-systems is powerful. On the one hand, Beaver is arguing that homosexuality has been figured in terms of absence, secrecy and slippage. On this model, lesbians and gays are coerced by the need to read into all manner of signs some sense of selfhood and identity. The reading of signs in this way has often been popularly translated into questions, such as 'Is s/he or isn't s/he?', or 'Have you heard about . . .?' The need to 'know' someone is lesbian or gay has often been disempowering for subjects still fearful of their own 'outing' or coming-out. Through the encounter with signs and representations, the homosexual subject attempts to visualise an identity and a position in the world. On the other hand, the homosexual, in popular media representation, is disturbingly invisible, someone who is able to pass, co-mingling with the crowd. On this model, the invisible homosexual is forced into visibility, constituted by those discourses which have the effect of naturalising the cultural contingencies of sex and gender. Adopting a similarly deconstructive strategy, Lee Edelman points out that the body of the lesbian and the gay man, now textualised, is, unlike its heterosexual counterpart, subjected 'to the alienating requirement that it be "read" ' (1994: 12).

Beaver goes on to point out how nineteenth-century discourses define the heterosexual, monogamous and married partnership as the ideal model of social and private life. The privilege accorded to heterosexual marriage made it possible to regard 'every other form of erotic relationship as *contre nature*, a threat to health as well as to society' (1981: 102). In other words, whilst sexuality is understood in the context of multiple sign-systems, the signs of a naturalised heterosexual order were the ones which came to predominate at the end of the nineteenth century. Beaver is careful to note that signs never operate outside of cultural politics and, following Jacques Derrida and Foucault, he argues that subjects use the language of the dominant in deconstructive or counter-discursive ways. However, because homosexuality has long been a taboo subject, it has relied on 'vicious stereotypes'. Beaver lists the now familiar taxonomy: 'angel-face, arse-bandit, . . . bent, . . . bugger, . . . bum boy, . . . poofter, . . . turd burglar, pervert' (ibid., 103). If the heterosexual is often figured in relation to the safe domains of marriage, family and children, reproductive sexual intercourse and health, the homosexual – following through this binary logic – is more usually associated with spinsterhood or bachelorhood, perverse sexual practices and disease.

In like vein to Beaver, Barbara Creed (1995) examines how 'lesbian bodies' have also been subjected to visual scrutiny and identification. She relates her observations to patriarchy's reliance on images of women as fluid, unstable and airy. Woman's body, in Creed's discussion, signifies the potential to return to a 'more primitive state of being', and 'her image is accordingly manipulated, shaped, altered' (1995: 87). But if woman's body, asks Creed, 'signifies the other, how, then, does the lesbian body differ from the body of the so-called "normal" woman?' (ibid., 88). She lists three stereotypes of the lesbian body: 'as active and masculinized'; as 'animalistic'; and as 'narcissistic'. 'Born from a deep-seated fear of female sexuality, these stereotypes refer explicitly to the lesbian body, and arise from the nature of the threat lesbianism offers to patriarchal heterosexual culture' (ibid.). Creed makes clear that there are no natural or biological reasons why lesbian bodies should be any different from bisexual or heterosexual ones, though culture has made the bodies of 'tribades, tomboys and tarts' into 'pseudo-males' (ibid., 101). The need to read and be read, to be visible and visualised, is of course vital to a politics which challenges systems of (sexual) representation. However, Marjorie Garber notes the 'double-edged' nature of sign-systems in lesbian and gay culture. 'The social semiotics of butch-femme . . . has often provoked homophobia', stirring up 'apologists in the gay and lesbian community to call for moderation' (1993: 140).

Televising Natural Sex?

Foucault's work more than any other has lent support to contemporary arguments which suggest that the words *sex*, *sexuality* and *gender* do not point to natural categories or experiences. There is no essentially sexed 'self' which is prior to the cultural creation of the self through the operation of representation. Judith Butler's *Gender Trouble* (1990) and *Bodies that Matter* (1993), and Eve Sedgwick's *Epistemology of the Closet* (1994) draw on and expand the work of Foucault, arguing that the relations between gender (the cultural expectations of what it means to be a woman or a man), and sexuality (the supposedly pre-cultural or 'natural' grounds on which gender is thought to be constructed), are neither direct nor continuous. In the case of Butler, gender and sexuality are as much about 'being' in the world in certain ways as they are performances required in cultures with rigid sex-gender divisions.

For both Butler and Sedgwick, sexuality is a cultural and provisional fact of life far more than it is a natural consequence of biology. Despite the cultural specificity of sexuality, it nonetheless stands in complex relation to systems of representation. However, if sexuality is not simply a natural category experienced in universal ways, it follows that terms such as 'gay', 'straight', 'feminine' and 'masculine' are not tied to sexuality or gender in straightforward ways. In the arguments of Butler and Sedgwick, there is no necessary or final truth of the body which makes it lesbian, gay, straight, queer, feminine or masculine. 'Starting with two sexes, as we must', writes Adam Philips towards the end of Butler's *The Psychic Life of Power*, 'locks us into a logic, a binary system that often seems remote from lived and spoken experience' (Philips, in Butler 1997b: 158). Similarly, Judith

Halberstam (1998) considers some of the 'experiences' of sex and gender in her important study, *Female Masculinity*. She details how gender attributes associated with men can be easily and subversively attached to women. Whilst there have always been more versions of womanhood than those which dominate mainstream cultures, Halberstam looks at the threats to masculinity and femininity posed by so-called 'butch' women. However, if there have always been more accounts of womanhood than those associated with the conventions of heterosexual and patriarchal femininity, Butler's and Halberstam's work also points out why masculinity and femininity have often come to seem determining, intractable and fixed notions of who subjects are or perceive themselves to be. It is in the context of a society whose institutions and discourses seemed firmly committed to rigid notions of heterosexual manliness and womanliness, that we consider sexuality and television.

Television representations of sexuality have been structured according to a number of assumptions. In the past, specific ethical, political, and therefore representational considerations meant that 'sex' was adjudged offensive, and homosexual sex was more offensive still. The laws governing relations among same-sex partners were far less liberal than for heterosexuals, and so the representation of same-sex relations was inflected by the politics of what could or could not be said or screened at any one point.[19] In Western societies, the sexual identity which has usually been privileged has been that associated with the demands of 'compulsory heterosexuality' (Rich 1980). Allied to this observation is the way sexual identity has been figured as the truth of the person rather than simply one aspect of subjectivity. Regardless of social class or gender, sexuality came to be seen as the single-most determining aspect of personal identity. Media output has often been underpinned by a *heteronormative* ideology.[20] Sitcoms and popular drama series have tended to rely on reversal of gender stereotypes in order to portray lesbian or gay characters. Lesbians are manly, and gay men are womanly or in drag, but always according to highly stereotyped gender imagery. The satirisation of gender stereotypes can often serve to undercut the 'serious' world in which such gender or sexuality is performed. The BBC's *Gimme Gimme Gimme* (BBC, 1999), for example, exemplifies material which, through its humour, explores how the culture of so-called 'marginal' groups relies on the complex inter-operation of the margins and the mainstream in order for both domains to make sense. Although Judith Butler's *Gender Trouble* has rightly drawn attention to the performative politics of drag and gender parody, drag, as John

Champagne argues, is double-edged, at once 'politically oppositional and reactionary' (1995: 122). However, regardless of the potential of gender transgressions, early television was governed by different sets of conventions regarding sexuality and broadcasting.

Standing in the Shadow

What can be said of the sexual subject or sexual cultures during this period? If few people had televisions, and not many programmes were broadcast, is it safe to conclude that the relationship between homo- or heterosexuality and television was of no serious consequence? The answer has to be yes and no, but mainly 'no'. In terms of representations of homosexuality, the first broadcast took the form of a discussion item on the current affairs programme *In the News* in 1954. This was followed by Granada's *Homosexuality and the Law: A Prologue* in 1957, and in 1964 the documentary *This Week* explored gay-male lifestyles. Terry Sanderson chronicles this period, noting that at the time, homosexuality was still illegal and so 'most of the participants were shown in silhouette. The broadcast caused a sensation, and the following year *This Week* followed it up with a programme about lesbians' (1995: 16).[21] The fact that documentaries devoted time to 'lifestyles' other than those grounded in heteronormative ideology is important. Invariably, however, the repeated sensationalisation of homosexuality also reinforced its status as a form of medical and social deviance. It was not until the 1970s and early 1980s that a few programmes began to address, represent and examine alternatives to heterosexual lives and cultures, though homosexuals were usually figured in problematic terms. Exceptions to this general rule include *Gays: Speaking Up* (Thames, 1978) and *Gay Life* (LWT, 1980–1).

By the late 1980s, programmes such as Channel 4's *Out on Tuesday* (14 February, 1989), alongside 'gay-theme' nights (on BBC and Channel 4) did begin to explore sexuality in ways which slowly dismantled the view that all homosexuals were the same. However, it was also during the 1980s that homosexuality was increasingly associated with the negative imagery used in government-sponsored safe-sex advertisements. Prior to the late 1970s, most programmes that were broadcast left viewers in no doubt about the importance of family values and consensual morality. In that sense, it is of some consequence that the dominant televisual version of sexuality was one which privileged heterosexual self-representation to the *apparent* exclusion of all others. Although there are no guarantees that programmes by or about homosexuals necessarily contest dominant values, it is safe to conclude that up until the 1970s, sexuality was mostly confined to the sphere of the family and the living room. From the middle of the 1950s to the late 1960s, television was still heavily committed to dramas, documentaries, sitcoms and children's programmes, which addressed audiences on the basis of an assumed heterosexuality. Opposite-sex marriage and the family were hegemonic, represented in dramas and soaps as the normative model of sexual relations. Stephen Wagg comments that the popularisation of television ownership throughout the 1950s and 1960s contributed to a general critique of family life. Television, which 'intruded in the home' also 'confronted the adult protectors of childhood dignity and innocence with their three greatest fears: sex, violence and commerce' (1992: 155). But this was never homosexual sex, the commerce was not 'pink', and the family viewing took place in a cultural climate pervaded by a thoroughly heteronormative ideology. Richard Dyer has argued that the dominant forms of identification set up by film and television were based around narratives which encouraged viewers to 'agree with [the medium's] idea of what heterosexual feelings are', implying that 'such feelings exist' (1993: 119). Patricia Juliana Smith, writing on popular media cultures of the 1960s, similarly argues that 'the sexual freedom the decade brought forth was primarily for the benefit of heterosexual males' (1999: 105).

The 'public service' ethos of the BBC, assurances about its educational, cultural and moral force (Scannell 2000), alongside a broad commitment to family values, the Commonwealth and (white) Christianity, undoubtedly bolstered a heterosexual consensus. This is not to claim that early television was knowingly homophobic; and nor should the hostility faced by 'out' homosexuals be overstated, though *The Naked Civil Servant* (Thames, 1975) is fairly accurate in its portrayal of the physical side to homophobic brutality. It is to suggest, however, that media institutions and practices interpellated audiences whose sexuality was rarely questioned. During the period under question, homosexuality was reported and visualised in terms of scandal or psychotic illness. Robert Corber (1997) details how in the United States and the West generally, male homosexuals were considered a national security risk, frequently associated with Soviet-style communism. Terms used today – bisexual, lesbian, gay, queer, transsexual, as well as the various sexual subcultures which those labels hide – were differently inflected in the Cold War 1950s and 1960s. Homosexuals were a group set apart. In the way that non-white subjects have traditionally been perceived using the generic term 'blacks', so lesbians, gays and bisexuals were classified simply as 'homosexual'. Representations of homosexual lives were invariably distilled through a lens which accorded visual privilege and priority to heterosexual practices. Dramas, sitcoms, police series and children's programmes positioned mothers and fathers, and husbands, wives and the family as both the dominant and regulatory models of identity. Despite the conflictual interpersonal relations which were grittily exposed in 'kitchen-sink' output of the time, these same dramas relied on heterosexual relations in order to stage their fictions of marriage, family life and work. In the way that Britain's Asian or Afro-Caribbean communities have found access to self-representation problematic (Malik 2002), so the homophobia which lesbians, gays and bisexuals experienced in the 1950s and 1960s took the form of an exclusion from representation altogether.

Inside and Outside

Of course, no media representation ever states the degree to which it is produced in the interests of heterosexuals (and is, to that extent, (hetero)sexist). However, the preceding observations aim to underline the material ways in which homosexual self-representation has been less than straightforward. Discussion of televisual representation is not simply concerned with the identity 'tokens' which occupy the space of the screen. It may be the case, for instance, that women have been in as many television dramas as men, but representation is concerned both with *who* is represented and with *why*, *when*, *where* and *how* the representation occurs. Larry Gross captures some of the arguments surrounding the politics of the symbolic and the representational in his essay 'What Is Wrong with This Picture? Lesbian Women and Gay Men on Television' (1994). 'Representation in the mediated "reality" of our mass culture is in itself power; certainly it is the case that nonrepresentation maintains the powerless status of groups that do not possess significant material or political power bases', argues Gross (1994: 143). In a sense, homosexuals have always been an implicit and necessary part of representation in the media but in terms of negation, absence, marginality and silence.

Yet self-representation is not simply a matter of images. And nor is democratic representation a case of ensuring that every programme includes sexualities which reflect the diversity of practices and experiences. Dramas produced and written by homosexuals do not necessarily resolve issues of misrepresentation. All representation is a form of distortion: the words and images of television refract all realities in particular ways.

Moreover, as Alexander Doty observes, film and television have always facilitated lesbian, gay and queer viewing strategies. 'Queer positions, queer readings, and queer pleasures are part of a reception space that stands simultaneously beside and within that created by heterosexual and straight positions' (1993: 15). Of course, it cannot be ignored that most televisual representation has occurred on the basis of heteronormative hegemony. But following through Doty's logic, visualisation – making something visible – is not solely concerned with whose sexuality is visualised on the television screen if all programmes are open to a range of readings.

Undoubtedly, representations occur 'in' some form of text. Texts – television dramas, films, literary fictions – not only construct meanings but also constitute the sites where debates about meaning occur. Whilst representations of sexuality also relate to the meanings attached to identity, it is clear that *how* identities are represented is not always undertaken in ways which attend to issues of parity and inclusion. The results of the Lesbian and Gay Broadcasting Project of 1985–6 reported that 'the proportion of lesbian/gay characters and issues' on television was 'profoundly low'. '. . . Our analysis [reveals] that, on television at least, over 90% of characterisation amounts to two types: the criminal and the sissy' (reported in Sanderson 1995: 18–20). To be objectified as a special case, sad victim or dangerous citizen might be at odds with forms of self-representation which valorise social-sexual difference, highlight the subject's context of victimisation, or expose how sexual citizenship has been historically denied to sexual minorities. David Miller (1991) has argued that representation of homosexuals in visual media has relied on the suggestive modes of connotation and allusion. As a dominant and enduring strategy in the representation of lesbian and gay lives, connotation visualises characters or events on the basis of implication, trace, inference, insinuation, hint and innuendo. Making a similar point, Dyer argues that 'sexuality, male or female, is not so much shown directly as symbolized. . . . Colours, textures, objects, effects of light, the shape of things, all convey sexuality through evocation, resonance, association' (1993: 112). Sometimes such inference is obscure and unclear, operating with codes that can be deciphered in positive and negative ways at the same time. Whilst Alfred Hitchcock films, for example, suggestively rely on male homosexuals in the construction of heterosexual-romance plots, these same homosexuals are both repudiated and demeaned in the triumph of marriage or opposite-sex love.

Homosexual characters of the past classically live alone as spinsters or bachelors and are obsessed by over-involved parents; mannerisms are often portrayed on the basis of gender reversals (e.g. women are figured in masculine ways; gay male voices are feminised); and lesbians and gays usually have medical, neurotic or psychiatric histories. During the 1960s, the life and career of singer Dusty Springfield was subject to all manner of suspicion in ways that the lives of contemporaries Lulu, Cilla Black and Sandie Shaw were not. The blend of convent schooling, single marital status, and appropriation of African-American music traditions were, on the one hand, signifiers whose overdetermining power pointed to a subject of dubious sexual persuasion. On the other hand, these same signs meant that Springfield was able to allude to a range of subjects and spectators, simultaneously addressing straight, lesbian and gay audiences. The tensions which 1960s television audiences were able to detect are reflected in Lucy O'Brien's account of the BBC series *Dusty*. Noting how Springfield was at the height of her career, O'Brien relates how the singer's 'family audience was firmly established, and anything threatening to compromise her image was quickly squashed' (1999: 98). Connecting issues of race and sexuality, Smith writes of Springfield's complex reworking of traditions in black music, where the visual signifiers allowed the singer to symbolise 'a displaced sexual freedom and power . . . subversively articulating unspeakable sexuality for a queer girl' (ibid., 108).[22]

Served Naked

During the 1970s, John Inman's Mr Humphries in BBC1's *Are You Being Served?* is more direct and self-referential about his sexuality; audiences are given obvious clues as to his fictional private life (he loves his mother, ballet and flamboyant clothes); and his camp antics, next to his interest in men's wear, index a man whose sexuality does not quite fit with 1970s macho manliness or style. Camp and drag, simultaneously transgressive and dissident, conformist and reactionary, have long been associated with gay male aesthetics. Titles from the 1973 episodes of *Are You Being Served?* ('Dear Sexy Knickers', 'Camping In', and 'Diamonds Are a Man's Best Friend') suggest the show's camp sense of humour as much as they satirise dominant accounts of the straight world of work and the heterosexual public sphere. In many ways, *Are You Being Served?* contests as much as it confirms the connotative rhetoric associated with female masculinity and male femininity. Inman's innuendo is blatant and, when compared to some mainstream comedy of the time, his humour is more challenging and contentious. Although his character is structured around mannerisms associated with camp and male effeminacy, it might be argued that there is nothing unduly problematic with such characterisation. It is seriously problematic, however, when it is set up as representative of gay life. Indeed, Humphries may well provoke some male audiences into the uncomfortable awareness that what constitutes maleness, masculinity or manliness is easily open to performative distortion and parody.[23] The bombastic Mrs Slocombe, in many ways Mr Humphries' 'straight man' in the double-act, serves to highlight the series' generic preoccupation with sex and gender symbolism. Mrs Slocombe, whose loud presence and humour are central to the show, is unashamed about the articulation and expression of *hetero*sexual desire. Whilst the comedic aspects of her character might seem to undercut the seriousness of her intentions, she represents an outspoken version of womanhood – and not just for heterosexual women! – in a period when many women were still confined by marriage, domesticity and the kitchen sink. Her outbursts, viewed through the devices of comedy, seem less threatening, yet this comic image, in the words of Dyer, articulates 'male fears and anxieties about female sexual energy, about the way it may test virility, about the way it challenges male supremacy' (1993: 116).

It was also during the 1970s that Thames Television adapted Quentin Crisp's autobiography *The Naked Civil Servant*. Verity Lambert and Barry Hanson's groundbreaking production of 1975 featured a flamboyant and outrageous John Hurt in the title role. Crisp is depicted as he was in life: camp, effeminate, outrageous and proud, and the hilarity of the book is exploited to the full in the Thames dramatisation. One of the effects of Mr Humphries' performances in *Are You Being Served?* is the disruption of norms associated with heterosexual manhood. A similar effect is achieved in *The Naked Civil Servant*, and Hurt's portrayal of Crisp expands the notions of sexuality and gender available to audiences during the 1970s. In the case of *Are You Being Served?*, the Grace Brothers' shop assistant is a vital part of the fictional world of the department store. One of the features of this comedy, however, is that Humphries is never exposed to the external realities beyond the shop. As a consequence, his behaviour is never modified to suit the constraints of a potentially antagonistic public environment, and is a necessary counter to other male characters' attempts at manly seriousness and decorum. However, the dramatic restaging of Crisp's life shows how his effeminacy and his flamboyance are central to the construction of the character's identity in a hostile Britain.

This Thames TV drama uses voice-over, 'live' action scenes, framing, monochrome backdrops and animated white script (along the lines of silent films) in the depiction of Crisp's life. Hurt's skin is whitened, serving to highlight the flaming henna-red hair, heavy mascara and bright lipstick. The portrayal of Crisp's arrogance and sarcasm is connected to his strategies of determination and resistance in the 'real' world, and the drama's representation of hostility and harassment is a reminder of a homophobic history. In some ways *The Naked Civil Servant* marks an important turning point to the degree that it begins to disrupt visual media's structuring of looks, gaze and spectatorship. *The Naked Civil Servant*, which Keith Howes sees as marking a 'quantum leap' (in Sanderson 1995: 17–18) in broadcasting history, is perhaps one of the first television productions to confront viewers with aspects of gay-male shame/pride, same-sex passion, and male–male voyeurism. Laura Mulvey's thesis that spectators are forced to identify with the male gaze is not so much overturned as it is complicated by a production in which the point of view is focused around a gay as opposed to a straight man. This is not to argue that there are viewing positions which are *essentially* lesbian or gay. Nor does the production's dramatisation of Crisp's life necessarily incite or repel particular kinds of viewers. However, the drama makes clear that Crisp belongs to a particular sexual minority whose norms and values differ from dominant models of intimacy. His personal history serves to reveal something of the subcultural spaces which homosexuals have appropriated in the interests of identity construction as much as how the protagonist's perceptions of the world were at odds with his heterosexual peers. It is worth recalling that the production was broadcast only six years after the Stonewall riots in New York. Many lesbians, gays and bisexuals were not 'out' or open about their sexuality. *The Naked Civil Servant* is important to the degree that it dramatises the story of a figure who was prepared to be open about his sexuality at a time when it was still an offence punishable by imprisonment. Crisp's autobiography makes clear that the author was less committed to gay liberation than he was presenting a case for sexual tolerance, one of the effects being the challenge the play poses to naturalised heterosexuality.[24]

It is important to stress that the questions and problems of representing lesbians and gays are not ones which concern the specificity or essential 'nature' of homosexuality. In a very obvious sense, the representation of *heterosexuality* is equally problematic, though culture has made its claims to naturalness seem compelling and essential. When historically dominant institutions (e.g. church, government, education, media) have often assumed that all subjects are heterosexual, then homosexuals will have to confront the problem of how best to re-present their (in)visibility. But if there is no essence to any sexuality other than the sign-systems which serve to make sex, gender and identity meaningful at any one point, then it is at the level of sign-systems – television, film, discourse – that groups will seek to exercise some degree of agency. *All* sexualities are invisible in that no one stable signifier points to a fixed referent, but when *some* sexualities are frequently misrepresented or just not represented at all, then the medium of television becomes an important and powerful site through which to contest dominant norms. The following sections consider some of the ways in which recent output has begun to rethink the representation of sexuality on television.

Homosexual or Queer? The Recent Present

In February, March and April 1999, and in February 2000, Channel 4 broadcast *Queer as Folk*. The series, which visualised a culture and space broadly associated with male same-sex desire, quickly established itself as a benchmark for similar programmes at the beginning of the twenty-first century. Its popularity and audience ratings suggest that it was watched by more than just gay men. Whilst lesbian, gay and bisexual audiences have never been ultimately denied all sorts of secret and queer identifications, *Queer as Folk* seems eager to make a once closeted world very public and very visible. The depiction of same-sex passion and intergenerational relationships, in the context of a subculture which was unashamed of its music and bars or the visibility of its lifestyle, made the straight and often compelling logic of the heterosexual world seem alien and indeed very queer. At times it seemed that a reversal had occurred whereby the 'straight world' in *Queer as Folk* was itself obscure and hidden. A number of themes and subplots served to disrupt some of the conventions of broadcasting, and for many *Queer as Folk* was something to be celebrated, a story, as Sally Munt writes, of 'pride and shame' (Munt 2000). Yet some of its story-lines (lesbian and gay parenting; 'under-age' sexual relations; internet pornography, chat rooms and rent boys; explicit reference to a range of gay-male sexual practices and routines; dysfunctional family life) undoubtedly challenged a number of viewers. Munt details some of the press response to the series (ibid., 532–3); and the *Becks* sponsorship of the series was quickly discontinued. The series has nonetheless influenced the kinds of series television channels are prepared to broadcast. The success of programmes such as *Metrosexuality* (2001), *Tinsel Town* (2002) and *Bob and Rose* (2001) is in part connected to the popularity of *Queer as Folk*. So what did the series capture and what did audiences consume? What is it that is visualised in *Queer as Folk*?

The Continuing Problems of Plural Identities

Central to the theoretical trajectories which inform lesbian, gay and queer studies is the question of identity, and there seems little doubt that *Queer as Folk* is in large part concerned with sexual identity. The series wastes little time introducing identities which audiences come to know as Vince (Craig Kelly), Stuart (Aidan Gillen) and Nathan (Charlie Hunnam). All three characters at some point exhibit degrees of pride and shame in relation to their identities, but unlike lesbian and gay stereotypes of previous generations, this series allows its characters to have some investment in their own agency and self-determination. These are not 'nice' gay boys from the hidden past, least of all Stuart! More interestingly, *Queer as Folk* seems to explore a culture in which sexuality and identity are understood in plural and fluid terms, where same-sex desire is only *one* marker of subjectivity. Of course matters of identity are not easily settled. The series, attentive to the politics of representing identities, exploits diverse images of lesbians and gay men, partly in order to contest the society in which these identities have often been rigidly fixed, and partly in order to demonstrate that perhaps there is no one identity which is ultimately representative.

From the outset, the series confronts the problems associated with fixing identity. At the end of Episode 1, Stuart rushes to the hospital where his child has just been born. Stuart is father to Romey's baby, though his identity as 'father' will be read as problematic in a society which continues to privilege heterosexual identity and marriage in relation to 'fatherhood'. Similarly, Romey's lesbian identity, certainly as far as some in the British Houses of Parliament are concerned, would cast doubt on her ability to mother the child she has just conceived. Next to Romey in the hospital ward are three of her friends. Russell Davies's script tell us that 'LISA's a classic lipstick lesbian; SIOBAHN is bald; SUZIE never says a word' (1999: 22). Signifiers of identity do matter, yet identity and self-identification are problematically multiple and complex. Whilst lesbians and gay men may share a homosexual past, the label 'homosexual' totalises same-sex experience and fails to register the differences which exist *within* and *amongst* lesbian and gay constituencies. One of the aims of queer theory is to blur and expand how we understand the relations between sexuality and other facts of identity (e.g., age, ethnicity and social class). Stuart's sexual desire is expressed in relationships which are interesting in terms of what they expose about age, social class and the cultural construction of bodies, as they are about same-sex practices among one version of gay 'manhood'. Using Bernard's advice to Nathan, the opening lines of the series make clear that there are no emblematic or ideal types:

> NATHAN: 'Scuse me, I mean, I'm just looking, but I don't – I mean, what's the best place to go?
>
> BERNARD: Depends what you're after. If you want bastards, go in there; if you want wankers, go in there; if you want selfish little mincing piss tart dick-heads; pick a building, any building, they're full of them,

Yet the buildings and spaces which the series constructs contain more than 'piss tart dickheads'. Stuart's encounters, for instance, are excited by a sense of danger and transgression (e.g. 'Greek God' (Episode 1), 'Goodfuk' (Episode 2)) and 'Big Cock City.com' (Series 2). These are arenas and experiences which are alien to the relatively 'safe' domain inhabited by Vince or short-term lover Cameron; and Romey and friends occupy a space whose distance from the world of Stuart serves to highlight his self-confident gay-male arrogance as much as it alludes to gender separatism and difference. Equally, the world of Alexander (Antony Cotton), Bernard (Andy Devine) and Hazel (Denise Black) serves to remind viewers of a 'queer' history in which straight women and gay men happily co-exist in the camp world of drag bars. Nathan's heterosexual mother, for example, finds this world an invaluable source of support in coming to terms with her son's sexuality. And in *Queer as Folk*, the functional families are ones which are brought together on the basis of need as opposed to marriage or convention.

The series' recognition of complexity shows how, unlike the industrial past, late-capitalist economies are eager to exploit 'gay villages'. The queerer and more sexually fragmented the culture, the more consumer capitalism is able to enlarge its market and profit bases. Yet *Queer as Folk* also makes clear that these queers also exercise some degree of limited agency. Alexander will be not be silenced or hidden from view, despite his parents' attempts to make him invisible in the town centre; ever-defiant Stuart confronts his nephew's bitter homophobia in the second series; and in the first series, Nathan refuses the comforts of family life, embracing instead the makeshift family of Hazel and Bernie. Such anger, directness and mutual support is largely absent from earlier broadcasting and the series invites audiences to explore a subculture in which homosexual self-nomination is more complex than some narratives have previously assumed. In many ways the recognition of such sexual complexity is, or can be, disturbing. One of the effects of such complication, for example, is that it can unsettle (or 'queer') those stabilising identity categories which helped shape lesbian and gay histories prior to and shortly after the Stonewall riots in June 1969. Within the context of Stonewall, identity politics was often grounded in rigid notions of sexuality and so a strong sense of identity became a necessary marker for subculture defending its rights. Lesbian, gay and bisexual, therefore, whilst they might be labels which reflect an identifiable constituency in particular spaces, are terms which also attest a particular time period. Sinfield writes that it may be necessary to acknowledge that 'gay' and 'lesbian' are 'historical phenomena and may now be hindering us more than they help us' (1998: 5). Whilst he is reluctant to embrace the queer-activist strategies of Peter Tatchell, Sinfield does acknowledge that there is no 'consensus about how les/bi/gay people are placed at the moment' (ibid., 195). But these are terms which have been used in order to construct specific images and representations. Whilst some critical perspectives on sexuality continue to use markers such as lesbian or gay, others adopt a mixture which incorporates queer.

Queer Theories

In recent criticism, 'queer' (as noun, verb and adjective) has been used to critique stabilising notions of a naturalised heterosexuality and gender. In many ways, however, 'queer' is an umbrella term, functioning to cast a shadow of uncertainty around lesbian, gay and bisexual identities. Perhaps more specifically useful in the deconstruction of sexuality is the work of Judith Butler. Taking lead from the poststructuralist work of Jacques Derrida, Michel Foucault and Jacques Lacan, her work has thrown doubt on stable notions of sexuality. Rather than seeing sex and gender in binary terms, Butler points to a range of desires, practices and identifications which obscure and blur the rigid distinctions associated with the sexual history of the recent past. Although she continues to use terms such as lesbian and gay, arguing for the strategic necessity of self-nomination, *Gender Trouble* and *Bodies That Matter* suggest that gender and sexuality are not simply grounded in a transparently sexed or gendered anatomy. Expanding Foucault's claim that sexuality is understood in relation to language and discourse, Butler shows how bodies are not simply pre-given forms upon which gender and sex are constructed. For Butler, the body per se does not speak outside cultural formations and representations.

Always questioning the assumptions underpinning normative (hetero)sexual practices, Butler's work shows how the simple binary heterosexual–homosexual rests on too simplistic a division of opposite-sex and same-sex practices. Her observations, similar to the work of Edelman and Sedgwick, move away from the notion of a lesbian body or a gay one to consider the processes of making meaning. Attentive to the difficulties of thinking sexuality outside of binary models, *Gender Trouble* and *Bodies That Matter* nonetheless begin to deconstruct the hetero-homosexual divide in an attempt to complicate notions of sexuality and power in contemporary life. If sexuality is not a clear matter, something whose boundaries are not rigid, then the visualisation of sexual identities will never simply be based on the meanings which signifiers or bodies are thought to guarantee. Queer theory, in its now various attempts to complicate how sexuality is configured and read, underscores the derivative and textual condition of any sexual identity. If the noun/adjective 'heterosexual' does not adequately define the sexual experiences of the majority, then lesbian and gay are terms which are thought to restrict how sexuality can be visualised and perceived. Halberstam's work, for example, points to the multiple ways women's physicality can be interpreted, generating readings which exceed many of the cultural conventions of the sex-gender system; and Evans and Gamman note how some gay men find 'images of lesbian women whom they mistake for "boys" as perversely attractive' (1995: 41).

Queer theory does not reject identity categories wholesale so much as it asks why they are useful, and for whom. To the extent that subjects can inhabit more than one site of sexual identification, then all subjects are potentially queer. Although queer has been used to group together non-heterosexual experiences, the term is used more generally to point to divergent desires and practices. Transvestite entertainer Eddie Izzard, for instance, does not really conform to hetero- or homosexual stereotypes, and neither is the production or consumption of his persona understood simply in relation to discrete bisexual, homosexual or heterosexual audiences. However, the adjective queer – as *Queer as Folk* shows – continues to be iterated in order to repudiate homosexuality whilst simultaneously endorsing the natural and compelling self-evidence of heterosexual identities. Driving Nathan to school at the end of Episode 1, 'kids have painted [on the jeep], in big white letters, a single word: QUEERS'. In contexts which also promote the sanctity of the family and the purity of the nation, queer continues to be vocalised in ways which accentuate the homophobia and misogyny attached to the history of the sign in question. By underlining the derivative, textual and relational nature of all identities, 'queer' signifies something more problematic about both identity and sexuality. But queer also casts doubt on strategies and representations which assume that *any* sexual identity is easily visualised on the basis of looks, gender stereotypes, facial expression, bodily gesture or voice. Simply, the knowledge – or secrets – that visualisation is thought to expose are seriously problematised.

All Queer Here?

Expanding the work of Foucault, Sedgwick has noted, after the late eighteenth century, how much cultural practice evidences that

> 'knowledge' and 'sex' became conceptually inseparable from one another – so that knowledge means in the first place sexual knowledge; and ignorance, sexual ignorance; and epistemological pressure of any sort seems a force increasingly saturated with sexual impulsion. (1993: 73)

Whilst *Queer as Folk* reflects the concerns of late twentieth-century cultures, where debates about sexuality and identity register a more problematic epistemology, and where sexuality has often been debated in spheres *considered* more honest than the late nineteenth century, there is a sense in which many of the characters live with secrets to do with sexuality. At the beginning of Episode 2, Nathan is at school, about to share his 'secret' with best friend Donna; Vince is at Harlo's supermarket, secretly lusting after two boys with trolleys; and Stuart is at the PR-advertising agency, preparing to have a brief encounter in the office toilet with a married man. All three scenes are concerned with secrecy and knowledge, (in)visibility and silence. One of the effects of secrecy is that it enables subjects to resist or refuse particular forms of association or identification. In which case, Vince's passing in the supermarket not only allows him, so he thinks, to cover his secret, but it also allows him to resist those discourses in other communities which would seek to expose the secret that is thought to be his identity. The effect of copying, passing and lying (seen in Vince's parody of the 'straight' man) ensures that nothing about identity in his work sphere, so he imagines, is tied to gayness. The passing and lying also have the effect of screening the 'knowledge' which is imagined as Vince's secret. However, because the lying/passing is bound up with a whole host of identity performances, screening can also be understood in a projective sense. Craig Kelly, the straight actor, is playing gay man Vince who is now playing the straight manager, Mr Vincent Tyler, who is also being read as available 'straight man' by work-mate Rosalie. Vince, in his soliloquial spaces, is able to project an identity whilst simultaneously rendering his work community invisible and deaf. If there is a secret, sexual knowledge, the people at work can neither see its presence nor hear its announcement. Yet these soliloquies, these private words and secret worlds, far from occluding all the other people in this scene, actually affirm the necessity of a public stage even though the mediations are thought to underscore a private sphere which is uniquely known only to Vince. On the queer stage, knowledge is now very much an open secret and everyone is involved even though Vince, on his stage at this point, is not 'out'.

Comically, the acting, passing and miming are not unique to Vince or to the other 'gay' characters. The staff who work in the supermarket are only too able to perform very queerly. Although the women at the supermarket mime the characteristics of the camp gay man, the series offers no original model which would either affirm or negate the quality or accuracy of their performance. For Vince or his work-mates, there is no original gay or straight which is available to be copied. If the women's gestures are successful, and they are hilariously so, then these copies exceed and supersede the authenticity assumed by the original. Later, in Episode 8, Nathan spots one of his homophobic classmates Christian, with girlfriend Cathy, in the New Union bar. Says Nathan's best friend Donna: 'He's out to impress. Canal Street, it's New York to the lower sixth.' Of course, for Christian to feel so at ease in the gay bar, he has had to assume that something will remain undetected. No one asks, for instance, to see his sexuality ID card! Not allowed to pass with such ease at school, Nathan is furious that heterosexual classmate Christian passes so unremarkably and insignificantly, as if invisible. Nathan takes a turn on the karaoke stage but refuses to sing.

> NATHAN: 'Cos that boy over there. Blue shirt, white T-shirt, dark hair, with the blonde girl. I'm in school with him, right, His name's Christian Hobbs. And Christian Hobbs, d'you know what he does? He finds a boy, and if that boy's a bit quiet, if he's a bit different, Christian Hobbs kicks his head in. He kicks them and he calls them queer. That boy there. He beats us up cos we're queer.

Cathy storms out utterly humiliated, leaving Christian in no doubt as to her views. Nathan orates his own self-confidence as much as he exposes the double operation of 'queer'. On the one hand people are 'queer' (old usage) if they are quiet or different, subject to bullying as a result; on the other hand, the quiet and unassuming Christian in the gay bar is read as gay, performing an identity before he expresses one. His body is also 'queer' (new usage), unable as it is to define the truth of Christian's desires. Rosalie, too, during Vince's party and after, lives temporarily with Vince's secret. But for these secrets to matter, or for the identity which is contained in the secret to assume vitality, audiences and characters are implicated in a variety of relational contexts. Although these contexts are about sex and sexuality, the same contexts are potentially open to multiple readings and interpretations to do with the body, adolescence, gender, community, fear, solidarity and friendship. The term 'queer', then, refers to a critical operation which aims to undo those identity categories which have been used to oppress subjects.[25] But its critical potential in relation to representation is also important. All representation is 'queer' (odd, peculiar, strange) to the extent that sexuality can never simply be visualised. Although cultures often require sexuality to be spoken, confessed, imagined and visualised as a discrete 'identity', the representations of sexuality point to the identity's many sources.

Queer as Folk shows how 'homosexuality' is often perceived as something the subject wants to forget, spoken in terms which specify not so much an identity as a performance which is required in a society where same-sex relationships are still linked to psychological maladaption. However, the series shows how queer subjects also resist, re-appropriating the terms of their own subjection. In the second series of *Queer as Folk*, Stuart is forced to confront his nephew's homophobia in front of the family:

> I'm queer, I'm gay, I'm homosexual, I'm a pouf, I'm a pufftah, I'm a ponce, I'm a bumboy, batty boy, backside artist, bugger. I'm bent, I am that arse bandit. I lift those shirts. I am a faggot arsed fudge-packing shit stabbing uphill gardener. . . . I fuck and am fucked. I suck and am sucked. . . . And I'm not a pervert. If there's one twisted bastard in this family it's this little blackmailer here. So congratulations, Thomas, I've just officially outed you.

Stuart's commanding response highlights the degree to which language and discourse constrain sexual subjects, underlining how words have been deployed in order to disgrace and humiliate lesbians and gays. Stuart's queer appropriation of this language – he outs his nephew as a pervert and not a homosexual – points to the ways in which symbolic resistance is one option in the reconstruction of potentially enabling forms of representation.

Chapter 5

The End of Representation? Television Drama and Postmodernism

With the television image – the television being the ultimate and perfect object for this new era – our own body and the whole surrounding universe become a control screen. . . . Each person sees himself at the controls of a hypothetical machine, isolated in a position of perfect and remote sovereignty, at an infinite distance from his universe of origin.

Jean Baudrillard, 'The Ecstasy of Communication'

5.1 Common Cultures and Values?

What are the differences between sitcoms, soap operas, and drama series of the 1950s and 1960s when compared with similar programmes now? Today's contexts of reception and production, with competing channels, programmes and schedules, next to the multi-generic nature of much television output, seem vastly different to the period in which the BBC and ITV were the only two channels to broadcast to the 'nation'. Yet was the coronation of Elizabeth II, for example, produced for a nation whose citizens shared a common culture? Or is this common culture harder to pin down, something more mythological than actual, a regulatory ideal as much as a material and bounded space? Compared with the early 1950s, the nation's 'way of life' today appears more pluralistic. The lives and cultures represented at the 2002 Golden Jubilee celebrations in London reflect a diversity which – even if only on the surface – was not evidenced at the coronation 50 years earlier. As a consequence of such plurality, are programmes produced and consumed on the basis of cultural difference or cultural sameness? Are audiences today dispersed and segmented in ways which 1950s audiences were not? Are news bulletins and current affairs programmes broadcast to a country whose multiple communities, subcultures and regional identities combine to form a unified audience? Or are programmes no longer produced or consumed on the basis of shared cultural identities?

In the 'postmodern' world, perhaps notions of shared cultures, values and identities are reminders of an earlier moment in twentieth-century history. The sorts of answers these questions invite depend on a number of variables. Studies by Charlotte Brunsdon (1983, 1987), Lynne Joyrich (1988, 1990, 1996), David Morley (1986, 1992), and Lynn Spigel (1992), show how age, ethnicity, gender, occupation, regional identity, sexuality and social class are factors which substantially inform how nations, television output and communities inter-operate one with each other. Moreover, questions of textuality, quality, form and genre, as G. W. Brandt (1993), John Caughie (2000) and Robin Nelson (1997) have noted, generate different questions. Theoretical perspectives will complicate questions and answers even further. Yet it is theoretical, pragmatic and socio-economic complications which have enlivened television broadcasting over the last 30 years. During this same period, a number of contradictory social, cultural and political variables have surrounded and informed television output and reception. This book has shown how textual analyses, television ethnographies and audience studies combine to enrich and enlarge how television drama is conceived. But psychoanalytic, queer, feminist and postcolonial critiques, as we have seen, repeatedly demonstrate that television is not a transparent medium. A summary of the changes in these areas provides an important historical and contextual backdrop for understanding some of the key developments which have taken place in relation to postmodernism, consumer capitalism and television studies.

Precarious Unity and Uncertain Disunity in (Post)modern Britain

British television during the period up until the mid-1970s was consumed within a culture and society still pledged, albeit problematically and precariously, to social welfare, free national health and state education, economic reform, and state planning. The same contexts governed literary, filmic and other media output. Despite much social upheaval during this period, state institutions such as education, the Church of England and the BBC relied on consensus values underpinned by liberal humanist 'common sense'. As the work of Sara Ahmed (1999), Paul Gilroy (1987, 1992), Stuart Hall

(1992a, 1993, 2000) and Sarita Malik (2002) suggests, notions of common sense, Britishness and national belonging were and are tied, albeit problematically, to whiteness, middle-class norms, and gender–sex divisions. Although Arnoldian values and Leavisite literary aesthetics were being contested in universities and the new polytechnics, a degree of political, social and institutional consensus continued to underpin a commitment to the notion of a common national culture. Popular cultures undoubtedly undermined the elitism of 'high' culture; alternative countercultures and subcultures had the effect of critiquing class; and the New Left was being mobilised as an alternative to 'old' Labour. Yet the vast majority of schools still relied on a canon of English literature; school assemblies promoted Christian values; and the predominance of Standard English, along with Received Pronunciation, were continuing signs of cultural and linguistic capital.

Much of the cultural consensus and later 'dissensus' (the term is used in Patricia Waugh's *The Harvest of the Sixties*, 1995[1]) was connected to the economy and to modes which entailed large-scale (Fordist) industrial production. The coalmining and steel industries, alongside shipbuilding and car manufacture, were highly labour intensive. However, the interventionist policies which had marked postwar economic consensus were challenged by monetarist and *laissez-faire* economic theories and practices which contributed to the erosion of primary-sector industries, the disintegration of communities and the gradual privatisation of the public sector. Alongside these changes in the economic domain, a number of developments in cultural and theoretical spheres served to undermine liberal-humanist values, particularly notions of individualism, agency and identity. Some of the names associated with these perspectives (Jean Baudrillard, Jacques Derrida, Frederic Jameson, Jacques Lacan and Jean-François Lyotard) are now well known, and their theoretical work is discussed later. These theories are often grouped under the now familiar terms 'postmodernism' and 'poststructuralism'. Of course no theory, postmodern or otherwise, serves as basis for dramatic, fictional or other creative practice. However, some of the issues expressed in dramatic work of the last 20 years reveal the ways in which creative and theoretical works articulate similar agendas. Postmodern theory's concerns with the problems of identity, language and communication have often been mirrored in fictional and dramatic texts which have explored ethnicity, gender and sexuality.

It was the strained and conflicting dialogues in the 1970s and 1980s between liberal humanism, on the one hand, and postmodernism and poststructuralism, on the other, which served to problematise theories of subjectivity, personal and national identity, and agency. On the economic front, a broad commitment to mixed-economy and interventionist models of welfare capitalism since 1945 was increasingly thrown into doubt by free-market 'anti-models' of economic 'liberation'. And the collectivist stress on labour and production of earlier periods was challenged by economic theories whose discourses emphasised consumerism, freedom and choice. In the UK, Margaret Thatcher's term of office, writes Patricia Waugh, 'was able openly to replace the goals of consensus with those of possessive individualism or enterprise' (1995: 20). In terms of cultural production, a number of television playwrights, film makers and writers reflected such tensions in their output. Alan Bleasedale, Hanif Kureishi, Verity Lambert, Mike Leigh, Phil Redmond, Fay Weldon and Jeanette Winterson chronicle how 'Britain' is not a country or a construct with a shared culture. *Boys from the Blackstuff* (1982) shows how cultures and communities were systematically destroyed as a result of free-market economics; *Oranges Are Not the Only Fruit* (1990) exposes the sex-gender system through the eyes of a lesbian whose dysfunctional family clings to religion in order to make sense of their own alienation from each other; and *The Buddha of Suburbia*'s (1993) exploration of ethnicity and class reveals the degree to which both categories complicate identity and desire.

These dramatic and creative works, sometimes more than the criticism or theory, have interrogated the uncertain harmony and the very definite conflict of the last 25 years. There is little doubt that the dominant discourses informing Britain's relatively optimistic consensus of the post-war years generated the promise of unity and integration. However, dramas by the above writers have supplemented dominant histories of childhood, the family, masculinity, sexuality, ethnicity and gender, proving effective in the deconstruction of 'official' national cultures of consent. A number of drama series from the 1980s and 1990s (e.g. *Cracker* (1993–), *Edge of Darkness* (1985), *GBH* (1991), *The Life and Loves of a She-Devil* (1986), *The Singing Detective* (1986) and *Tutti Frutti* (1987), work with a blend of realism, surrealism, gothic, action-thriller and horror. Caughie notes how in some dramas, there is a 'gradual, sometimes almost imperceptible intrusion of madness – of individuals and institutions – and the transformation of realism into the surreal' (2000: 205). Troy Kennedy Martin's *Edge of Darkness* (BBC, 1985), whilst drawing on realist traditions, is a definite move away from naturalism. The drama, part political critique of the Thatcher–Reagan years, and part action drama, deploys, in the words of

Andrew Lavender, strategies associated with 'controversial realism', the 'poetic' and 'mystical' (in Brandt 1993: 104–5). *Life and Loves of a She-Devil* (BBC, 1986) similarly departs from realist modes, the BBC drama exploiting Weldon's novelistic fusion of gothic, fantasy, surrealism and horror. The drama's feminist agenda addresses issues of women's roles and domesticity, exploring how traditionally marginalised subjects are able – or not – to subvert liberal-humanist values. Its gothic heroine resists the dominant versions of what it means to be a mother, wife, lover and wage-earner. Both the drama and the novel depart from the conventions of realism, a disengagement which also signals a shift away from narrative strategies traditionally associated with patriarchy. Yet there remain contradictions, and there are no obvious breaks between one period and another.

Much of the naturalist/realist, modernist and experimental drama since the late 1970s casts a contradictory shadow over the political unity and cultural coherence thought to typify the period before 1974. However, as Waugh notes generally of the last 40 years, the period before this reveals 'a profound disaffection with the inadequacies of consensus', and the 1980s 'respond similarly to the brutal acquisitiveness of the Thatcher years' (1995: 20). It is within – and often against – this disjunctive cultural context that televisual interventions have operated to undermine singular and totalised versions of what it means to be 'British'. Sometimes this has been done in formats which mix genres in satirical and humorous ways. *Da Ali G Show* (2000), *Goodness Gracious Me* (1998) and *Gimme Gimme Gimme* (1999) partly demonstrate how ethnicity and sexuality impact on national and personal identity, satirising earlier versions of race and sex which often failed to visualise Britain's *other* half. *The Day Today* (1994), *Brass Eye* (1997–2001) and *The League of Gentlemen* (1999–) call into doubt notions of community, family and consensus morality. However, the interrogation of Britain's cultural homogeneity, or the deconstruction of identity enacted in experimental, innovative or loosely 'postmodern' output, stands in contrast to the realist and social-realist dramas.

5.2 Television Drama and Postmodernism

Television in Postmodern Conditions

Jean-François Lyotard's *The Postmodern Condition: A Report on Knowledge* (1984) is a useful source to begin a discussion of the relations between cultural heterogeneity and the viewing contexts of postmodernity.

His work points to a number of changes in social, economic and cultural practices which have contributed to the emergence of what he calls the 'postmodern condition'. If modern societies are broadly characterised by cohesion, centralisation and containment, then postmodern societies are characterised by disintegration, decentralisation and dispersal. Lyotard's work highlights the status and function of knowledge, contrasting the period of Enlightenment and modernity, when the authority of scientific knowledge was grounded in its ability to present itself as *the* truth, with the postmodern period, where the status of knowledge is more doubtful and contradictory. Central to Lyotard's position is his argument that the grand or master narratives of the past have now ceded their power to micro or small narratives. Grand narratives, which explain the world and human history on the basis of key doctrines, are now forced to compete with other, perhaps more compelling accounts of the past and present. In Lyotard's version of postmodern theory, 'modern' accounts of history are geared towards some form of synthesis. Conflict – of a personal or social kind – is always resolved because totalising or grand explanations set the terms for how conflict arises and how it will be resolved. Freudian psychoanalysis, for example, promises psychic resolution on the basis of therapy; classical Marxist theory points to revolution as the way to overcome class conflict; and capitalism is structured around a grand narrative whose self-justifying rationale is the creation of private wealth. In all these models the individual subject inhabits a society which, though imperfect, can nonetheless be changed. Knowledge and science make sense in relation to social progress and advancement. In the modern period, science 'legitimates itself with reference to a metadiscourse' argues Lyotard (1984: xxiii). Societies grounded in the discourses of reason, science and truth are 'modern'.

Postmodern theories do not abandon the discourse of truth so much as demonstrate how truths are relative and contingent. In postmodern society truth is useful in terms of its functions, but truth production is not solely tied to the grand narratives of religion or science. Lyotard's postmodern society is marked by fragmentation, libidinal anarchy, diversity and eclecticism. In comparison to modernity, the sources of power and truth are fractured and dispersed. Language seems to lose its denotative function, becoming a game of desire, one linguistic regime competing with another. The multifaceted and eclectic character of contemporary culture, where styles, fashions and tastes are never really 'in' or 'out', is mirrored in the way television organises its programmes, schedules and output. Television time is always 'now'; studios and technology can recreate the past in an instant; and the multi-channel world afforded by satellite or digital means the possibilities of 'now' are as multiple and as instantaneous as the channels to which audiences can subscribe. Advertising and music videos are visually stunning, creating their own worlds and characters; soap-opera plots are discussed at Prime Minister's Questions; and programmes dealing with crime and justice dramatise burglaries, assault and murder. Compared with the early days of British broadcasting, the range of images, genres and styles accessed with just five channels is enormous. American televisual space-time, according to Jean Baudrillard and Pierre Bourdieu, seems more real than chronological time; yet time and space are deformed and splintered by televisual technologies; and it is thought that multi-generic programmes leave audiences with the remnants and scraps of endlessly recycled material.

Pierre Bourdieu's (1998) critique of contemporary programmes attends to what he sees as the depoliticising tendencies of popular television in France. Whilst Bourdieu's work remains broadly sociological, his insights into postmodern media cultures are useful to this current outline. Like Jameson (see below), Bourdieu notes '[t]elevision's power of diffusion' (1998: 44), and its ability to make 'everything ordinary' (ibid.). In a social space where television images are as central and as symbolically dominant as the West, and where 'pure entertainment [and] mindless talk show chatter' (ibid., 3) are privileged above 'analysis, in-depth interviews [and] serious documentaries' (ibid.), then the '[c]onstant, permanent relationships of inequality' (ibid., 40) are in danger of being elided. Whilst Bourdieu does not share a nostalgia for the 'paternalistic pedagogical television of the past' (ibid., 48), he nonetheless sees in contemporary television 'a populist spontaneism [whose] demagogic capitulation to popular tastes' (ibid.) is as much a threat to the 'democratic use' (ibid.) of television as the one posed in the paternalistic 1950s and 1960s. Throughout Bourdieu's study, he stresses the impact of televisual images on audiences as well as the 'symbolic weight' attached to 'national media' and 'especially the symbolic dominance of American television, which serves a good many journalists as both a model and a source of ideas, formulas, and tactics' (ibid., 41).

Jürgen Habermas (1985), a theorist whose work belongs to the tradition of the Frankfurt School, is also wary of postmodern theory. For Habermas, the projects of modernity and Enlightenment are as yet unfulfilled and incomplete. Theorists of postmodernity such as Lyotard, seen by Habermas as conservative and reactionary, fail to acknowledge the ways in which communication and dialogue need not be incommensurable or impossible. 'In everyday communication, cognitive meanings, moral expectations, subjective expressions and evaluations must relate to one another' (1985: 11). He argues that the blurring of the boundaries between life and art, and 'fiction and praxis' (ibid.) is politically hazardous. To 'declare everything to be art' is nothing short of 'nonsense' (ibid.). He stresses the importance of a public sphere in which a 'rationalized everyday life' (ibid.) is still an attainable goal. Keen to understand the origins of fragmentation in society rather than its cultural manifestations in film or fiction, Habermas thinks that 'instead of giving up modernity and its project as a lost cause, we should learn from the mistake of those extravagant programs which have tried to negate modernity' (ibid., 12).

The Viewing Contexts of Postmodernity[2]

Despite these conflicting appraisals of postmodernity, there is some measure of agreement as to the features which typify the viewing contexts of postmodernity, and these may be summarised as follows.

Multi-channel world: Up until recently, the two main channels available to British audiences were BBC and ITV. ITV, on the one hand, whilst still fairly regulated, was associated with commerce and advertising, and companies such as Granada served specific regions and/or produced programmes for national broadcast on the independent network. Tony Warren's *Coronation Street*, for example, was Granada's and ITV's pioneering soap opera. *World of Sport*, *This Week* and *Crossroads* (the first version), are other examples of ITV's local/national coverage. On the other hand, the BBC, whose revenue is directly linked to the licence fee, was able to resist the demands of the free market and tended to produce programmes which were not as tied to audience ratings, popularity, or the constraints of commercialism. Throughout the 1990s, and with increased deregulation, the channels, private companies, production companies and investors which now have stakes in television broadcasting far exceed anything imagined when Channel Four interrupted the duopolistic status quo in 1982. In addition to deregulation, technological developments of the last 20 years (e.g. cable, digital, satellite, online-interactive and pay-per-view) have increased the pressure on the BBC and ITV. The BBC, partially enabled by deregulation, and alert to the possibilities of domestic and international markets, has responded with some success, expanding into America and Europe, offering 24-hour news services, enlarging its market share at home, and investing in productions usually associated with ITV. More competition and more channels do not mean that audiences necessarily have opportunities to access cultural, ethnic or social diversity. However, one of the features of postmodern culture is the degree to which the 'grand narratives' of the past have been penetrated by the local – but where the interests of global and consumer capitalism are never far away.

Old and new media: Siune and Hultén (1998) have compared what they refer to as 'the old media' – or media more associated with modernity – with the new media, whose features and functions are more attuned to the seemingly dispersed spheres of the postmodern condition. Their separations point out the ways in which the *old* media are closely related to the aims of Fordist production and how the *new* media are more focused on consumer, consumption, competition, and the market. The old media is associated with monopoly whereas the new media is more attuned to the demands of capitalistic competition in international markets. Television is local and global at the same time. If the media of the recent past was publicly funded and thus able to work with some sense of 'democracy' or public service, then the media of today is forced to operate on the basis of 'profit'; broadcasting companies are forced to survive in contexts more ruthless than the period up the 1980s. Citizens make way for consumers, and the contexts of the neighbourhood and the nation now make sense only within the global concerns of consumer capitalism (Siune and Hultén 1998: 36).

Plural screens and multiple images: The media technologies associated with modernity produced visual images which were accessed in four principal ways: painting, photography, film and, latterly, television. The emergence of new technologies in postmodernity means that digital photography, PC/Internet monitors, video games, video recorders and camcorders, DVDs, mobile phones, e-mail, fax, pay-per-view, and satellite subscription services compete one with another in the production, representation, distribution and consumption of images. Again, whilst there is nothing specific to technology which makes it necessarily or essentially postmodern, the uses to which the technology is put ensure that no one source or channel can position itself as the authoritative arbiter of truth. The making of a documentary about New York City Fire Service by a French production team provided an account of 11 September 2001 which complemented the accounts provided by CNN and SKY-News. Other video footage adds to the many images which are accessed in programmes concerned with the events of September 11. However, none of these sources on their own are able to account fully for the meanings associated with the events on that particular date.

Fluid schedules and formats: Up until the 1970s, television usually finished around midnight and closed down for about seven hours. Moreover, the day often concluded with an epilogue or religious (Christian) thought; and stations played the National Anthem. Viewing occurred in relation to fixed spaces (most households owned one TV set, which was located in the living room), and the form, genre and structure of programmes were more rigidly defined than today. The *Radio Times*, for instance, listed only BBC programmes and provided information which was considered educational and informative. Both the BBC and ITV programmed and timetabled according to fairly standardised viewing patterns and behaviour. Relatively fixed notions of childhood, family, gender, ethnicity and age meant that programmes catered in limited ways, at set times, and with little flexibility. Some formats did not exist (e.g. reality television, docu-soaps); and the formats that did exist were broadcast as discrete entities. Documentaries, dramas and soap operas are now produced in composite formats, so that docu-soaps, drama-docs and docu-dramas are as popularly consumed as their earlier versions. A recent BBC advertisement, which promotes licence-fee payments by direct debit, is very similar to BBC2's *The Office* (2001), itself a pastiche of multiple other genres. Whilst it would be inaccurate to claim that channels have blurred absolutely the factual and the fictional, the 'modern' period of television was geared more towards clearer if rather fixed distinctions.

Realism and naturalism; experimentation and reflexivity: Hans Bertens's *The Idea of the Postmodern* (1995) summarises some key points in relation to the idea of postmodernism and representation. He distinguishes between an empirical and a postmodern perspective. The empirical view holds that 'language can represent reality', that language is 'transparent, a window on the world, and knowledge arises out of our direct experience of reality, undistorted and not contaminated by language' (1995: 6). Both realism and naturalism are to some degree grounded in an empiricist view of the world. In such a framework, there is no doubt that reality can be depicted. Realist and naturalist modes are able represent the truth of the world in fictional and non-fictional ways. Postmodern theory rejects such empiricism and 'gives up on language's representational function and follows poststructuralism in the idea that language constitutes, rather than reflects, the world' (ibid.) Bertens, noting the influences of Derrida's and Lacan's poststructuralism, argues that knowledge is always 'distorted by language, that is, by the historical circumstances and the specific environment in which it arises' (ibid.). Importantly for this current discussion, there is no subjectivity or sense of selfhood which is outside of language or representation. In the postmodern world, television celebrities become role models; talent shows promise fame; and adverts construct identities as much as they promote products and commodities. 'The autonomous subject of modernity, objectively rational and self-determined, likewise gives way to the postmodern subject which is largely . . . determined within and constituted by language' (ibid.).

Television, Postmodernism and Programme Style

In the preceding section, 'postmodern' and 'postmodernism' have been deployed in periodising ways. But the terms have also been used in contrast to the related notions of 'modern' and 'modernism'. The latter terms are often used to describe early twentieth-century avant-garde writing, art and drama; and 'postmodern' has been popularly used since the late 1970s to describe contemporary cultures. Modern(ist) culture is often, though not always, imagined as autonomous, something produced by an 'artist' whose output was not tied to the limitations imposed by the economy. Postmodern(ist) culture borrows eclectically from other sources, more associated with late-capitalist consumer cultures, where the distinctions between so-called high and so-called popular culture are blurred. The eclecticism of postmodern culture is captured in Rice and Waugh's very useful summary:

> The diversity and multiplicity of styles at play in contemporary culture leads to a condition characterized by fragmentation and by an emphasis on surface appearance. . . . Postmodernism extends the reign of the signifier into culture in general and poses a more radical 'loss' of the signified; it casts doubt on the function and ability of language to organize and control meanings in the socio-cultural domain; it recasts the role of the social mass as held within the reason of ideology; and it emphasizes consumption, seeing it as a play which constantly eludes the rational explanation of theory. (1989: 259–60)

If postmodern culture is noted for its eclecticism, then postmodern texts classically usurp and rearrange other material. By way of initial outline, postmodern texts often (a) expropriate sources, figures and images from other media; (b) rework earlier media constructions in allusive and playful ways; (c) revisualise and reconstruct reality as both multiple and fragmentary;

(d) undermine and/or threaten textual, thematic and narrative coherence; (e) operate with a plural as opposed to a singular logic; (f) foreground the signifier over the signified; (f) blur formal, generic and stylistic boundaries; (g) confuse the sense of space and time, so that recognisable or familiar landscapes seem incomplete and hyperreal; (h) threaten notions of the fully formed or whole 'character', offering instead fluid, split or fractured 'subjects'; (i) bewilder viewers' attempts to impose one reading on the text; (j) obscure the distinctions between high and popular culture; (k) seem inconclusive and open-ended.

Ultimately there are no great breaks or ruptures in how one period is described in comparison to another, though for many critics, television has come to play a central role in postmodern theory. Television, as commodity, consumer good and transmitter of images and sounds, is seen by theorists Jean Baudrillard and Frederic Jameson as typically postmodern. For Jameson (1985), television technology is associated with the effacement and erosion of high culture by mass culture. His account of postmodern culture is twofold. On the one hand, Jameson uses the notions of parody and pastiche in order to explore postmodern cultural practices, arguing that late-capitalist or consumer culture is typified by pastiche. Whilst both terms involve mimicry of other styles, parody has the effect of mocking and satirising the person or object imitated. Unlike parody, which 'capitalizes on the uniqueness of . . . styles and seizes on their idiosyncrasies' (1985: 113), pastiche mixes styles eclectically, drawing from sources in similar vein to parody, but 'without the satirical impulse, without laughter. . . . Pastiche is blank parody, parody that has lost its sense of humor' (ibid., 114).

On the other hand, television, alongside postmodern media in general, is part of a schizophrenic (in the sense of blurred, split and multiple) experience of time. Taking a lead from the work of Jacques Lacan, Jameson suggests that postmodernism and schizophrenia are marked by a similar breakdown of the relationship between signifiers. Whilst structuralist accounts of meaning rely to some degree on the interrelationships between words, meaning and extralinguistic reality (words really do point to things in the material world), postmodern and poststructuralist accounts argue that signifiers point not to stable meanings of objects in the world but to more signifiers. An historical sense of the material realities or referents of the past and present is problematised by postmodern media, which generate a sense of isolation, discontinuity and incoherence. By erasing or obscuring a sense of the past, certain television programmes, and particularly videotexts, are able to produce the sense of a permanent and endless present moment. As with the person experiencing schizophrenia, so television might provide 'an undifferentiated vision of the world in the present' where temporal continuities break down (ibid., 120). Postmodern culture, Jameson argues, does not produce 'monumental' texts as modernism did, but 'ceaselessly reshuffles the fragments of preexistent texts' (ibid.).

It is the power that symbols and images seem to have in relation to the mediation and construction of reality which also concerns Baudrillard. He, too, draws on American mass culture to stage his argument, developing his points around the notions of 'simulation', also the title of his 1983 book. Baudrillard is often seen as someone who theorises away all notions of reality. In the capitalist world, media technologies, ultimately in the service of profit, determine reality. Along similar lines to Marshall McLuhan, Baudrillard suggests that the medium is the message. But in Baudrillard's version, there is not much meaning left in the message, no certainty that the message arrives, and the message directs us to more and more messages, more and more images. In the postmodern world, images, languages and signs constitute reality as much as they refract, or reflect at an angle, a world 'out there'. In his very influential *Simulations* (1983), Baudrillard argues that contemporary cultures are based around images for which there are no longer any originals. The spatial and temporal zones generated by film, television and advertising are taken as the 'real' as opposed to the mediated world. In modern or early twentieth-century cultures, the sign was linked to an extra-textual reality, and representation functioned to reflect objective or subjective realities.

In the hyperreal and simulated space of postmodernism, images have little or no connection to any extra-textual referent. The image-creating potential of television is singled out in Baudrillard's work, where factual and fictional programmes are no longer clearly differentiated (a criticism also made by Bourdieu). Simulation entails the 'generation by models of a real without origins or reality: a hyperreal' (1983: 2). However, one of the consequences of the simulated world is that the distinction between fact and fantasy, truth and error, and the material and the immaterial no longer seem to matter. The 'dissolution of TV into life [and] the dissolution of life into TV' (ibid., 55) is how Baudrillard describes the blurred distinctions generated by American television and media technologies. The accuracy and influence of Baudrillard's assessment is considered later. However, the work of critics such as Baudrillard, Jameson and Lyotard serves to inform the following summary of the key stylistic features of postmodernist style.

Textual realities: Many theorists have noted how postmodernism does not abandon realism as *one* possible mode of representation. Rather, postmodern texts deploy realism in combination with other modes in order to focus on the mediated and textual nature of representation and reality. As early as 1977, Roland Barthes's 'Inaugural Lecture' ([1977] 1993a) to the Collège de France captured some the debates surrounding realism and mediation. 'The real is not representable, and it is because men try to represent it by words that there is a history of literature' (1993a: 465). Barthes's argument is not a rejection of extra-textual reality so much as it is one which attends to the problematic nature of the constitution and representation of reality. But following Baudrillard, filmic and televisual realities are the 'real' world. In the hyperreal space of postmodernism images 'the real is no longer real' (Baudrillard 1983: 25). Michael Ryan describes hyperreality as a situation where 'cultural signs become instead active agents in themselves, creating and evoking new substances, new social forms, new ways of acting and thinking, new attitudes' (1988: 560).

Multi-discursive terrain: No one discourse or genre serves to structure meaning in any resolute way. Whilst some critics conclude that postmodernism is marked by indeterminacy, Peter Nicholls suggests that an 'unresolvable *contradiction*' (1996: 52; emphasis in original) is a more prominent feature of postmodern texts. These contradictions often occur as a result of the blending and blurring of the discourses of popular with high culture, fact with fiction, and genre with genre. The discourses of science, philosophy, religion, ethics and art contend one with each other in textual compositions which provide no code or narrative point of view from which to conclude final meaning. Barthes again captures some of the mood of postmodernism in his 'The Death of the Author' (1977). The text is viewed as a 'multidimensional space in which a variety of writings, none of them original, blend and clash' (ibid., 146). Barthes's stress on inauthenticity as opposed to originality highlights the ways in which postmodern texts are not so much new or innovative as they are reworkings of the 'innumerable centres of culture' (ibid.) and history. Postmodernism, as Lyotard has suggested, is not so much a break with modernism as it is its disruptive and contradictory, unruly partner.

Temporal confusion: Often postmodern texts confuse time and space in ways not observed in realist and naturalist work. Even those modernist works which blend the chronological with the psychological and the subjective experience of time do so on the basis of dimension and depth as opposed to confusion or inexactness. Dick Hebdige suggests that in postmodern conceptions of time, 'the past is played and replayed as an amusing range of styles, genres [and] signifying practices to be combined and recombined at will. The then (and the there) are subsumed in the Now' (1989: 277). Notions of time and temporality are problematised in the work of Baudrillard and Lyotard. Their work describes how postmodern cultures revive signs, images and perspectives connected to the past, but where no one past is privileged above another. History is not so much rejected (past images inform the present) so much as it is deconstructed. Images clash and compete with each other; dream-like states confuse the psychological and subjective with the objective and the social; the domains of fact and fiction no longer seem to be differentiated; and little premium is placed on making sense of the text's different sites of meaning. Jameson describes postmodernism as the 'transformation of reality into images, the fragmentation of time into a series of perpetual presents' (Jameson 1985: 125).

Fractured subjects and selves: Freud's work is interested in how the self is composed of a conscious and unconscious domain, linked to the notions of id, ego and superego. His work suggests that selfhood is tripartite rather than unitary, but this is quite different to the fractured and split subject posited in Lacanian and poststructuralist theory. In the postmodern world, argues Jeffrey Weeks, selfhood is a 'necessary fiction' (*Invented Morality*, 1995), constructed from language and discourse. Lacanian notions of the self posit its illusory, imaginary and relational status. And Judith Butler's *Gender Trouble* (1990) contends that whilst one might be born a woman or man, with an anatomy which is judged female or male, it is culture and society which (en)genders the body and establishes identity. A girl is not born girl but is immediately subjected to a process of 'girling' (pink clothes, certain names and not others, etc.); boys are similarly made into boys. Whilst identity in postmodern discourse is not something which is fixed, neither is it something which we simply choose. The powerful fixing of identity through gender and sex, as Butler shows, succeeds precisely because identity seems natural, as if established at birth. Her work shows how a complex inter-operation of the social and the psychic (Lacan), with the discursive and linguistic (Foucault), serves to construct a subject which has no final anchorage or grounds. Anthony Elliott argues that the emphasis on the 'illusory nature of the self . . . in poststructuralist psychoanalysis fits neatly with the postmodern emphasis on surfaces, images and fragments' (2002: 34).

5.3 Two Case Studies

Postmodernism and postmodernity, then, are periodising terms which are deployed in discussions about style and contemporary cultures, and knowledge and society respectively. On the one hand, postmodernity refers to the period after modernity; on the other hand, postmodernism refers to the period after modernism. How might these terms further assist in the exploration and understanding of recent television drama? Whilst television, as noted, is often discussed in relation to the conditions of postmodernity, is it safe to assume that dramatic texts are similarly postmodern? Is it possible for realist texts to appeal in credulous ways in conditions where form, genre and content are often thrown into doubt? The texts chosen for the case study reflect popular American as well as experimental British output. David Lynch's *Twin Peaks* is chosen in order to reflect an American television drama (and film) which has obtained popular cult following in America, Britain and Europe.[3] Its postmodern status is additionally confirmed by the web sites and conferences devoted to the endless meanings which this American series is able to generate. American output (e.g. *Twin Peaks*, *Miami Vice*, *Buffy*) has been condemned and celebrated in Britain and the United States, and so a consideration of some of this criticism serves to enlarge earlier arguments. *Sophie's World* (1995) is chosen as a counter to some of the negative criticisms associated with postmodern and experimental television. The BBC2 production from the mid-1990s started its life as a novel, written by Norwegian Jostein Gaader. The sales and translations of the novel attest its popular status, though the television version sees Paul Greengrass and Mike Poole draw on a number of stylistic strategies of postmodernism, further complicating the novel's own styles and devices.

Twin Peaks *(1989): 'All the characters in a dream may be yourself' (Log Lady)*

David Lynch's *Twin Peaks* is often cited as a piece which exemplifies many of the stylistic features of postmodern film and television drama. For that reason, it is a helpful text to use in order to understand postmodern style. However, it also raises important questions about the context and ethics of television viewing, linking with issues raised in earlier discussion about television and postmodernity. On one level, the drama tells of the events surrounding the murder of Laura Palmer. There is, of course, nothing particularly unusual about a murder in a TV series; using detective genres in order to incite a dramatic narrative is very common; and having a key detective (in this case FBI agent Dale Cooper, (played by Kyle MacLachlan) work on the crime is part of the business of popular television. Using key characters and locations week after week is also standard in television drama, a strategy audiences do not normally question. On a second level, the drama is concerned with family violence; on another plane, viewers are invited to consider personal isolation, dysfunctional communities and social alienation; and on yet a fourth level, it is possible to understand *Twin Peaks* as a television spectacle, a programme which relies on media representations and texts of popular culture. Following through this final claim, it might be argued that *Twin Peaks* is indeed the real (i.e. postmodern real) world. Access to reality is always mediated, never immediate, and always on the basis of texts which confusingly point to other texts.

The series is definitely confusing and also bemusing. Audiences surely do want to know what happened to Audrey, Pete and Thomas Eckhardt in the bank vault. Week by week, viewers are left wondering what exactly the conjunction of the planets was about and who was speaking through Sarah to Major Briggs. Do we ever discover the ultimate significance of the telepathic Log Lady? Yet viewers are not totally defamiliarised by the landscape, terrain, spatial dimensions, time, people, clothing, domestic interiors and those other facets of film and television which generate a sense of familiarity and some degree of certainty. However, its soap-opera references, and its allusions to film noir, Hitchcock films, traditions of gothic suspense and a host of other television series, actors and styles begin to cast doubt on the fixtures and fittings of Lynch's world. Yet whilst Lynch's fictional world contests its own *illusions* (the 'reality' of one dramatic fiction is used to undermine another), the multiple *allusions* nonetheless contribute to Lynch's murder investigation and the world of *Twin Peaks* in general. Yet this is an unusual murder investigation when the series begins to explore far more than the circumstances or motives which led to Laura's death. Surrounding Lynch's take on the crime genre is a part-playful, part-disturbing investigation of a world which seems to have abandoned modernity's commitment to the certainties of reason, logic and causality.

Twin Peaks' allusions point as much to popular media culture as they hint at Christian and Buddhist spirituality, the Tibetan *Book of the Dead*, eternal salvation and damnation, and communication between human and extraterrestrial life forms. A chain of sometimes obvious – and sometimes obscure – binary oppositions (e.g. darkness and light, two mountain peaks, two versions of certain episodes, guilt and innocence) ties viewers into the many readings which *Twin Peaks* allows. The dialectical aspects of the drama are suggested by some of the episodes: 'Masked Ball', 'Laura's Secret Diary', 'Rest in Pain', 'The One-Armed Man', 'Double Play', and 'Slaves and Masters'. The series itself is a co-production, and some of the episodes were co-written with Mark Frost. But these double and oppositional features are also tied into the way the series pairs its characters. The character of *Laura* Palmer, murder victim in the series, is inspired by the 1950s film noir of the same name. Harry S. Truman, the *Twin Peaks'* sheriff, directly references a former US president; Dale Cooper similarly refers to a key figure of the Northwest USA; and James Dean, rebel and romantic celebrity-hero of mid-century American culture, clearly underpins the construction of James Hurley. Why play inter-textually and self-reflexively in the way that *Twin Peaks* appears to do?

Twin Peaks rejects the fixity of the historical past, constructing characters who are obviously composite, rooted in other fictional representations more than tangible histories. But in the place 'Twin Peaks' (and in *Twin Peaks*!) there is no *history* in a singular sense. The series points to North American histories and cultures, but *Twin Peaks* is unable to decide which histories constitute the truthful versions of a past. Laura, for instance, is both fictionally 'real' and essential to the plot of *Twin Peaks*, but she is constructed on the basis of other fictional identities. *Twin Peaks* – the place, its people and its history – necessarily reflects America in that it is, very simply, not about alien experiences in a country on another planet. But perhaps that is part of Lynch's aim. America is not culturally or socially homogeneous and so any representation cannot avoid some kind of distortion. Lynch's reflection is alienating to the degree that all states, America included, alienate their citizens. If *Twin Peaks* does alienate its audiences, then such a claim has to be understood in the context of a society which frequently alienates (or distorts the views of) many of its citizens. Recent campaigns around cultural citizenship in the West resonate a politics which is about inclusion and democracy in ways which much state-organised politics are not. In that sense, Lynch's postmodern output is meaningful in the context of a society in which some groups have always been hidden from official history.

Similarly, in the way that *Twin Peaks* is derived from numerous sources, so America is itself derivative, composed out of many competing narratives. Like *Twin Peaks*, the United States relies in part on its popular media texts for its domestic and global sense of identity, and yet America, again resembling *Twin Peaks*, is always open to more than one reading. If *Twin Peaks* seems to take audiences down bizarre routes in the field of *fictional* detection, then such oddities have to be understood alongside some of the *actual* circumstances of America's *factual* detection. The curious details surrounding J. F. Kennedy's assassination, the Watergate affair, or the re-count in Florida during the presidential election of 2000, make the world of *Twin Peaks* seem realist by comparison.

Twin Peaks' mixture of the conventions of crime-murder thrillers and whodunit mysteries with elements which draw on surrealist and magical-realist stylisation serve to complicate further the endless double-coded references and textual allusions. This multi-generic format is intended, in line with postmodern aesthetics, to be read in ironic terms: 'knowing audiences' are knowingly entertained, going along with the competing genres, amused by and pondering the possibilities *Twin Peaks* raises. The irony and pastiche are themselves double-coded, working not only to undercut the realities of the series' fictional world ('Is there *really* a world like the one in *Twin Peaks*?'), but also reminding viewers that we have been compelled in our 'real' time by the fictional realities of this world. We tune in each week, work through as many allusions as make sense or interest us, possibly conclude that the series is a waste of time by Episode 6, and tune in for a bit more the following week. Is the world reflected in North American postmodern drama meaningless, simply playing with signs for audiences whose only motivation is *Twin Peaks*' double-coded and ironic criss-crossing of discourses? Or is the postmodern world which is reflected in the drama the world as it is experienced at the end of the twentieth century: dislocated, irrational and nightmarish?

In dramas which conform to fairly obvious and standard generic conventions (authored-text material, novel-in-performance output such as *Middlemarch* (1994), police series, or hospital dramas), the sequencing of events, character relations, location and timing combine with the genre to construct certain expectations about meaning. *Middlemarch* is a novel and a television drama which is concerned with industrial change in nineteenth-century Britain; in the television version, we know that characters are costumed in periodising ways; actors necessarily fake sincerity; and we recognise that present-day location details are disguised in order to furnish a sense of a specific past. We also know that the fictional world of the novel and the drama is just that – a fiction. However, and unlike *Twin Peaks*, neither version invites readers/viewers to consider reality as discontinuous, fluid, or what poststructuralists would label 'decentred'. The causal and objective world of the *Middlemarch* story is not called into doubt by the form or genre: the fiction seems faithful to the reality it represents. *Twin Peaks*, on the other hand, offers something which is both multiple and doubtful, and viewers do not willingly suspend their disbelief. Perhaps the job of a drama such as *Twin Peaks* is as much to expose the fragmented aspects of everyday life as it is to show how the world of everyday life is a media fabrication, often disguising the ideology which secures its naturalised status. Popular dramas such as *The Darling Buds of May* (1991), *Heartbeat* (1991) and *Hetty Wainthrop Investigates* (1996) present the world in causal and connected ways; the sphere of the everyday is invariably presented in idealised and optimistic terms; and the characters who people these series seem naturally good, communicative and communitarian; if characters aren't 'good', then they are made to see the immoral errors of their ways.

For many people the everyday world represented in such dramas *is* the alien world. Packaged in forms and genres which often leave the world uninterrogated, some dramas present the world as seamless, where people connect around common values. Yet the world of the mundane and the everyday can, for some, be boring, demanding and estranging. By drawing attention to its status as drama, *Twin Peaks* might well be inviting viewers to consider the ethics of television viewing. Alternatively phrased, *Twin Peaks* and *Sophie's World* (below) are concerned to investigate why we watch television drama in the first instance. In many ways, both *Twin Peaks* and *Sophie's World* distrust the common-sense ethics surrounding some versions of everyday life. In *Twin Peaks*, the streets and venues of everyday life are not blissfully domestic, familial or inviting. Rather, the world of everyday life, which surely does include crime, murder and disconnection, is seen in the drama to be hazardous. Perhaps, then, in postmodern television, dramas do point to a *real* world but in so doing expose how the world is *made to seem real* by textuality itself. But it is the series' endless textual allusions and its boundless semiosis, where surface is everything and meaning-making becomes futile, which have led some critics to cast doubt on the claims of postmodernist and experimental work.

Nelson argues that postmodernity is characterised by 'semiotic overload' (1997: 169). Citing the work of Lawrence Grossberg, he is concerned by the visual, stylistic, verbal, and imagistic excesses of television. In Nelson's view, the many channels and the 'resultant "surfacing" arising from an inability to settle on any one programme, together with the bricolage and paratactical principles of construction where narrative is less important than the style of the images and surface is all' (ibid.) can result in televisual 'non-sense'. Nelson suggests that it 'remains arguable as to whether the intertextual play of texts and a flexible subjectivity is unrestrainedly liberating' (ibid.). It is important not to overlook the ' "realist" disposition of the popular audience' (ibid., 168). He goes on to argue that although 'there may be potential in the play of signification of a postmodern aesthetic, its powers of liberation cannot be assumed in advance' (ibid., 171). Moreover, there is 'no simple assurance that the playfulness of active readers will be free from entrenched reactionary attitudes' (ibid.). Finally, although 'postmodernism encourages the abandonment of holist attempts to make sense of the world' (ibid., 174), subjects are inherently predisposed to 'make sense of their own, increasingly privatised lives. In this context a demand is created for some stability, however illusory' (ibid.).

In many respects, Nelson's concerns about postmodern television and its output might well be justified. Programmes which conjure (manipulate?) viewers' nostalgia, or which abandon the 'sense-making' opportunities of the medium in favour of an endless free-floating play of the superficial, need the counterbalance, as Dorothy Hobson reports, of television drama, which provides some sense of 'stability in our lives. We have enough change forced upon us' (Hobson, cited in Nelson 1997: 174). Yet it needs to be asked quite how many programmes are as postmodern as Nelson's chapter seems to imply. Moreover, viewing figures for certain dramas (*Buffy*, 1997; *Byker Grove*, 1989; *Queer as Folk*, 1999; or *Tinsel Town*, 2000) suggest that audiences are far from unable to settle on recent output. The televisual postmodernism that Nelson describes is arguably not as dominant or as pervasive as his book seems to suggest. G. W. Brandt's *British Television Drama in the 1980s* devotes only one part of one chapter to a discussion of postmodernism (1993: 227–8). John Caughie's recent book (2000) ignores – more or less – so-called postmodern or experimental output in favour of 'quality' and 'modernist' drama (Caughie's terms). John Corner's work (1998, 1999) focuses attention more on notions of image and the power of images than it does on postmodernism, style and television.

Perhaps the more interesting questions are concerned with who 'watches'[4] experimental or postmodern output, who writes and produces it, and why realist modes are abandoned or reworked in favour of material which is more composite in character. It is interesting to observe that, with the exception of one essay,[5] the accounts in Brandt, Caughie and Nelson make little reference to material which considers the (postmodern) cultural politics of identity. Whilst macro-political debates can never be ignored, the personal and public politics of gender, ethnicity and sexuality arise partly in response to the failure of national and global politics to represent the interests of *all* subjects. Social exclusion is linked to abysmal economic policies, as it is a result of outmoded models of subjectivity. It might be the case that those groups traditionally marginalised from dominant or mainstream representations will produce and write creative works in ways which serve to challenge both form and genre. If realist drama is able to critique social conditions, then it needs to be asked whose social conditions are under scrutiny, how the critique functions, and which groups never quite seem to fit into the formal constraints of realist output. The realist and naturalist dramas of the last 35 years have often been silent on matters of gender, race and sexuality. Feminist commentary in the field strongly maintains that realist and naturalist modes have very definite roots in a patriarchal organisation of society. Moreover, when dramas and other fictions have sought to challenge the mainstream, then the modes of melodrama, fantasy, gothic, horror, detection and first-person narrative have been chosen over and above those broadly associated with realist formats. During the nineteenth century, for instance, it was often the carnivalesque, excessive and gory world of music hall and melodrama which called into question social as well as dramatic conformity.

There is little doubt that one of the key functions of drama is its ability to critique social life. But the modes of that critique are not fixed. And there are no guarantees that drama on its own will change lives or cultures. Nelson praises the 1990s *Our Friends in the North* as a drama which 'tries to unmask the complexity of experience lived through time' (1997: 241). He sees the production as something which mixes the personal with 'broader political issues such as police corruption', exploring in addition the 'housing problems of Newcastle's badly-built, modernist high-rise and the Rachmanite scandals of the rented housing sector' (ibid.). Nelson's assessment of *Our Friends* is not in doubt and he is surely right to point out the importance of the series in terms of its understanding of local history and politics. However, if this is a drama which 'purports to be giving a true (albeit fictional) account of cultural and political change in the UK over the last thirty years' (ibid., 241), it is also a drama whose account of life in and around Newcastle is also only ever partial and incomplete. Many of the high-rise flats still exist, and many groups who live in the properties (the elderly, young single people, lesbians and gay men, those new to the region) have categorically stated at local housing management committees that to pull them down would be to uproot communities once more. *Our Friends* has the effect of demonstrating that for many people collectivist politics and its politicians continue to fail the diverse needs of the electorate. Although 'critical realism may be . . . more productive of a dialogic exchange with potential for cognitive reorientation than critical postmodernism' (ibid., 248), there are no guarantees about the directions or conclusions of 'cognitive reorientation'. In making a similar argument, Peter Flannery uses social realism in *Our Friends* to good effect. But other dramatic modes avail themselves to a critique which details cultural and social diversity in ways that *Our Friends* does not.

Sophie's World *(1995)*

How radical is postmodernism in relation to the critical potential of social realism? Do films or television dramas really allow audiences to occupy a range of critical positions in ways that realist output does not? Do dramas which have adopted some of the stylistic features associated with postmodernism (e.g. the popular *Miami Vice*; the experimental *Sophie's World*) suggest a more critical or reactionary phase in television drama? Or is television output that is attentive to postmodern style simply a means of tinkering with signs and signifiers in cynical and sarcastic ways? New fashions and styles make money – in all spheres of life. Whilst programmes might seem to celebrate and promote cultural diversity, television is also big business, ultimately tied to markets, consumer trends and political ideologies. Earlier discussion in this book show how work by critics such as Ien Ang and David Morley points to audience surveys and ethnographies which demonstrate that television consumption is an active and interactive operation. But to what extent are form and genre endowed with resistant and critical potential? What is the function of agency? Is human agency literally 'self-created', as John Fiske seems to imply, or is it always tied to structures such as the economy, work, discourses and institutions?

Discussing the 1980s series *Miami Vice*, Fiske (1987) argues for a postmodernism which is disruptive and oppositional, something which deregulates the controlling power of discourse and (televisual) image: '[I]n rejecting sense, postmodernism is rejecting the social machine and its power to regulate our lives and thinking' (1987: 254). As noted earlier, postmodernism, as opposed to postmodern theory per se, is often associated with a blurring of the distinction between the domain of the real and the domain of the represented. 'Images are more imperative than the real', argues Fiske (ibid.). Stressing image and surface more than content and substance, postmodernism is thought to complicate how 'material' reality is figured and comprehended. In a loosely Baudrillardian sense, Fiske argues that '[postmodernism] refuses categories . . . [and] denies distinctions. . . . It refuses neat generic differences. . . . The postmodern style crosses genre boundaries as easily as those of gender and class' (ibid.). Moreover, what counts as personal experience, selfhood and psychological interority are bypassed in favour of notions of identity as a series of masks and masquerade, where subjects *perform* roles rather than *express* a true or authentic self. 'The self is a shifting transient identity, literally self-created' (ibid., 259). Whilst some binary models of identity emphasise the relative independence of agency and structure, where subjects negotiate on the basis of struggle, some postmodern accounts point to the free play of language and signifying practices. Lyotard, for instance, observes how subjects are caught up in a range of language games and micro-narratives. The modern period, with its macro-narratives of time, chronology, linear progress and causality is contrasted by postmodern versions of time, which point to fluidity and discontinuity. '[Postmodern] culture', argues Fiske, 'signals the death of authenticity, any underlying "true" meaning of gender *or of anything else*' (ibid.; emphasis added).

It is issues of selfhood and identity which are thematised in the BBC2 adaptation of Jostein Gaarder's *Sophie's World*. The drama begins with Sophie (Jessica Marshall-Gardiner) walking home from school with her friend Joanna. A narrator's voice – Gaader's – reassures audiences of the ordinariness of such an activity, his spoken English strongly reminiscent of the Nordic accentuation associated with popular Disney versions of fairy-tales. Once 'home', a place adorned with a white picket fence and free-standing letter box reminiscent of Lynch's *Blue Velvet*, Sophie begins to receive odd letters. 'Who are you?', the first letter pretentiously inquires. Audiences know – or think they know – that this is Sophie Amundsen. She stares into the mirror and tells herself that she is who she is supposed to be. But in postmodern worlds, knowledge is understood in relation to uncertainty, irony and disbelief. Her hilarious but deeply caring mother (Twiggy Lawson), rightly annoyed by Sophie's investigations, is in no doubt that her daughter is, after all, Sophie Amundsen. But the letters mount up and, as a result, Sophie begins a correspondence course to find out more.

Central to her learning is Alberto Knox (Paul Greengrass), who becomes mentor, father, adviser, joker and at times student to Sophie. Using the history of ideas to structure *his* narrative, Knox explains how the self and the world are best initially understood using a classical method which draws on cognition (reason) and feelings (the senses). This quickly proves a limited account and so the journey to find alternative ways of understanding ourselves and the world involves Alberto's comic explanations of various philosophical narratives and language games. Ultimately, Sophie seems to know who she is but is confused by the different meanings attached to this knowledge. This play on knowledge and identity is, as Fiske has noted, central to much postmodern debate, and the stylistically composite *Sophie's World* is clearly alert to the sorts of issues raised in the work of Lyotard (above). In the opening sequences of the drama, viewers are confronted by a pair of hands typing on a keyboard. The camera then moves from the hands to a man's face as he winks knowingly at the camera. Is this the author of *Sophie's World*? Do we need to know that Gaader wrote this novel? Or is the story more important than the author?

Audiences' knowledge of *Sophie's World* is at once certain and equivocal. 'Sophie Amundsen was on her way home from school with her friend Joanna', reports the voice of Gaader. But these late-twentieth-century school students are now seen next to an opening set which resembles an adventure-film depiction of a seventeenth-century explorer's study, bedecked with skull, pseudo-scientific implements, charts and other equipment. On arrival at Sophie's house, audiences quickly realise that it seems to be made from cardboard, like the nearby forest and the set in general. In highlighting the constructed status of reality, the BBC2 version of *Sophie's World* makes no attempt to hide the programme's televisual status. The sets allude to the winding yellow road of *The Wizard of Oz*, video and amusement arcades, children's programmes (ITV's *Rainbow* and the BBC's *The Magic Roundabout*), news and documentaries, and television and recording studios. Alberto Knox is at once a peripatetic teacher-philosopher, a circus compère, a sleuth and children's entertainer. Sophie spends her time with Alberto or with her mother in the kitchen. The only part of the 'home' we see is in fact the kitchen; in Sophie's postmodern world, the space associated with cooking, cleaning and domesticity continues to be gendered and is still inhabited by women! The kitchen window looks to the cardboard forest, and the IKEA-style kitchen recalls the set and antics of *Absolutely Fabulous*. Twiggy plays the role of mother, drawing on characters from the latter series with a mixture of the Abigail of Mike Leigh's *Abigail's Party* (1977). We never see the husband or father; Sophie's 'real' UN-soldier father is absent, though Alberto doubles as father and is seen in military uniform via television screens.

Television screens are used throughout the drama, often to project multiple versions of Alberto or to broadcast news reports and images of war. The opening of the drama uses recent military maps of former Yugoslavia and Sarajevo, reminding audiences of the present time of the production and the drama's first television broadcast; computer screens, word processors, music and graphics achieve a similar effect. Viewers are then confronted by a man's hands, typing on the word processor. Is this the author of *Sophie's World*? Or is this the pair of hands typing the graphics that tells us we are in this world? Such images and allusions point to *how* knowledge is constructed as opposed to a knowledge or history which awaits discovery. Whilst the colonising explorers of modernity were thought to uncover monumental truths, enlightening whole civilisations with their knowledge, the televisual set of *Sophie's World* immediately points to the political status of postmodern knowledge. Knowledge is constructed to achieve certain ends, an assertion which is equally true of the imperial past. It is personal knowledge which is foregrounded as important in the drama, but only ever against a backdrop of maps pointing to Western Europe. The microcosmic and intimate sphere of Sophie's domain only makes sense in the context of the global and international dimensions in which all knowledge takes shape.

The map of Yugoslavia is a reminder of how knowledge is never impartial, often tied to the nation, geo-political arrangements and state institutions. At the beginning of the twentieth century, it was ethnic conflict which ensured that this part of Europe was headlined in Britain. And the socialist reconstruction of Yugoslavia after the Second World War under Marshall Tito was, by the end of the twentieth century, in the process of some considerable destruction and turmoil. Sophie's access to this 'knowledge' is via television screens, news reports, and the information imparted by documentaries. Yet the very fact that Alberto and Sophie can have the discussions they do implies a history and context much bigger than the micro-space of the forest or the IKEA kitchen. Knowledge, like the television image, is mediated, always reflected at an ideological angle, and bound to codes and practices which govern how knowledge of both self and world may be accessed. But the actual and fictional news broadcasts of war serve a political function in the drama. Although Alberto and his tutee might seem to be isolated in Sophie's world, contemporary society in the West ensures that the world mediated by television is never far away. Alberto and Sophie discuss philosophical method, ethics and existential angst, but the news screens interrupt the dialogue, showing how the history of peoples and ideas is never constructed in a vacuum or forest but is often formulated within and against the backdrop of genocidal repression. Some people clearly exercise more agency than others in Gaader's postmodern world.

The themes of personal and collective agency are strongly foregrounded in both the novel and the drama. Both Alberto and Sophie learn that they are not free agents in any straightforward sense. And the screen images of war in Europe force questions about action, ethics and responsibility. The limited nature of agency is not a new observation: Marx and Freud highlighted the degree to which economic and psychic structures govern action. But how seriously can one take the drama's references to war and politics in a piece that abandons realism in favour of the magical, multi-generic and surreal elements of postmodernism? Many of the labels which have become associated with postmodernism concern the text's indeterminacy as opposed to certainty, fluidity rather than fixity, and its decentred over and above its structured and hierarchical construction. On the one hand, *Sophie's World* seems to celebrate parody and pastiche, irony and satire, self-consciousness and reflexivity, and a general mood of playfulness and obscurity. On the other hand, the drama draws on the recognisable world of popular music, the familiar faces of newsreaders, advertising, and other television programmes, cancelling out some of its own obscurity.

Conclusions: Back to the Beginning? Narratives, Stories and Selves

It is within and against this world that Alberto and Sophie construct for themselves a sense of identity. But it is in this same world that identity is seen to possess the characteristics of fiction. As this book has repeatedly underlined, identity is bound up in histories and narratives; and selfhood, like narrative, is seen to evolve. If Sophie's mother relies on the narratives of popular romance in order to fashion a sense of self, her daughter rejects this, selecting other texts. There is more than one narrative available to Sophie, implying the potential for agency and choice. The BBC version of Gaader's text reveals how the sense of agency and choice seems enabling as much as it is constraining. As with many of the characters in *Queer as Folk*, Sophie knows she cannot be who she wants to be. At birth she was given an identity and a name, something she confirms when she looks in the (Lacanian) mirror. But Sophie – at 15 – is also clearly *more* than the girl who was born into a specific context and past. Wrestling with the problems of identity with Alberto, Sophie begins to acknowledge that identity is as much about fixity and exclusion (she wonders who Hilde and Albert Knag are) as it is the illusion of choice and self-determination.

What Alberto and Sophie do realise is that it is Albert Knag who writes the book about Sophie Amundsen for his daughter Hilde's pleasure. In other words, Sophie and Alberto are themselves fictions within a fiction. Fictional status is not immaterial, and nor can it be dismissed as simply illusory. Rather, it points to the material structures, the boundaries and systems of power which all narrative entails. In the work of Michel Foucault (2000c), subjects have freedom and power, but within certain parameters. He writes that part of the job of 'resistance' is to 'bring to light the power relations, locate their position, find out their point of application and the methods used' (2000c: 329). Note that for Foucault, knowing the source of power or oppression is not necessarily to overturn oppression, at least not in any immediate or self-evident way. Rather he points to the various networks of power which criss-cross and transect human relations. To begin to understand something of the functioning and operation of power, subjects are in a position to dismantle and resist such power. 'In order to understand what power relations are about, perhaps we should investigate the forms of resistance and attempts made to dissociate these relations' (ibid.).

It is precisely the relations of (narrative) power which preoccupy the characters in *Sophie's World*. Hilde's father ensures that Sophie and Alberto become aware of their recreative and performative duties, but neither of Knag's creations are able fully to comprehend the source of power so much as the force of power in human relationships. Of course it is the fictional Knag who is in control, but only ever within a novel controlled by Gaader (now controlled by the BBC). It is Knag who authorises the fiction, but always with reference to his audience, Hilde; and it is Knag who organises the structure and agency, but which is ultimately authorised by Gaader. In order to understand each other, Sophie and Alberto are forced to draw on discourses and narratives which pre-date and thus predetermine their own encounter. Alberto draws on philosophy, popular song, rhyming couplets and slips of the tongue in order to communicate with Sophie. Sophie reworks Alberto's language into something which is meaningful to her. Sophie's own discourse quickly becomes something her mother is unable to follow. Sophie's mother frequently offers advice found in the romantic fictions she reads. Consoling and persuading Sophie, her mother ultimately attempts to explain the world in relation to the romantic young man she imagines is sending the letters and who will provide some kind of provisional end to Sophie's current quest.

The drama's apparent playfulness with truth, power and agency can be understood in relation to three observations whose common thread is narrative. Firstly, audiences begin to gauge the absolute importance of agency and truth, angry that for some of the time we are led to believe that Sophie and Alberto were more than fictions within a fiction. But the drama makes it clear that subjects can never exercise absolute agency or self-determination. In a sphere where actions are subject to the constraints of others, then self-determination will sometimes appear more fictional than actual. Secondly, the sources of power are often blurred in an environment which relies on the televisual image for the dissemination of data. Thinking that she exercises power in her world, Sophie pursues her quest for self-discovery. Yet she relies on signifiers – mediated images, words and letters in order to understand herself. Similarly, audiences rely on images brought to the screen by newsreaders, editors and media controllers. In the way that Sophie questions the reliability of her sources, so audiences wonder how reliable the BBC, ITV and the other channels are in representing world events such as war. Thirdly, by abandoning the conventions of realism, *Sophie's World* begins to ask questions about the causal world associated with such narratives. Those dramas of the 1980s and 1990s which adopt broadly realist strategies rightly highlight the causes and effects of unemployment, gender division and racism. But they are dramas which constitute only *one* way of representing or seeing the spectrum of human experience.

Increasingly the world is understood in terms of what is seen in representations, advertising, consumption, the media etc. This deregulated and privatised terrain is not cause for celebration. But dramas such as *Sophie's World* let viewers see the serious power media and image have in controlling lives. To acknowledge that society and social relations are figured and often experienced in fragmentary and transitional terms is not to revel uncritically in such disconnection. Freedom and agency in *Sophie's World* are tied to all sorts of conditions. Their actions are not only dependent one upon the other, but relate to discourses which at once give a sense of identity at the same time as they constrain and constrict Sophie's and Alberto's behaviour.

Enough Truths for a Few More Narratives

Nelson and others have pointed to critical realism as an important way of seeing the world. In many respects, Nelson's claims are endorsed in these concluding observations. However, perhaps postmodernist output has the potential to disrupt how the world is seen. Chapter 2 of this book discussed Barthes's claim that all narratives shape how the world is depicted. His work also draws attention to the differences between *what* and *how* something is seen. In many respects, postmodern and experimental drama wrestles with similar problems. Foucault captures something of the problematic relationship between what is seen and how it is seen when he writes that 'people cling to ways of seeing, saying, doing, and thinking, more than to what is seen, to what is thought, said, or done' (2000b: 242).

Towards the end of Nelson's study, he cites *Twin Peaks* as a 'kind of *both/and text*' (1997: 236; emphasis ours). Nelson means that the text is both modernist and postmodernist. By being postmodernist, *Twin Peaks* provides 'fun [and] a range of pleasures to its audiences' (ibid., 237). As with ITV's *Heartbeat*, *Twin Peaks* offers 'discrete pleasures for the semi-attentive viewer selecting appealing morsels from an extensive menu' (ibid.). By 'modernist', Nelson means that *Twin Peaks* also possesses the 'distinctive authorial signature' (ibid., 236). But this is an interesting interpretation of drama. On the one hand, postmodernist texts are trivial on Nelson's reading, offering pleasures and fun, but where the 'politics of [postmodern] pleasure' (ibid., 237) is somehow 'problematic' (ibid.). Modernist texts, on the other hand, are authored, qualitatively different, more serious, and presumably engage *fully* attentive viewers. They are, by implication, more politically engaged, though the specific political details are not fully stated. But there are no guarantees that authored dramas, politically engaged material, critical realist work, or obviously didactic dramas – all work which this current book has discussed – necessarily operate to activate a personal or collective politics. Brecht's work, for instance, whilst critiquing capitalism, failed to offer any workable model of democratic socialism. This is not to suggest that Brecht's work is impaired as a result. And nor is it to argue that realist – or in Brecht's case, modernist – works should not set out to challenge those structures (capitalist or otherwise) which deny and negate human agency.

However, it is to suggest that dramas can only ever be seen as *one* element in a whole network of political action. To judge a creative work solely on the basis of its manifest politics, important though that is, is to fail to acknowledge the degree to which audiences (re)use texts. On one level, *all* texts are political, and never neutral, reflecting the world from a particular viewpoint. But what audiences *do* with *all* television drama can never be foreclosed in advance of that usage. Letters to newspapers suggest that

Queer as Folk was greeted as something which exposed male homophobia as much as it stereotyped gay men as camp and lesbians as marginal and aggressive. *Boys from the Blackstuff* and *GBH*, though criticised for their sexism, nonetheless attack the politics of the right and the left, the dramas exposing monetarism and municipal corruption respectively. But they also ask questions about motivation, intention and agency, offering no easy solutions to the psychology of behaviour or problems of identity.

Interestingly, the realist *Boys from the Blackstuff* and the experimental *Sophie's World* are dramas which investigate the sources and impact of power on identity and behaviour. Both are concerned with governments and governmentality. For different reasons and in different ways, both dramas expose the importance of identity as well as the ways in which identities are easily manipulated and violated. And both expose how the sense of 'our' own uniqueness and subjectivity come to seem illusory in consumer-capitalist and postmodern terrain. Concerns about postmodern subjectivity are part of a much wider debate. Sean Homer observes that 'the singularity of history, the unity of society, the primacy of class and the autonomy of the subject' have been 'undermined or at least thrown into doubt. . . . Universalism, essentialism and rationalism have irreversibly dissolved' (1998: 18). Jameson's critique is useful to the degree that it points out that the death of the 'bourgeois individual' subject (an individual whose integrity invariably elided class, ethnicity and gender) is an important reminder that this subject 'never really existed in the first place' (1985: 115). Discourses of individual uniqueness and personal identity have often been used to control subjects. Hal Foster similarly complicates how 'we' might understand the loss of 'our' sense of uniqueness and self-certainty by qualifying just who this subject was:

> For what is this subject that, threatened by loss, is so bemoaned? Bourgeois perhaps, patriarchal certainly – it is the phallocentric order of subjectivity. For some, for many, this is indeed a great loss – and may lead to narcissistic laments. . . . But for others, precisely for Others, this is no great loss at all. (1984: 77)

Indeed, many *others* – for reasons which include class, ethnicity and gender – may have always sensed that subjectivity or selfhood was somehow composite, designed from fragments of dominant, marginal, mainstream or subcultural texts and narratives. The conceit of individual autonomy – that subjects are able to act freely, with agency, and in self-determining ways – is a conceit of the few rather than the many. Though dominant discourses might seem to promise individual autonomy, Sophie Amundsen learns that identity is understood in terms which often exceed her own self-perceptions, contingent upon how she is figured by others as much as how she attempts to fashion an identity for herself.

This book has suggested that television dramas remain a principal means of accessing and critiquing human experience. Television dramas provide pleasure; they purport to deal with 'reality' and the truth of 'how things are'; and television dramas are fantasies, always reflecting a world at an angle. But fantasies and fictions are not ignorant of 'reality' so much as ways of seeing or framing reality. The ways of seeing and narrativising how the world is experienced will continue to be plural: experience is not a universal category. Nor is experience necessarily unique, somehow offering the final truth of self. The messages of drama which are finally received on the screen – whether in realist or postmodernist modes – are not necessarily the ones which are sent. The pleasures, for example, which Sophie gets from seeing herself in narrative have to be measured against the structures which also impede her progress and contain the possibilities of who she imagines herself to be. Yet the pleasures of dramatic narratives are never simply ones which serve personal ends. As this book has argued, viewing pleasures are intensely political, never too far removed from institutional, textual and ideological structures. Television dramas inscribe and incite audiences. On the basis of narratives, the truths of television dramas are affirmed, questioned or rejected by the range of identities who constitute the 'audience'. But there is not one truth to tell. And because truths are invariably packaged in narratives, then there is not one approach to the truth of television drama. For these reasons, television drama will continue to be a vital part of television output as well as television, media and cultural studies.

Notes

Chapter 1 Representing Television Drama

1. Williams first uses this term in 1954 in *Preface to Film*, but develops it most fully in *The Long Revolution* (1965). See also Williams (1965). In his writing on television he uses it both in relation to 'television as cultural form' and in his discussion of specific programmes.
2. See Section 3.2, and Sue Thornham, *Passionate Detachments* (1997: Ch.2).
3. For this interpretation see, for example, Terence Hawkes, *Structuralism and Semiotics* (1977: 114–15).
4. According to Roman Jacobson, both metaphor and metonymy are figures of 'equivalence' since they propose similarities between two apparently unlike entities. See Hawkes (1977: 76–8).
5. See Baudrillard's *Seduction*, which emphasises this parallel (1990: 8).
6. Writing about the British *Wednesday Play* anthology series of the 1960s, for example, Madeleine Macmurraugh-Kavanagh notes its producers' view of 'the relationship between viewer and image [as] one of the female audience as passive recipient of the male message-system' (2000: 152).
7. See for example the definitions of documentary offered by the founder of the British documentary movement, John Grierson (1966), and the assertion by Michael Balcon of Ealing Studios that 'documentary' is 'not a label to be lightly attached to films of a specific, factual type; it is an attitude of mind toward film making' (1969: 130).
8. For an account of this 1940s critical discourse of the British 'quality film' see John Ellis (1996) and Andrew Higson (1986).
9. Brandt quotes Philip Abrams, in Denys Thompson (ed.), *Discrimination and Popular Culture* (1964), in outlining this charge. Abrams argues that television can be defined as a 'universal, continuous, public service . . . for domestic consumption'. These characteristics, argues Abrams, work together, so that

'continuity . . . serves to compound the trivialising tendencies of universality' (Abrams in Thompson 1964: 52, 58, cited in Brandt 1981: 3, 4).

10. See for example Albert Hunt's essay on Alan Plater (Brandt 1981: 153).
11. The reference point for Griffiths is therefore not Brecht but Georg Lukács (see Section 2.3). For a fuller discussion of this debate in relation to British television drama see John Caughie (2000: Ch. 5).
12. See Griffiths (1976). For critical use of the term see particularly John Tulloch (1990).
13. The quotation is from the essay by Edward Braun, who was also a contributor to Brandt's first collection.
14. Caughie begins by identifying the kind of television drama which concerns him as 'serious television drama', but then refers to it simply as 'television drama' – a move that tends to make his arguments self-confirming.
15. For this term see Benedict Anderson (1983).
16. See, for example, Hollows and Jancovich (eds), *Approaches to Popular Film* (1995), and, in relation to television, Robert C. Allen's edited collection, *Channels of Discourse, Reassembled* (1992). In relation to the latter, John Caughie (2000: 9) objects that the approach taken by Allen's contributors is more suited to film.

Chapter 2 Stories and Meanings

1. See Fiske (1987: 128–30).
2. See summaries included in the work of Graeme Burton (2000), Patricia Holland (1997), Nick Lacey (2000) and James Watson (1998).
3. Closer comparisons of form can be achieved by comparing Waters's written text with the BBC version.
4. For a detailed breakdown of Kozloff's model, see Burton (2000: 116–17).
5. See Tony Bennett's and Janet Woollacott's *Bond and Beyond* (1987), which considers how popular narrative fiction may or may not have seduced readers and film-goers into thinking that the 'figure of Bond' is 'a popular hero' (1987: 1).
6. 'Lesbian' is itself contentious to the degree that it is primarily a twentieth-century identity category.
7. Worries over agency in any act of reading or viewing are discussed by Nelson (1997: 2–3). However, the text itself can be seen to raise problems which incite agency or acts of interpretation.
8. See also Altman's influential essay from 1984, pp. 216–26.
9. See, for example, Philip Schlesinger (1978), James Curran et al. (1986); and Greg Philo (1996).
10. *Ideologiekritik* is broadly understood here as the aim of critically exposing the workings of ideology in culture and cultural forms; see Mulhern 2000 in particular.

11. No specific text of Foucault's is recommended as 'essential' reading, though *The Order of Things* (1973), *The Archaeology of Knowledge* (1989) and *Discipline and Punish* (1995) are concerned with some of the ideas in this part of the chapter.
12. See, for example, the essays collected in *Ethics* (2000a), especially 'Technologies of the Self' (223), and 'The Ethics of the Concern of the Self' (281).
13. See Section 3.1 for further discussion of this.
14. For a fuller discussion of this point, see Chapter 1. Tony Garnett, producer of many of the *Wednesday Plays* of the 1960s, provides an example of this, when he recalls a discussion with the writer Jim Allen, who began his television career writing for that most paradigmatic and 'feminised' of television genres, soap opera. Garnett told Allen that 'he'd got to choose between being a serious writer and writing on *Coronation Street* because he couldn't do both . . . And when I say *Coronation Street* I mean every serial like that, which runs on and on forever' (Hudson 1972).
15. The terms 'documentary drama' and 'drama-documentary' have a confusing history. John Caughie (1980) distinguishes between the two, but most often they are used interchangeably (see Kerr 1990), and will be here.
16. Grierson first coined the term 'documentary' in his review of Robert Flaherty's film *Moana* in 1926.
17. See especially, but far from exclusively, *Up the Junction* (trans. 3 November 1965, dir. Loach, story editor Garnett), *Cathy Come Home* (trans. 16 November 1966, dir. Loach, prod. Garnett), *The Lump* (trans. 1 February 1967, dir. Gold, prod. Garnett), *In Two Minds* (trans. 1 March 1967, dir. Loach, prod. Garnett), *The Big Flame* (trans. 19 February 1969, dir. Loach, prod. Garnett).
18. Williams chooses *The Big Flame* as his example in his 'Lecture on Realism' (1977).
19. See Murdock (1980), and Buscombe (1980).
20. In Loach's view, the kinds of 'truth' which the television documentary is permitted to show are, however, heavily circumscribed by the institution of television.
21. See Kerr (1990) for an account of some of these attacks.
22. Sandford reports that 'As a result of the film and certain meetings which we held in Birmingham afterwards, this town, and others, ceased their practice of separating three or four hundred husbands per year from their wives and children' (1984: 19); see also Kerr (1990: 80).
23. See discussion of *The Royle Family*, Section 2.2.

Chapter 3 Power and Subjectivity

1. The essay is reprinted in a modified form and with a shortened title in Hall et al. (eds), *Culture, Media, Language* (1980: 119–38), but without the section on television drama.

2. See Introduction to this volume, and Section 2.3.
3. See Alan Clarke, 'This is not the boy scouts' (1986).
4. See Madeleine Macmurraugh-Kavanagh's account (2000: 40).
5. This is the phrase used by *A Man from the Sun*'s writer, John Elliott (1992: 88). Elsewhere this group is referred to as the Dramatised Documentary Group or Unit (see Goodwin and Kerr 1983: 3).
6. For conflicting views on these claims, see Caryl Doncaster, one of the key members of the BBC's Dramatised Documentary Group, in Goodwin and Kerr (1983: 9) and John Elliott (1992: 88).
7. See Tulloch (1990).
8. See Lola Young (1996: 84–114) for a discussion of this.
9. This term, used to express white British fears during the 1950s, has been picked up recently by Stuart Hall (1992a, 1993), who, quoting Salman Rushdie's *Imaginary Homelands*, offers it instead as a celebratory term – in 'a love-song to our mongrel selves'.
10. The phrase is from Benedict Anderson. See Anderson (1983) and Hall (1992: 292–5).
11. See Lavery et al. (1996: 1–21); also Jodi Dean (1997: 68).
12. The term comes from the French sociologist Pierre Bourdieu (1986: 176–7). As James Donald (1985: 132) points out, however, whilst the term is useful, Bourdieu does not really explain either the *power* or the *pleasures* of these emotional 'investments'.
13. See Madan Sarup (1992: 64).
14. See the 1964 essay, 'Fantasy and the Origins of Sexuality', by Jean Laplanche and Jean-Bertrand Pontalis, which draws together Freud's work on this concept and which makes the case for its importance (Laplanche and Pontalis 1986).
15. See Freud, 'Psychoanalysis and Legal Evidence', in Freud (1959: 108).
16. Boyd is literally a parental investigator in the series. His own son, Joe, disappeared at the age of 16, and many of Boyd's investigations are seen to repeat the process of searching for his son.

Chapter 4 Gender and Sexuality

1. The pilot script for the series was developed as early as 1974, reportedly inspired by Molly Haskell's observation in *From Reverence to Rape* that there had never been a female buddy movie. The pilot did not go out until 1981, however, broadcast on CBS as a made-for-TV movie. See D'Acci (1987).
2. The police series and the sitcom have been the two genres which have attracted most feminist analysis in terms of theories of ideology or hegemony. Whilst the sitcom has most usually been seen as a genre which serves hegemonic interests by voicing women's dissent within an overall structure that

renders it non-threatening and consensual (Brunsdon et al. 1997), the woman-centred detective series has tended to be seen as ideologically disruptive (Skirrow 1985; Brunsdon 1987; Gamman 1988; Clark 1990; Thornham 1994).

3. See Section 3.2; and Thornham (1997; Ch. 2).
4. Such arguments fail to take into account either the very different uses which spectators may make of these constructions, or the actual ways in which narrative works (see Section 2.1).
5. See Alcock and Robson (1990) for this reading of *Cagney and Lacey*, and Thornham (1994) on *Prime Suspect*.
6. In Patricia Mellencamp's chapter on *The George Burns and Gracie Allen Show* and *I Love Lucy*, she draws explicit parallels between US political and military strategies which aimed at 'containment' of both external and internal 'enemies' and the domestic ideological strategies aimed at women (1986: 81).
7. The tabloid spread which we see recalls not only Alison Halford's press treatment but also that of another professional woman who opposed a masculine police hierarchy at the end of the 1980s, Dr Marietta Higgs. The tabloid representation of Tennison as an 'obsessive' and isolated woman, juxtaposed with family snaps of the 'innocent' and 'hounded' Marlow, parallel the accusations of 'conspiracy' and 'obsession' against Higgs and the pleas on behalf of 'innocent' (male) parents in the Cleveland child abuse case of 1987. See Campbell (1988) for further details.
8. See Charlotte Brunsdon (1997) for discussion of the confusions surrounding these terms.
9. For a more comprehensive list and categorisation, see Dow (1996).
10. The extent to which (like their 1970s forerunners, *Charlie's Angels* or *Wonder Woman*, 1976–9) they also fuel male fantasies has, of course, been much debated. See Pender (2002) and Moseley and Read (2002).
11. Denotes series 4, episode 7.
12. Danae Clark (1990) uses this phrase of *Cagney and Lacey* to describe the series' replacement of a model of spectatorship in which women are eroticised objects of the male gaze to one in which women both reverse the gaze and share a structure of looks which establishes a primary identification with each other and an ironic distance from the patriarchal world which they observe.
13. In 4.2. For this aspect of 1970s feminist activism, see Thornham (2000: Ch. 7).
14. The series makes great play of Carrie's 'addiction' to that most fetishised of objects, the high heeled shoe.
15. Diane Negra points out the 'almost laughable uniformity of the WASP surnames of the four female protagonists (Hobbes, Bradshaw, York and Jones)' (forthcoming: 22). Although racism is critiqued, as for example in the representation of Trey's mother's horror at the idea that he and Charlotte might adopt a Chinese baby, it is a matter of individual prejudice and style (Trey's mother is old-fashioned and narrow-minded), not structural inequality.

16. In an unusual and rather uncomfortable reference to a politics of the public sphere, Carrie comments in 'Bay of Married Pigs' (1.3) that 'maybe the fight between marrieds and singles is like the war in Northern Ireland: we're all basically the same, but somehow we just wound up on different sides'.
17. See also Lynne Joyrich's important contribution to the study of sexuality, viewing and television (2001).
18. See the work of Epstein and Straub (1991) and Sinfield (1994, 1998).
19. Summaries of historical context can be found in David Hugh (1997), Neil Miller (1995) and Colin Spencer (1995).
20. The term *heteronormative* is associated with Michael Warner (1993). It refers to the ways in which institutions, discourses and media texts, for example, make heterosexuality seem the most coherent, dominant and therefore privileged version of sexual identity.
21. Sanderson's book remains an invaluable source and summary.
22. Sometimes a subject's sexuality has not been open to the potentially liberating readings that Springfield's performances ambivalently facilitated. See Medhurst (2000), for discussion of Gilbert Harding's *Face to Face* interview.
23. See Stuart Hall's comments on Inman/Humphries in Curran and Seaton, (1985).
24. With the exception of *The Naked Civil Servant*, and the BBC's 1990 dramatisation of Jeanette Winterson's *Oranges Are Not the Only Fruit*, the vast majority of television output up until the 1990s was not given over to cultures other than a one which figured heteronormativity as dominant. A few series did include minor lesbian or gay characters. Examples include *The Roads to Freedom* (BBC, 1970); *Porridge* (BBC, 1974–8); *Angels* (1976–82); London Weekend Television's *Agony* (1979–81); *Tenko* (BBC, 1981–4); *Brookside*, Channel 4's first soap (1982); BBC1's *EastEnders*.
25. See Butler's summary (1993: 223–42).

Chapter 5 The End of Representation?

1. Waugh's chronicling of this period, though dealing predominantly with literary studies, nonetheless proves very useful for anyone studying creative and imaginative output against the backdrop of the last 40 years.
2. Useful summaries and discussions are found in Burton (2000: 39–40, 161–3, 291–302), Creeber (2001: 43–6), Holland (1997: 247–60); and summary and detailed discussion in Nelson (1997: 50–98).
3. See David Lavery (1995), for a collection of essays on this production.
4. The phrase 'watching television', as David Morley points out (1986), inadequately describes audience–programme relations.
5. See Liz Bird and Jo Eliot, 'The Life and Loves of a She-Devil', in Brandt (ed.) (1993).

References

Adorno, T. W. and Horkheimer, M., *Dialectic of Enlightenment* (London and New York: Verso, 1997).

Ahmed, S., ' "She'll wake up one of these days and find she's turned into a nigger": Passing through Hybridity', *Theory, Culture and Society*, 16: 2 (1999), pp. 87–106.

Alcock, B. and Robson, J., 'Cagney and Lacey Revisited', *Feminist Review*, 35 (1990), pp. 42–53.

Allen, R. C. (ed.), *Channels of Discourse* (London and New York: Routledge, 1987).

Allen, R.C. (ed.), *Channels of Discourse, Reassembled* (London: Routledge, 1992).

Althusser, L., *Essays on Ideology* (London: Verso, 1984).

Altman, R., 'A Semantic/Syntactic Approach to Film Genre' (1984), in R. Altman, *Film/Genre* (London: British Film Institute, 1999).

Altman, R., 'Television Sound', in T. Modleski (ed.), *Studies in Entertainment* (Bloomington and Indianapolis: Indiana University Press, 1986), pp. 39–54.

Altman, R., *Film/Genre* (London: British Film Institute, 1999).

Anderson, B., *Imagined Communities* (London: Verso, 1983).

Ang, I., *Watching Dallas* (London: Methuen, 1985).

Ang, I., 'Melodramatic Identifications: Television Fiction and Women's Fantasy', in M. E. Brown (ed.), *Television and Women's Culture* (London: Sage, 1990), pp. 75–88.

Bakhtin, M. M., *The Dialogic Imagination: Four Essays*, trans. C. Emerson and M. Holquist (Austin, TX: University of Texas Press, 1981).

Bakhtin, M. M., *Speech Genres and Other Late Essays*, trans. V. W. McGee, ed. C. Emerson and M. Holquist (Austin, TX: University of Texas Press, 1986).

Balcon, M., *Michael Balcon Presents . . . A Lifetime of Films* (London: Hutchinson, 1969).

Barthes, R., *S/Z*, trans. R. Miller (New York: Hill and Wang, 1974).

Barthes, R., *Image–Music–Text*, trans. S. Heath (London: Fontana, 1977).

Barthes, R., 'Inaugural Lecture, Collège de France' [1977], in S. Sontag (ed.), *A Roland Barthes Reader* (London: Vintage, 1993a), pp. 457–78.

Barthes, R., 'The Pleasure of the Text' [1975], in S. Sontag (ed.), *A Roland Barthes Reader* (London: Vintage, 1993b), pp. 404–14.

Bathrick, S., '*The Mary Tyler Moore Show*: Women at Home and at Work', in J. Feuer et al. (eds), *MTM: 'Quality Television'* (London: British Film Institute, 1984), pp. 99–131.

Baudrillard, J., *Simulations* (New York: Semiotexte(e), 1983).

Baudrillard, J., 'The Ecstasy of Communication', in H. Foster (ed.), *Postmodern Culture* (London: Pluto, 1985), pp. 126–34.

Baudrillard, J., *Seduction,* trans. B. Singer (Basingstoke: Palgrave Macmillan, 1990).

Baudrillard, J., *Simulacra and Simulation*, trans. S. F. Glaser (Ann Arbor: University of Michigan Press, 1994).

Beaver, H., 'Homosexual Signs: In Memory of Roland Barthes', *Critical Inquiry*, 8: 1 (Autumn 1981).

Benjamin, W., *Understanding Brecht,* trans. A. Bostock; intro. S. Mitchell (London: New Left Books, 1973).

Bennett, T. and Woollacott, J., *Bond and Beyond* (London: Macmillan, 1987).

Bertens, H., *The Idea of the Postmodern: A History* (London and New York: Routledge, 1995).

Bhabha, H. (ed.), *Nation and Narration* (London: Routledge, 1990).

Bignell, J., Lacey, S. and Macmurraugh-Kavenagh, M. (eds), *British Television Drama: Past, Present and Future* (Basingstoke: Palgrave Macmillan, 2000).

Bird, L. and Eliot, J., 'The Lives and Loves of a She-Devil', in G. W. Brandt (ed.), *British Television Drama in the 1980s* (Cambridge: Cambridge University Press, 1993), pp. 214–33.

Bondebjerg, I., 'Public Discourse/Private Fascination: Hybridization in "True-Life-Story" Genres', *Media, Culture & Society*, 18: 1 (1996), pp. 27–45.

Bordwell, D., *Making Meaning: Inference and Rhetoric in the Interpretation of Cinema* (Cambridge, MA: Harvard University Press, 1989).

Bourdieu, P., 'The Aristocracy of Culture', in R. Collins et al. (eds), *Media, Culture and Society: A Critical Reader* (London: Sage, 1986), pp. 164–93.

Bourdieu, P., *On Television and Journalism* (London: Pluto, 1998).

Bourne, S., *Black in the British Frame: Black People in British Film and Television, 1896–1996* (London: Cassell, 1998).

Brandt, G. W. (ed.), *British Television Drama* (Cambridge: Cambridge University Press, 1981).

Brandt, G. W. (ed.), *British Television Drama in the 1980s* (Cambridge: Cambridge University Press, 1993).

Brown, M. E., *Television and Women's Culture: The Politics of the Popular* (London: Sage, 1990).

Brown, M. E., *Soap Opera and Women's Talk: The Pleasures of Resistance* (London: Sage, 1994).

Brunsdon, C., '*Crossroads*: Notes on Soap Opera', in E. A. Kaplan (ed.), *Regarding Television* (Los Angeles, CA: University Publications of America, 1983), pp. 76–83.

Brunsdon, C., 'Men's Genres for Women', in H. Baehr and G. Dyer (eds), *Boxed In: Women and Television* (London: Pandora, 1987), pp. 184–202.

Brunsdon, C., 'Text and Audience', in E. Seiter et al. (eds), *Remote Control: Television, Audiences & Cultural Power* (London: Routledge, 1989), pp. 116–29.

Brunsdon, C., 'Television: Aesthetics and Audiences', in P. Mellencamp (ed.), *Logics of Television* (London: British Film Institute, 1990), pp. 59–72.

Brunsdon, C., 'Identity in Feminist Television Criticism', *Media, Culture and Society*, 15: 2 (1993), pp. 309–20.

Brunsdon, C., *Screen Tastes* (London: Routledge, 1997).

Brunsdon, C., 'Structure of Anxiety: Recent British Television Crime Fiction', *Screen*, 39: 3 (1998), pp. 223–43.

Brunsdon, C., D'Acci, J. and Spigel, L. (eds), *Feminist Television Criticism: A Reader* (Oxford: Oxford University Press, 1997).

Burton, G., *Talking Television: An Introduction to the Study of Television* (London: Edward Arnold, 2000).

Buscombe. E., 'Creativity in Television', *Screen Education*, 35 (1980), pp. 5–17.

Buscombe. E. (ed.), *British Television: A Reader* (Oxford: Oxford University Press, 2000).

Butler, J., *Gender Trouble: Feminism and the Subversion of Identity* (New York and London: Routledge, 1990).

Butler, J., *Bodies That Matter: On the Discursive Limits of Sex* (New York and London: Routledge, 1993).

Butler, J., *The Psychic Life of Power: Theories in Subjection* (Stanford, CA: Stanford University Press, 1997).

Butler, J., *Excitable Speech: A Politics of the Performative* (New York and London: Routledge, 1998).

Caldwell, J. T., *Televisuality: Style, Crisis, and Authority in American Television* (New Brunswick, NJ: Rutgers University Press, 1995).

Callinicos, A., *Theories and Narratives: Reflections on the Philosophy of History* (Cambridge: Polity Press, 1997).

Campbell, B., *Unofficial Secrets* (London: Virago, 1988).

Casey, B., 'Genre', in Kenneth McLeish (ed.), *Key Ideas in Human Thought* (London: Bloomsbury, 1993).

Caughie, J., 'Progressive Television and Documentary Drama', *Screen*, 21: 3 (1980), pp. 9–35.

Caughie, J., 'Popular Culture: Notes and Revisions', in C. MacCabe (ed.), *High Theory/Low Culture* (Manchester: Manchester University Press, 1986), pp. 156–71.

Caughie, J., *Television Drama: Realism, Modernism, and British Culture* (Oxford: Oxford University Press, 2000).

de Certeau, M., *The Practice of Everyday Life* (Berkeley, CA: University of California Press, 1984).

Champagne, J., *The Ethics of Marginality: A New Approach to Gay Studies* (Minneapolis: University of Minnesota Press, 1995).

Clark, D., '*Cagney & Lacey*: Feminist Strategies of Detection', in M. E. Brown (ed.), *Television and Women's Culture* (London: Sage, 1990), pp. 117–33.

Clarke, A., ' "This is not the boy scouts": Television Police Series and Definitions of Law and Order', in T. Bennett et al. (eds), *Popular Culture and Social Relations* (Milton Keynes: Open University Press, 1986), pp. 219–32.

Corber, R. J., *Homosexuality in Cold War America: Resistance and the Crisis of Masculinity* (Durham, NC: Duke University Press, 1997).

Corner, J., 'Presumption as Theory: "Realism" in Television Studies', *Screen*, 33: 1 (1992), pp. 97–102.

Corner, J., *Television Form and Public Address* (London: Edward Arnold, 1995).

Corner, J., *The Art of Record: A Critical Introduction to Documentary* (Manchester: Manchester University Press, 1996).

Corner, J., *Studying Media: Problems of Theory and Method* (Edinburgh: Edinburgh University Press, 1998).

Corner, J., *Critical Ideas in Television Studies* (Oxford: Oxford University Press, 1999).

Cowie, E., *Representing the Woman: Cinema and Psychoanalysis* (Basingstoke: Palgrave Macmillan, 1997).

Creeber, G. (ed.), *The Television Genre Book* (London: British Film Institute, 2001).

Creed, B., 'Lesbian Bodies: Tribades, Tomboys and Tarts', in E. Grosz and E. Probyn (eds), *Sexy Bodies: The Strange Carnalities of Feminism* (London: Routledge, 1995), pp. 86–103.

Crisp, Q., *The Naked Civil Servant* (London: Penguin, 1997).

Culler, J., *Barthes* (London: Fontana, 1983).

Curran, J. and Seaton, J., *Power without Responsibility: The Press and Broadcasting in Britain* (London: Methuen, 1985).

Curran, J., Ecclestone, J., Oakley, G. and Richardson, A. (eds), *Bending Reality: The State of the Media* (London: Pluto, 1986).

D'Acci, J., 'The Case of Cagney and Lacey', in H. Baehr and G. Dyer (eds), *Boxed In: Women and Television* (London: Pandora, 1987), pp. 203–25.

Davies, R. R., *Queer as Folk: The Scripts* (London: Channel 4 Books, 1999).

Dean, J., 'The Truth is Out There: Aliens and the Fugitivity of Postmodern Truth', *Camera Obscura* (1997), pp. 42–75.

Derrida, J., *Of Grammatology*, trans. G. C. Spivak (Baltimore, MD, and London: Johns Hopkins University Press, 1976).

Derrida, J., *Writing and Difference*, trans. A. Bass (London: Routledge & Kegan Paul, 1978).

Derrida, J., 'Differénce', *A Derrida Reader: Between the Blinds*, ed. P. Kamuf (New York: Columbia University Press, 1991a).

Derrida, J., 'Signature Event Context', *A Derrida Reader: Between the Blinds*, ed. P. Kamuf (New York: Columbia University Press, 1991b).

Derrida, Jacques, 'Speech and Phenomena', *The Derrida Reader: Between the Blinds*, ed. P. Kamuf (New York: Columbia University Press, 1991c).

Doane, M. A., *The Desire to Desire: The Woman's Film of the 1940s* (Basingstoke: Palgrave Macmillan, 1987).

Donald, J., 'Anxious Moments: *The Sweeney* in 1975', in M. Alvarado and J. Stewart (eds), *Made for Television: Euston Films Limited* (London: British Film Institute, 1985), pp. 117–35.

Doty, A., *Making Things Perfectly Queer: Interpreting Mass Culture* (Minneapolis: University of Minnesota Press, 1993).

Dovey, J., 'Reality TV', in G. Creeber (ed.), *The Television Genre Book* (London: British Film Institute, 2001), pp. 134–7.

Dow, B., *Prime Time Feminism: Television, Media Culture, and the Women's Movement since 1970* (Philadelphia, PA: University of Pennsylvania Press, 1996).

Dunn, I., 'Making it Happen: The Making of the Lesbian and Gay Community in Scotland', in E. Healey and A. Mason (eds), *Stonewall 25: The Making of the Lesbian and Gay Community in Britain* (London: Virago, 1994), pp. 111–21.

Dyer, R., *The Matter of Images: Essays on Representation* (London: Routledge & Kegan Paul, 1993).

Eagleton, T., *Ideology: An Introduction* (London: Verso, 1991).

Eagleton, T., *The Idea of Culture* (Oxford: Blackwell Publishers, 2000).

Edelman, L., *Homographesis: Essays in Gay Literary and Cultural Theory* (New York and London: Routledge, 1994).

Elliott, A., *Psychoanalytic Theory: An Introduction* (Basingstoke: Palgrave Macmillan, 2002).

Elliott, J., Interview, in J. Pines (ed.), *Black and White in Colour: Black People in Television since 1936* (London: British Film Institute, 1992), pp. 85–91.

Ellis, J., *Visible Fictions* (London: Routledge & Kegan Paul, 1982).

Ellis, J., 'The Quality Film Adventure: British Critics and the Cinema, 1942–1948', in A. Higson (ed.), *Dissolving Views: Key Writings on British Cinema* (London: Cassell, 1996), pp. 66–93.

Ellis, J., 'Television as Working Through', in J. Gripsrud (ed.), *Television and Common Knowledge* (London: Routledge & Kegan Paul, 1999), pp. 55–70.

Epstein J. and Straub, K. (eds), *Body Guards: The Cultural Politics of Gender Ambiguity* (New York and London: Routledge & Kegan Paul, 1991).

Evans, C. and Gamman, L., 'The Gaze Revisited, or Reviewing Queer Viewing', in P. Burston and C. Richardson (eds), *Queer Romance: Lesbians, Gay Men and Popular Culture* (London: Routledge & Kegan Paul, 1995), pp. 13–56.

Faludi, S., *Backlash: The Undeclared War Against Women* (London: Chatto & Windus, 1992).

Feuer, J., 'The Concept of Live Television: Ontology as Ideology', in E. A. Kaplan (ed.), *Regarding Television* (Fredrick, MD: University Publications of America, 1983), pp. 12–22.

Feuer, J., 'Narrative Form in American Network Television', in C. MacCabe (ed.), *High Theory/Low Culture* (Manchester: Manchester University Press, 1986), pp. 101–14.

Feuer, J., 'Genre Study and Television', in R. C. Allen (ed.), *Channels of Discourse, Reassembled* (London: Routledge & Kegan Paul, 1992), pp. 138–59.

Feuer, J., 'The Gay and Queer Sitcom (*Will and Grace*)', in G. Creeber (ed.), *The Television Genre Book* (London: British Film Institute, 2001), pp. 70–3.

Fiske, J., *Introduction to Communication Studies* (London: Methuen, 1982).

Fiske, J., *Television Culture* (London: Methuen, 1987).

Fiske, J., 'Moments of Television: Neither the Text nor the Audience', in E. Seiter et al. (eds), *Remote Control: Television, Audiences & Cultural Power* (London: Routledge & Kegan Paul, 1989), pp. 56–78.

Flitterman-Lewis, S., 'Psychoanalysis, Film and Television', in R. C. Allen (ed.), *Channels of Discourse, Reassembled* (London: Routledge & Kegan Paul, 1992), pp. 203–46.

Foster, H., '(Post)modern Polemics' , *New German Critique*, 33 (1984), pp. 67–79.

Foucault, M., *The Order of Things: An Archaeology of the Human Sciences* [1966] (New York: Vintage, 1973).

Foucault, M., *The Archaeology of Knowledge* [1969] (London: Routledge, 1989).

Foucault, M., *Discipline and Punish: The Birth of the Prison* [1975] (New York: Vintage, 1995).

Foucault, M., *The History of Sexuality*, vol. 1: *An Introduction* [1976], trans. R. Hurley (New York: Random House, 1978).

Foucault, M., *The Foucault Reader*, ed. P. Rabinow (London: Penguin, 1984).

Foucault, M., *Ethics: Essential Works of Foucault, 1954–1984*, vol. 1, ed. P. Rabinow (London: Penguin Books, 2000a).

Foucault, M., *Aesthetics: Essential Works of Foucault, 1954–1984*, vol. 2, ed. J. D. Faubion (London: Penguin Books, 2000b).

Foucault, M., *Power: Essential Works of Foucault, 1954–1984*, vol. 3, ed. J. D. Faubion (London: Penguin Books, 2000c).

Freud, S., 'Psychoanalysis and Legal Evidence', in S. Freud, *The Standard Edition of the Complete Psychological Works of Sigmund Freud*, vol. 9, ed. J. Strachey (London: Hogarth Press, 1959), pp. 99–114.

Freud, S., 'Some Psychical Consequences of the Anatomical Distinction between the Sexes', in S. Freud, *On Sexuality* [1925], Pelican Freud Library, vol. 7 (Harmondsworth: Penguin, 1977) pp. 323–43.

Friedan, B., *The Feminine Mystique* (London: Penguin, 1965).

Friedman, A., *Writing for Visual Media* (Burlington, MA: Focal Press, 2001).

Gaader, J., *Sophie's World* (London: Phoenix House, 1996).

Gamman, L., 'Watching the Detectives: The Enigma of the Female Gaze', in L. Gamman and M. Marshment (eds), *The Female Gaze: Women as Viewers of Popular Culture* (London: The Women's Press, 1988), pp. 8–26.

Garber, M., *Vested Interests: Cross-Dressing and Cultural Anxiety* (London: Penguin Books, 1993).

Garnett, T., 'Drama Forum – November 1997', in www.world-productions.com/ Tony Garnett Reference Library.

Garnett, T., 'Contexts', in J. Bignell, S. Lacey and M. Macmurraugh-Kavenagh (eds), *British Television Drama: Past, Present and Future* (Basingstoke: Palgrave Macmillan, 2000), pp. 11–23.

Genette, G., *Narrative Discourse* (Ithaca, NY: Cornell University Press, 1980).

Geraghty, C., *British Cinema in the Fifties* (London: Routledge & Kegan Paul, 2000).

Gianetti, L., *Understanding Movies* (Englewood-Cliffs, NJ: Prentice Hall, 1993).

Gilbert, W. S., 'The Television Play: Outside the Consensus', *Screen Education*, 35 (Summer 1980) pp. 35–44.

Gilroy, P., *There Ain't No Black in the Union Jack* (London: Routledge, 1987).

Gilroy, P., 'The End of Antiracism', in J. Donald and A. Rattansi (eds), *'Race', Culture and Difference* (London: Sage, 1992), pp. 49–61.

Gledhill, C., 'Genre', in Pam Cook (ed), *The Cinema Book* (London: British Film Institute, 1985), pp. 58–109.

Gledhill, C., 'The Melodramatic Field: An Investigation', in Gledhill, *Home is Where the Heart Is: Studies in Melodrama and the Woman's Film* (London: British Film Institute, 1987), pp. 5–39.

Gledhill, C., 'Pleasurable Negotiations', in E. D. Pribram (ed.), *Female Spectators* (London: Verso, 1988), pp. 64–89.

Gledhill, C., 'Genre and Gender: The Case of Soap Opera', in S. Hall (ed.), *Representation: Cultural Representations and Signifying Practices* (London: Sage, 1997), pp. 337–84.

Goodwin, A. and Kerr, P. (eds), *Drama-Documentary*, BFI Dossier 19 (London: British Film Institute, 1983).

Grierson, J., *Grierson on Documentary*, ed. F. Hardy (London: Faber & Faber, 1966).

Griffiths, T., 'Trevor and Bill: On Putting Politics before *News at Ten*', interview, *The Leveller* 1 (1976).

Griffiths, T., 'Countering Consent: An Interview with John Wyver', in F. Pike (ed.), *Ah! Mischief: The Writer and Television* (London: Faber & Faber, 1982), pp. 30–40.

Gripsrud, J., 'Television, Broadcasting, Flow: Key Metaphors in TV Theory', in C. Geraghty and D. Lusted (eds), *The Television Studies Book* (London: Edward Arnold, 1998), pp. 17–32.

Gross, L., 'What is Wrong with this Picture? Lesbian Women and Gay Men on Television', in R. J. Ringer (ed.), *Queer Words, Queer Images: Communication and the Construction of Homosexuality* (New York: New York University Press, 1994), pp. 143–56.

Grossberg, L., 'The In-Difference of Television', *Screen*, 28: 2 (1987), pp. 28–45.

Grosz, E., *Jacques Lacan: A Feminist Introduction* (London: Routledge & Kegan Paul, 1990).

Habermas, J., 'Modernity – An Incomplete Project', in H. Foster (ed), *Postmodern Culture* (London: Pluto, 1985), pp. 3–15.

Halberstam, J., *Female Masculinity* (Durham, NC: Duke University Press, 1998).

Hall, S., *Encoding and Decoding in the Television Discourse*, Occasional Paper no. 7 (Birmingham: CCCS, 1973).

Hall, S., *Television as a Medium and its Relation to Culture*, Occasional Paper no. 34 (Birmingham: CCCS, 1975).

Hall, S., 'Culture, the Media and the "Ideological Effect" ', in J. Curran, M. Gurevitch and J. Woollacott (eds), *Mass Communication and Society* (London: Edward Arnold, 1977), pp. 315–48.

Hall, S., 'Encoding/Decoding', in Hall et al. (eds), *Culture, Media, Language* (London: Hutchinson, 1980), pp. 119–38.

Hall, S., 'Media Power and Class Power', in J. Curran et al. (eds), *Bending Reality: The State of the Media* (London: Pluto, 1986), pp. 5–14.

Hall, S., 'Minimal Selves', ICA Documents 6, *Identity, The Real Me: Postmodernism and the Question of Identity* (London: ICA, 1987), pp. 44–6.

Hall, S., 'Cultural Identity and Diaspora', in J. Rutherford (ed.), *Identity* (London: Lawrence & Wishart, 1990), pp. 222–37.

Hall, S., 'The West and the Rest: Discourse and Power', in S. Hall and B. Gieben (eds), *Formations of Modernity* (Cambridge: Polity, 1992a), pp. 275–320.

Hall, S., 'Cultural Studies and Its Theoretical Legacies', in L. Grossberg, C. Nelson and P. Treichler (eds), *Cultural Studies* (New York & London: Routledge, 1992b) pp. 277–94.

Hall, S., 'Culture, Community, Nation', *Cultural Studies,* 7: 3 (1993), pp. 349–63.

Hall, S., 'Signification, Representation, Ideology: Althusser and the Post-Structuralist Debates', in J. Curran et al. (eds), *Cultural Studies and Communications* (London: Edward Arnold, 1996), pp. 11–34.

Hall, S., 'Who needs "Identity"?', in P. du Gay, J. Evans and P. Redman (eds), *Identity: A Reader* (London: Sage, 2000), pp. 15–30.

Hallam, J., 'Power Plays: Gender, Genre and Lynda La Plante', in J. Bignell et al. (eds), *British Television Drama: Past, Present and Future* (Basingstoke: Palgrave Macmillan, 2000), pp. 140–9.

Haskell, M., *From Reverence to Rape: The Treatment of Women in the Movies* [1974] (Chicago and London: University of Chicago Press, 1987).

Hawkes, T., *Structuralism and Semiotics* (London: Methuen, 1977).

Heath, S., 'Representing Television', in P. Mellencamp (ed.), *Logics of Television* (London: British Film Institute, 1990), pp. 267–302.

Heath, S. and Skirrow, G., 'An Interview with Raymond Williams', in T. Modleski (ed.), *Studies in Entertainment* (Bloomington and Indianapolis: Indiana University Press, 1986), pp. 3–17.

Hebdige, D., 'The Bottom Line on Planet One' [1985], in P. Rice and P. Waugh (eds), *Modern Literary Theory: A Reader* (London: Edward Arnold, 1989), pp. 260–81.

Hennessy, R., *Profit and Pleasure: Sexual Identities in Late Capitalism* (Routledge: New York and London, 2000).

Hermes, J., *Reading Women's Magazines* (Cambridge: Polity Press, 1995).

Higson, A., ' "Britain's Outstanding Contribution to the Film": The Documentary-Realist Tradition', in C. Barr (ed.), *All Our Yesterdays: 90 Years of British Cinema* (London: British Film Institute, 1986), pp. 72–97.

Hodge, R. and Kress, G., *Social Semiotics* (Cambridge: Polity Press, 1988).

Holland, P., *The Television Handbook* (London: Routledge & Kegan Paul, 1997).

Hollows, J. and Jancovich, M. (eds), *Approaches to Popular Film* (Manchester: Manchester University Press, 1995).

Homer, S., 'Psychoanalysis, Post-Marxism and the Subject: From the Ethical to the Political', in *Journal of the Universities Association for Psychoanalytic Studies*, vol. 1 (Spring 1998), pp. 18–28.

Honigman, J. (ed.), *Handbook of Social and Cultural Anthropology* (Chicago, Il: Rand McNally, 1973).

Hudson, R., 'Television in Britain: Description and Dissent', from *Theatre Quarterly*, 2: 6 (1972), in www.world-productions.com/Tony Garnett Reference Library.

Hugh, D., *On Queer Street: A Social History of British Homosexuality, 1895–1995* (London: HarperCollins, 1997).

Hurd, G., 'The Television Presentation of the Police', in T. Bennett et al. (eds), *Popular Television and Film* (London: British Film Institute, 1981), pp. 53–70.

Hutson, A. et al., *Big World, Small Screen: The Role of Television in American Society* (Lincoln and London: University of Nebraska Press, 1992).

Huyssen, A., 'Mass Culture as Woman: Modernism's Other', in A. Huyssen, *After the Great Divide: Modernism, Mass Culture and Postmodernism* (Basingstoke: Palgrave Macmillan, 1986), pp. 44–62.

Iser, W., *The Act of Reading: A Theory of Aesthetic Response* [1976] (London: Routledge and Kegan Paul, 1978).

Jameson, F., 'Postmodernism and Consumer Society', in H. Foster (ed.), *Postmodern Culture* (London: Pluto, 1985), 111–25.

Jauss, H. R., *Toward an Aesthetic of Reception* (Brighton: Harvester, 1982).

Johnston, C., 'Women's Cinema as Counter-Cinema', in C. Johnston (ed.), *Notes on Women's Cinema* (London: Society for Education in Film and Television, 1973), pp. 24–31.

Johnston, C. Dorothy, 'Arzner: Critical Strategies', in C. Penley (ed.), *Feminism and Film Theory* [1975] (London: Routledge, 1988), pp. 36–45.

Joyrich, L., 'All that Television Allows: TV Melodrama, Postmodernism and Consumer Culture', *Camera Obscura*, 16 (1988) 141–7.

Joyrich, L., 'Critical and Textual Hypermasculinity', in P. Mellencamp (ed.), *Logics of Television* (London: British Film Institute, 1990), pp. 156–72.

Joyrich, L., *Re-viewing Reception: Television, Gender, and Postmodern Culture* (Bloomington: Indiana University Press, 1996).

Joyrich, L., 'Epistemology of the Console', *Critical Inquiry*, 27 (2001), pp. 439–67.

Kaplan, E. A., *Women and Film: Both Sides of the Camera* (New York and London: Methuen, 1983).

Kermode, F., *The Sense of an Ending: Studies in the Theory of Fiction* (London: Oxford University Press, 1967).

Kerr, P., 'F for Fake? Friction over Faction', in A. Goodwin and G. Whannel (eds), *Understanding Television* (London: Routledge, 1990), pp. 74–87.

Kilborn, R., 'New Contexts for Documentary Production in Britain', *Media, Culture & Society*, 18: 1 (1996), pp. 141–50.

Kilborn, R. and Izod, J., *An Introduction to Television Documentary* (Manchester: Manchester University Press, 1997).

Kirkham, P. and Skeggs, B., '*Absolutely Fabulous*: Absolutely Feminist?', in C. Geraghty and D. Lusted (eds), *The Television Studies Book* (London: Edward Arnold, 1998), pp. 287–98.

Kozloff, S. R., 'Narrative Theory and Television', in R. C. Allen (ed.), *Channels of Discourse, Reassembled* (London: Routledge & Kegan Paul, 1992), pp. 67–100.

Kracauer, S., *Theory of Film* (Oxford: Oxford University Press, 1965).

Kuhn, A., *The Power of the Image: Essays on Representation and Sexuality* (London: Routledge & Kegan Paul, 1985).

Kuhn, A. (ed.), *Alien Zone: Cultural Theory and Contemporary Science Fiction Cinema* (London: Verso, 1990).

Kureishi, H., *The Buddha of Suburbia* (London: Faber & Faber, 1990).

Lacan, J., *Écrits: A Selection* [1977], trans. A. Sheridan (London and New York: Routledge, 1989).

Lacey, N., *Narrative and Genre: Key Concepts in Media Studies* (Basingstoke: Palgrave Macmillan, 2000).

Laing, S., 'Raymond Williams and the Cultural Analysis of Television', *Media, Culture and Society*, 13: 2 (April 1991), pp. 153–69.

Laplanche, J. and Pontalis, J-B., 'Fantasy and the Origins of Sexuality' [1964], in V. Burgin, J. Donald and C. Kaplan (eds), *Formations of Fantasy* (London and New York: Routledge, 1986), pp. 5–34.

Larsen, P., 'Imaginary Spaces: Television, Technology and Everyday Consciousness', in J. Gripsrud (ed.), *Television and Common Knowledge* (London: Routledge & Kegan Paul, 1999), pp. 108–21.

de Lauretis, T., *Alice Doesn't: Feminism, Semiotics, Cinema* (Basingstoke: Palgrave Macmillan, 1984).

Lavender, A., ' "Edge of Darkness": Troy Kennedy Martin', in G. W. Brandt (ed.), *British Television Drama in the 1980s* (Cambridge: Cambridge University Press, 1993), pp. 103–18.

Lavery, D. (ed.), *Full of Secrets: Critical Approaches to 'Twin Peaks'* (Detroit, MI: Wayne State University, 1995).

Lavery, D., Hague, A. and Cartwright, M. (eds), *'Deny All Knowledge': Reading the X-Files* (London: Faber and Faber, 1996).

Leavis, F. R., 'Mass Civilisation and Minority Culture', in J. Storey (ed.), *Cultural Theory and Popular Culture: A Reader* (Hemel Hempstead: Harvester Wheatsheaf, 1994), pp. 12–20.

Leavis, Q. D., *Fiction and the Reading Public* (London: Chatto & Windus, 1978).

Livingstone, S. M., *Making Sense of Television: The Psychology of Audience Interpretation* (London: Pergamon, 1990).

Loach, K., *The Navigators* (Channel 4 television 2002).

Lovell, T., 'Ideology and *Coronation Street*', in R. Dyer et al., *Coronation Street* (London: British Film Institute, 1981), pp. 40–52.

Lukács, G., 'Narrate or Describe', in *Writer and Critic* (London: Merlin Press, 1970), pp. 110–48.

Lyotard, J.-F., T*he Postmodern Condition: A Report on Knowledge* (Manchester: Manchester University Press, 1984).

MacCabe, C., 'Realism and the Cinema: Notes on some Brechtian Theses', *Screen,* 15: 2 (1974), pp. 7–27.

MacCabe, C., 'Theory and Film: Principles of Realism and Pleasure', *Screen*, 17: 3 (1976), pp. 7–27.

MacCabe, C., '*Days of Hope:* a Response to Colin McArthur', in T. Bennett et al. (eds), *Popular Television and Film* (London: British Film Institute, 1981), pp. 310–13.

Macdonald, D., 'A Theory of Mass Culture', in J. Storey (ed.), *Cultural Theory and Popular Culture: A Reader* (Hemel Hempstead: Harvester Wheatsheaf, 1994), pp. 29–43.

Macherey, P., *A Theory of Literary Production* (London: Routledge & Kegan Paul, 1978).

Macmurraugh-Kavanagh, M., 'Too Secret for Words: Coded Dissent in Female-Authored *Wednesday Plays*', in J. Bignell et al. (eds), *British Television Drama: Past, Present and Future* (Basingstoke: Palgrave Macmillan, 2000), pp. 150–61.

Macmurraugh-Kavenagh, M., 'What's All This Then? The Ideology of Identity in *The Cops*', in B. Carson and M. Llewellyn-Jones (eds), *Frames and Fictions in Television* (Exeter: Intellect Books, 2000), pp. 40–9.

Malik, S., *Representing Black Britain: Black and Asian Images on Television* (London: Sage, 2002).

Marcuse, H., *One Dimensional Man* (London: Abacus, 1972).

McArthur, C., 'Historical Drama', in T. Bennett et al. (eds), *Popular Television and Film* (London: British Film Institute, 1981), pp. 288–301.

McGrath, J., 'TV Drama: the Case against Naturalism', *Sight and Sound*, 46: 2 (Spring 1977), pp. 100–5.

McGrath, J., 'TV Drama: Then and Now', in J. Bignell et al. (eds), *British Television Drama: Past, Present and Future* (Basingstoke: Palgrave Macmillan, 2000), pp. 64–7.

McGuigan, J., *Cultural Populism* (London: Routledge & Kegan Paul, 1992).

McLuhan, M., *Understanding Media* (London: Routledge and Kegan Paul, 1964).

Medhurst, A., 'Every Wart and Pustule: Gilbert Harding and Television Stardom', in E. Buscombe (ed.), *British Television: A Reader* (Oxford: Oxford University Press, 2000), pp. 248–64.

Mellencamp, P., 'Situation Comedy, Feminism and Freud: Discourses of Gracie and Lucy', in T. Modleski (ed.), *Studies in Entertainment* (Bloomington and Indianapolis: Indiana University Press, 1986), pp. 80–95.

Mercer, C., 'Complicit Pleasures', in T. Bennett et al. (eds), *Popular Culture and Social Relations* (Milton Keynes: Open University Press, 1986), pp. 50–68.

Metz, C., 'The Imaginary Signifier', *Screen*, 16: 2 (1975), pp. 14–76.

Miller, C. R., 'Genre as Social Action', *Quarterly Journal of Speech*, 70 (1984), pp. 151–67.

Miller, D. A., *The Novel and the Police* (Berkeley and Los Angeles, CA: University of California Press, 1988).

Miller. D., 'Anal Rope' in D. Fuss (ed.), *Inside/Outside: Lesbian Theories, Gay Theories* (New York and London: Routledge, 1991), pp. 119–41.

Miller, J., *Seductions: Studies in Reading and Culture* (London: Virago, 1990).

Miller, N., *Out of the Past: Gay and Lesbian History from 1869 to the Present* (London: Vintage, 1995).

Modleski, T., 'The Rhythms of Reception: Daytime Television and Women's Work', in E. A. Kaplan (ed.), *Regarding Television* (Los Angeles, CA: University Publications of America, 1983), pp. 67–75.

Modleski, T., *Loving with a Vengeance: Mass-Produced Fantasies for Women* (London: Methuen, 1984).

Modleski, T., 'The Terror of Pleasure: the Contemporary Horror Film and Postmodern Theory', in T. Modleski (ed.), *Studies in Entertainment* (Bloomington and Indianapolis: Indiana University Press, 1986a), pp. 155–66.

Modleski, T., 'Femininity as Mas(s)querade: a Feminist Approach to Mass Culture', in C. MacCabe (ed.), *High Theory/Low Culture* (Manchester: Manchester University Press, 1986b), pp. 37–52.

Modleski, T., *Feminism without Women: Culture and Criticism in a 'Postfeminist' Age* (London: Routledge & Kegan Paul, 1991).

Morley, D., *The 'Nationwide' Audience* (London: British Film Institute, 1980).

Morley, D., *Family Television* (London: Comedia, 1986).

Morley, D., *Television, Audiences and Cultural Studies* (London: Routledge & Kegan Paul, 1992).

Morse, M., 'An Ontology of Everyday Distraction: The Freeway, the Mall, and Television', in P. Mellencamp (ed.), *Logics of Television* (London: British Film Institute, 1990), pp. 193–221.

Moseley, R. and Read, J., ' "Having it *Ally*": Popular Television (Post-)Feminism', *Feminist Media Studies*, 2: 2 (2002), pp. 231–49.

Mulhern, F., *Culture/Metaculture* (London and New York: Routledge & Kegan Paul, 2000).

Mulvey, L., 'Visual Pleasure and Narrative Cinema' [1975], in L. Mulvey, *Visual and Other Pleasures* (Basingstoke: Palgrave Macmillan, 1989), pp. 14–26.

Munt, S., 'Shame/Pride Dichotomies in *Queer as Folk*', in *Textual Practice*, 14: 3 (2000), pp. 531–46.

Murdock, G., 'Authorship and Organisation', *Screen Education*, 35 (1980), pp. 19–34.

Neale, S., *Genre* (London: British Film Institute, 1980).

Neale, S., 'Questions of Genre', *Screen*, 31: 1 (1990), pp. 45–66.

Neale, S., 'Studying Genre', in G. Creeber (ed.), *The Television Genre Book* (London: British Film Institute, 2001), pp. 1–2.

Neale, S., 'Westerns and Gangster Films Since the 1970s', in S. Neale (ed.), *Genre and Contemporary Hollywood* (London: British Film Institute, 2002), pp. 27–47.

Negra, D., ' "Quality Postfeminism?" Sex and the Single Girl on HBO', forthcoming in *Genders*.

Nelson, R., *TV Drama in Transition: Forms, Values and Cultural Change* (Basingstoke: Palgrave Macmillan, 1997).

Nicholls, P., 'The Belated Postmodern: History, Phantoms, and Tony Morrison', in S. Vice, (ed.), *Psychoanalytic Criticism: A Reader* (Cambridge: Polity Press, 1996).

Nichols, B., *Representing Reality* (Bloomington and Indianapolis: Indiana University Press, 1991).

Nichols, B., *Blurred Boundaries: Questions of Meaning in Contemporary Culture* (Bloomington and Indianapolis: Indiana University Press, 1994).

O'Brien, L., *Dusty: A Biography of Dusty Springfield* (London: Sidgwick & Jackson, 1999).

Paget, D., *No Other Way to Tell It: Dramadoc/docudrama on Television* (Manchester: Manchester University Press, 1998).

Pender, P., ' "I'm Buffy, and You're . . . History": the Postmodern Politics of *Buffy*', in R. V. Wilcox and D. Lavery (eds), *Fighting the Forces: What's at Stake in 'Buffy the Vampire Slayer'* (Oxford: Rowman & Littlefield, 2002), pp. 35–44.

Philips, A., 'Keep It Moving', in J. Butler (ed.), *The Psychic Life of Power: Theories in Subjection* (Stanford, CA: Stanford University Press, 1997), pp. 151–9.

Philo, G., *Glasgow University Media Group Reader: News, Industry, Economy, War, and Politics* (London: Routledge & Kegan Paul, 1996).

Plummer, K., *Telling Sexual Stories: Power, Change and Social Worlds* (London and New York: Routledge & Kegan Paul, 1995).

Posener, J., *Spray it Loud* (London: Pandora, 1982).

Potter, D., *Waiting for the Boat: Dennis Potter on Television* (London: Faber & Faber, 1984).

Prince, G., *A Dictionary of Narratology* (Lincoln: University of Nebraska Press, 1987)

Pringle, A., 'A Methodology for Television Analysis with Reference to the Drama Series', *Screen,* 13: 2 (1972), pp. 116–26.

Probyn, E., 'New Traditionalism and Post-Feminism: TV Does the Home', *Screen*, 31: 2 (1990), pp. 147–59.

Propp, V., *Morphology of the Folktale* (Austin, TX: University of Texas Press, 1968).

Radway, J., *Reading the Romance: Women, Patriarchy, and Popular Literature* (London: Verso, 1987).

Reid, E. C., 'Viewdata: the Television Viewing Habits of Young Black Women in London' [1989], in H. Baehr and A. Gray (eds), *Turning It On: A Reader in Women and Media* (London: Edward Arnold, 1996), pp. 138–56.

Rich, A., 'Compulsory Heterosexuality and Lesbian Existence', in *Signs: Journal of Women in Culture and Society*, 5: 4 (1980), pp. 631–60.

Rice, P. and Waugh, P. (eds), *Modern Literary Theory: A Reader* (London: Edward Arnold, 1989).

Rimmon-Kenan, S., *Narrative Fiction: Contemporary Poetics* (London: Routledge & Kegan Paul, 1983).

Roscoe, J. and Hight, C., Faking It: *Mock-documentary and the Subversion of Factuality* (Manchester: Manchester University Press, 2001).

Rosenfelt, D. and Stacey, J., 'Second Thoughts on the Second Wave', in K. V. Hansen and I. J. Philipson (eds), *Women, Class and the Feminist Imagination* (Philadelphia, PA: Temple University Press, 1990), pp. 549–67.

Rowe, K., 'Roseanne: Unruly Woman as Domestic Goddess', *Screen*, 31: 4 (1990), pp. 408–19.

Ryan, M., 'Postmodern Politics', in *Theory, Culture & Society*, 5: 2–3 (1988), pp. 559–76.

Said, E., *Culture and Imperialism* (London: Chatto & Windus, 1983).

Sanderson, T., *Mediawatch: The Treatment of Male and Female Homosexuality in the British Media* (London: Cassell, 1995).

Sandford, J., 'Edna and Cathy: Just Huge Commercials', in *Drama-Documentary*, BFI Dossier 19 (London: British Film Institute, 1984), pp. 16–19.

Sarup, M., *Jacques Lacan* (Hemel Hempstead: Harvester Wheatsheaf, 1992).

Saussure de, F., *Course in General Linguistics* (London: Fontana/Collins, 1974).

Scannell, P., 'Public Service Broadcasting: the History of a Concept', in E. Buscombe (ed.), *British Television: A Reader* (Oxford: Oxford University Press, 2000), pp. 45–62.

Schlesinger, P., *Putting Reality Together: BBC News* (London: Constable, 1978).

Schlesinger, P., Murdock, G. and Elliott, P., *Televising 'Terrorism': Political Violence in Popular Culture* (London: Comedia, 1983).

Sedgwick, E. K., *Epistemology of the Closet* [1990] (London: Penguin, 1994).

Seiter, E. et al., ' "Don't treat us like we're so stupid and naïve" – Towards an Ethnography of Soap Opera Viewers' [1989], in H. Baehr and A. Gray (eds), *Turning It On: A Reader in Women and Media* (London: Edward Arnold, 1996), pp. 138–56.

Seiter, E., 'Making Distinctions in Television Audience Research', in *Cultural Studies*, 4: 1 (1990), pp. 61–84.

Shubik, I., *Play for Today: The Evolution of Television Drama* (Manchester: Manchester University Press, 2000).

Silverman, K., *The Subject of Semiotics* (Oxford: Oxford University Press, 1983).

Sinfield, A., *The Wilde Century: Effeminacy, Oscar Wilde and the Queer Moment* (London: Cassell, 1994).

Sinfield, A., *Gay and After* (London: Serpent's Tail, 1998).

Siune, K. and Hultén, O., 'Does Public Broadcasting Have a Future?', in D. McQuail and K. Siune (eds), *Media Policy: Convergence, Concentration, Commerce* (The Euromedia Research Group, London: Sage, 1998), 23–37.

Skirrow, G., '*Widows*', in M. Alvarado and J. Stewart (eds), *Made for Television: Euston Films Limited* (London: British Film Institute, 1985), pp. 174–84.

Smith, J., 'There's Only One Yorkshire Ripper', in *Misogynies* (London: Faber & Faber, 1989), pp. 117–51.

Smith, P. J., ' "You don't have to say you love me": The Camp Masquerades of Dusty Springfield', in P. J. Smith (ed.), *The Queer Sixties* (New York: Routledge, 1999), pp. 105–26.

Soper, K., 'Relativism and Utopianism: Critical Theory and Cultural Studies', in N. Aldred and M. Ryle (eds), *Teaching Culture: The Long Revolution in Cultural Studies* (London: NIACE, 1999), pp. 66–8.

Spencer, C., *Homosexuality: A History* (London: Fourth Estate, 1995).

Spigel, L., *Make Room for TV: Television and the Family Ideal in Postwar America* (Chicago, IL: University of Chicago Press, 1992).

Spivak, G. C., 'Translator's Preface', in Jacques Derrida, *Of Grammatology* (Baltimore, MD: Johns Hopkins University Press, 1976), pp. ix–lxxxvii.

Spivak, G. C., *In Other Words: Essays in Cultural Politics* (London: Routledge & Kegan Paul, 1987).

Stam, R., Burgoyne, R. and Flitterman-Lewis, S., *New Vocabularies in Film Semiotics* (London: Routledge & Kegan Paul, 1992).

Stam, R., *Film Theory* (Oxford: Blackwell Publishers, 2000).

Storey, J., *Cultural Theory and Popular Culture: An Introduction* (Harlow: Prentice Hall, 2001).

Thompson, D. (ed.), *Discrimination and Popular Culture* (Harmondsworth: Penguin, 1964).

Thornham, S., 'Feminist Interventions: *Prime Suspect I*', *Critical Survey*, 6: 2 (1994), pp. 226–33.

Thornham, S., *Passionate Detachments: An Introduction to Feminist Film Theory* (London: Edward Arnold, 1997).

Thornham, S., *Feminist Theory and Cultural Studies* (London: Edward Arnold, 2000).

Thornham, S., ' "A Good Body": The Case of/for Feminist Media Studies', *European Journal of Cultural Studies*, 6: 1 (2003), pp. 75–94.

Todorov, T., *The Fantastic: A Structural Approach to a Literary Genre,* trans. R. Howard (Ithaca, NY: Cornell University Press, 1975).

Todorov, T., 'The Typology of Detective Fiction', in D. Lodge (ed.), *Modern Criticism and Theory: A Reader* (New York: Longman, 1988), pp. 137–44.

Tulloch, J., *Television Drama: Agency, Audience and Myth* (London: Routledge & Kegan Paul, 1990).

Tulloch, J. and Alvarado, M., *Doctor Who: The Unfolding Text* (London: Macmillan, 1983).

Turner, G., 'Genre, Format and "Live" Television', in G. Creeber (ed.), *The Television Genre Book* (London: British Film Institute, 2001), pp. 6–7.

Vogler, C., *The Writer's Journey: Mythic Structure for Storytellers and Screenwriters* (London: Pan, 1999).

Vološinov, V. N., *Marxism and the Philosophy of Language* [1929], trans. L. Matejka and I. T. Titunik (Cambridge, MA, and London: Harvard University Press, 1996).

Wagg, S., ' "One I made earlier": Media, Popular Culture and the Politics of Childhood', in D. Strinati and S. Wagg (eds), *Come on Down? Popular Media Culture in Post-war Britain* (London: Routledge & Kegan Paul, 1992), pp. 150–78.

Warner, M. (ed.), *Fear of a Queer Planet* (Minneapolis: University of Minnesota Press, 1993).

Warner, M., *No Go the Bogeyman: Scaring, Lulling and Making Mock* (London: Chatto & Windus, 1998).

Waters, S., *Tipping the Velvet* (London: Virago, 1999).

Watson, J., *Media Communication: An Introduction to Theory and Process* (Basingstoke: Palgrave Macmillan, 1998).

Waugh, P., *The Harvest of the Sixties* (Oxford and New York: Oxford University Press, 1995)

Webster, W., *Not a Man to Match Her: The Marketing of a Prime Minister* (London: The Women's Press, 1990).

Weeks, J., *Invented Moralities: Sexual Values in an Age of Uncertainty* (Cambridge: Polity Press, 1995).

White, E., *The Flâneur* (London: Bloomsbury, 2001).

White, H., *Metahistory* (Baltimore, MD: Johns Hopkins University Press, 1975).

White, M., 'Ideological Analysis and Television', in R. C. Allen (ed.), *Channels of Discourse, Reassembled* (London: Routledge & Kegan Paul, 1992), pp. 161–202.

Wilcox, R. and Williams, J. P., ' "What do you think?" *The X-Files*, Liminality, and Gender Pleasure', in D. Lavery, A. Hague and M. Cartwright (eds), *'Deny All Knowledge': Reading the X-Files* (London: Faber & Faber, 1996), pp. 99–120.

Williams, L., 'Film Bodies: Gender, Genre and Excess', in S. Thornham (ed.), *Feminist Film Theory: A Reader* (Edinburgh: Edinburgh University Press, 1999), pp. 267–81.

Williams, R., *The Long Revolution* (Harmondsworth: Penguin, 1965).

Williams, R., *Keywords: A Vocabulary of Culture and Society* (London: Fontana, 1976).

Williams, R., 'A Lecture on Realism', *Screen*, 18: 1 (1977), pp. 61–74.

Williams, R., *Raymond Williams on Television*, ed. A. O'Connor (London: Routledge, 1989).

Williams, R., *Television: Technology and Cultural Form* (London: Routledge, 1990).

Williams, R. and Orrom, M., *Preface to Film* (London: Film Drama 1954).

Women and Film, 'Overview', *Women and Film*, 1 (1972), pp. 3–6.

Woodward, K., 'Concepts of Identity and Difference', in K. Woodward (ed.), *Identity and Difference* (London: Sage, 1997), pp. 7–61.

Young, L., *Fear of the Dark: 'Race', Gender and Sexuality in the Cinema* (London: Routledge, 1996).

Yousaf, N., *Hanif Kureishi's 'The Buddha of Suburbia'* (New York and London: Continuum, 2002).

Zipes, J., 'A Second Gaze at Little Red Riding Hood's Trials and Tribulations', in J. Zipes (ed.), *Don't Bet on the Prince: Contemporary Feminist Fairy Tales in North America and England* (Aldershot: Gower, 1989), pp. 227–60.

Programme Index

The Professionals (1977–83), ITV1 UK
Queer as Folk (1999–2000), Channel 4 UK
Rhoda (1974–8), CBS USA
Roseanne (1988–97), ABC USA
The Royle Family (1998–2000), BBC UK
Sex and the City (1998–2004), Channel 4 UK
Silent Witness (1996–2003), BBC1 UK
The Singing Detective (1986), BBC1 UK
Sophie's World (1995), BBC2 UK
Star Trek (1966–), NBC/BBC UK
The Sweeney (1975–8), ITV1 UK
This Week (1956–92), UK
Thin Air (3–4 November 2002), BBC1 UK
Til Death Do Us Part (1966–75), BBC1 UK
Tinsel Town (2000–), BBC2 UK
Tipping the Velvet (2002), BBC2 UK
Tutti Frutti (1987), BBC2 UK
Twin Peaks (1989), ABC USA
Waking the Dead (2000–), BBC1 UK
The Wednesday Play (1964–70), BBC UK
Widows (1983), ITV1 UK
The X-Files (1993–2002), Channel 4 UK
Z Cars (1962–78), BBC UK

General Index
